Caste, Race and Discrimination

Caste, Race and Discrimination

Discourses in International Context

EDITED BY
SUKHADEO THORAT
UMAKANT

INDIAN INSTITUTE OF DALIT STUDIES, NEW DELHI

RAWAT PUBLICATIONS
Jaipur and New Delhi

ISBN 81-7033-892-1

Published in association with
Indian Institute of Dalit Studies
D/25-D, South Extension, Part II, New Delhi 110 049
Phone: 011-51643981/82 Fax: 011-51643982
E-mail: iids@dalitstudies.org
Website: www.dalitstudies.org

Published by
Prem Rawat for *Rawat Publications*
Satyam Apts., Sector 3, Jawahar Nagar, Jaipur 302 004 (India)
Phone: 0141 265 1748 / 7006 Fax: 0141 265 1748
E-mail: info@rawatbooks.com
Website: www.rawatbooks.com

New Delhi Office
4858/24, Ansari Road, Daryaganj, New Delhi 110 002
Phone: 011-23263290

Typeset by Rawat Computers, Jaipur
Printed at Chaman Enterprises, New Delhi

Contents

Foreword ix
MARTIN MACWAN

Acknowledgements xi

Introduction xiii
SUKHADEO THORAT AND UMAKANT

UN and Dalit Intervention

1 UN Bodies and the Dalits: A Historical Review of Interventions 3
N. PAUL DIVAKAR AND AJAI M.

2 (UN) Touchables in Durban 31
MARTIN MACWAN

Is Caste Race?

3 The Official Position 43
SOLI J. SORABJEE

4 Race and Caste 49
ANDRÉ BÉTEILLE

5 Caste Is Not Race: But, Let's Go to the UN Forum Anyway 53
DIPANKAR GUPTA

6 Dalits and Durban — 57
P. RADHAKRISHNAN

7 Caste Consciousness: Initiate an Open Discussion in Durban — 65
ANDRÉ BÉTEILLE

8 Caste, Race, Politics — 69
DIPANKAR GUPTA

9 Caste in the Mirror of Race — 85
D.L. SHETH

10 Race and Caste: Anthropological and Sociological Perspectives — 97
T.K. OOMMEN

11 Silence of the Lambs: Durban and the Indian Elite — 110
SUBHASH GATADE

12 UN Conference Against Racism: Is Caste Race? — 120
AMBROSE PINTO

Caste, Race and Discrimination

13 Hidden Apartheid — 133
TEESTA SETALVAD

14 Discrimination that Must be Cast Away — 142
SWAMI AGNIVESH AND VALSON THAMPU

15 We, the Other People — 149
K.G. KANNABIRAN

16 Annihilating Caste — 153
MARI MARCEL THEKAEKARA

17 Durban, Caste and Indian Democracy — 156
KANCHA ILAIAH

18 Caste, the Academy and Dalit Women — 160
KALPANA KANNABIRAN

19 India's Apartheid — 164
RAJEEV DHAVAN

20 Debate on Discrimination: Casteism is Racism of Another Sort — 168
ARJUN SENGUPTA

21 Facing Up to the Facts — 172
KULDIP NAYAR

22 Caste, Race and Human Rights — 176
M.N. PANINI

Caste, Race and Internationalisation

23 The UN, Racism and Caste 187
GAIL OMVEDT

24 Caste and the World Conference Against Racism 194
DAVID HASLAM

25 Racial Discrimination as a Grave Violation of Human Rights 199
P.N. BHAGWATI

26 Caste at Durban: Why and How 207
A.S. NARANG

27 UN's Record on Caste Rights 211
SIRAJ M. SAIT

Dalit Discourse

28 Regaining Our Lost Faith 227
PRAKASH LOUIS

29 Caste and the UN Meet 237
KANCHA ILAIAH

30 Politics of Representation 241
GOPAL GURU

31 The Race for Caste: Prolegomena to the Durban Conference 250
SHIV VISVANATHAN

32 Durban and Dalit Discourse 265
SHIV VISVANATHAN

Discriminated Groups in Asia and Africa

33 Caste Discrimination 283
SMITA NARULA

34 Caste and Social Origin: Descent-Based Discrimination in Asia 292
SUKHADEO THORAT AND UMAKANT

Post-Durban Reflections

35 What Next for India's Dalits? 313
MARI MARCEL THEKAEKARA

36 Post-Durban Reflections: Color Line – Caste Line 317
N. PAUL DIVAKAR

37 Caste at the World Conference Against Racism 322
PETER N. PROVE

Sources of Articles 326

Contributors 329

Appendix: Statement by the National Human Rights Commission, India at WCAR 334
JUSTICE K. RAMASWAMY

Index 337

Foreword

I feel deeply honoured to introduce the first publication of Indian Institute of Dalit Studies (IIDS) on the historical debate on caste and race or casteism and racism in the context of UN's World Conference Against Racism (WCAR). WCAR has been an important vehicle to raise caste discrimination as the major form of human rights violation on the global platform. The debate itself speaks volumes on the visibility that the question of caste discrimination enhanced both nationally and internationally. This volume is an important contribution of IIDS, especially for upcoming Dalit generation, and all those who are engaged in the struggle against caste discrimination, and who are likely to fall prey to generational distortion of the history.

This book, in fact, is the outcome of the different positions taken by the Dalit activists, the government and its representatives at the various forums of the United Nations, for their persistent and fierce opposition to the inclusion of caste discrimination in the agenda of WCAR, without which neither the greater visibility that the issue has attained nor the long-term inclusion of the issue that has penetrated the attention of the UN was possible.

IIDS is deeply committed to the philosophy of open debate and this is evident from the fact that the volume has included articles with diverse views. Academic tolerance is a greater value, which is nurtured by IIDS. The volume leaves it to the readers to find their own judgement.

Prof. Sukhadeo Thorat, the Director of IIDS and Dr. Umakant along with all the team members deserve congratulations from all of us to make this publication possible.

Martin Macwan
Chairperson
Indian Institute of Dalit Studies

Acknowledgements

This volume contains both published and unpublished papers. The published papers are collected from various sources, like research journals, newspapers, and other sources within and outside India. Indeed, it was a time-consuming and tedious job. However exception apart this tedious job was made relatively easy by cooperation and support from a number of persons, editors of newspapers and copyright owners. Therefore, we are grateful to all of them.

We offer our sincere gratitude to the following:

- The Editor of *Economic and Political Weekly* for granting us the permission to publish four articles, by Shiv Visvanathan, Ambrose Pinto, and M.N. Panini.
- The Editor of *Mainstream* for allowing us to publish articles by A.S. Narang and by Subhash Gatade.
- The Editor of *Seminar* to allow us to publish as many as seven articles by Soli J. Sorabjee, Smita Narula, Martin Macwan, Prakash Louis, Gopal Guru, Dipankar Gupta, and D.L. Sheth.
- The Editor of *The Hindu* to allow us to publish as many as 14 articles by André Béteille, Gail Omvedt, Swami Agnivesh and Valson Thampu, K.G. Kannabiran, Mari Marcel Thekaekara,

Kancha Ilaiah, Kalpana Kannabiran, Rajeev Dhavan, P. Radhakrishnan, and Kuldeep Nayar.

- The Editor of *Times of India* for allowing us to publish articles by Dipankar Gupta, Arjun Sengupta, and André Béteille.
- The Editor of *PUCL Bulletin* for giving permission to publish an article by Justice P.N. Bhagwati.
- The Editor of *Communalism Combat* also deserves our thanks for granting us the permission to publish one article by Teesta Setalvad.
- The Editor of *Dalit International Newsletter* for granting permission to publish articles by David Haslam, N. Paul Divakar and Peter N. Prove.
- The National Human Rights Commission to give permission to publish an article by T.K. Oommen.
- Siraj M. Sait, N. Paul Divakar and Ajai M. for allowing us to publish their papers.

We are also thankful to those who have helped us in a number of ways by taking efforts to dig out papers from their collected records. We are particularly thankful to Martin Macwan (former Convener of NCDHR), Paul Divakar (first Convener of NCDHR), Ruth Manorama, Henri Tiphagne, Vincent Manoharan, Aloysius Irudayam, Vimal Thorat, David Haslam, Smita Narula, Rikke Norhlind, Walter Hahn, Gerard Oonk, Peter Prove, Tim Gill and many others.

Thanks are also due to Pramod Dabral of IIDS for typing the lengthy manuscript. We are also thankful to Pranit Rawat of Rawat Publications who agreed to publish this volume in a short span of time.

Sukhadeo Thorat
Umakant

Introduction

SUKHADEO THORAT AND UMAKANT

The NGOs and social organisations in India, USA and Canada have frequently used the international forums like UN's Sub-Commission on Promotion and Protection of Human Rights and Committee on Elimination of Racial Discrimination (CERD) to address the issue of human rights violations of Dalits and similar groups. The interventions in UN bodies have brought the Dalit organisations, the representatives of the Indian government and UN bodies, particularly the CERD, together where each one of them took different position on the issue of human rights violations associated with caste and untouchability-based discrimination and exclusion. Similarly, the groups from Nepal and Japan have also tried to address the issue of discrimination associated with caste and social origin in the international bodies. However, the differences among the three constituents, namely, the NGOs, governments and the CERD, remained confined to close-door discussions and rarely became a subject of discussion in wider public domain.

The World Conference Against Racism, Racial Discrimination, Xenophobia and Related Intolerance (WCAR), held at Durban, South Africa in 2001, however, brought the issues from the close-door discussions in international bodies into public domain in India, Nepal and also Japan. In India, the discussion in the public domain was induced by the decision of various organisations to take the issue of caste and untouchability-based discrimination on the agenda of UN conference in Durban. Among the several organisations, the National Campaign on Dalit Human Rights (NCDHR) – a collective of Dalit NGOs – other organisations and NGOs, academicians, activists and large number of supporters spearheaded the national campaign in India for inclusion of the issue of caste and untouchability-based discrimination in the Durban conference.

This decision of NCDHR and other organisations to include the issue of caste discrimination, under the purview of descent-based discrimination in the international forum, invited diverse and wide-spread reactions and viewpoints by various constituents, namely, the government, national human rights bodies, other organisations, NGOs, activists, academicians, press and other sections of Indian society. Reams and reams of paper was devoted to discuss this issue in English and regional press. Never in our view so much has been written by various sections of Indian society on the issue of caste and problem of Dalits in such a narrow span of time in the recent history. Given the significance of the issue and seriousness with which the Indian civil society had responded through writings on one of the most important problems that we faced today, the Indian Institute of Dalit Studies decided to put together the selected writings, if not all, published within and outside India in books, journals, newspapers, memorandums and other sources before and after the Durban conference. The literature included in this volume is indeed immensely rich, insightful and reflective of the contemporary thinking of the government, human rights organisations, academic world, civil society organisations and the public at large. It provides a good insight as to how the different constituents perceive the problem of caste discrimination in general and of the low-caste untouchables in particular.

The book contains thirty-seven papers, small as well as long ones, besides an introduction, which covers a number of issues. It is rather difficult to capture the range of issues and various shades of opinions expressed in these papers. In the introduction, therefore, we present and touch up the central issues that are the focal points of discussions. Among several issues, some of the main issues that these papers address include: Is caste race? What are the similarities and differences between caste and race? Does the issue of caste discrimination falls under the purview of discrimination-related provisions of UN? Should Dalits in India also use international forums to address the issue of caste and untouchability-based discrimination? Are such interventions justified and necessary? Since the legal provisions in India are in place, should not the Dalit organisations address the issue locally? Since the Indian government is signatory of a number of UN charters on human rights, should it not be made accountable internationally for continuing discrimination of Dalits and for failure of criminal justice system in providing safeguards to Dalits? Besides these issues, some of the papers also highlight the continuing discrimination of Dalits. Some papers have discussed the limitations of UN framework for explicitly and clearly not addressing the issue of discrimination in Asia and African countries arising out of institutions of caste/untouchability, social origin and the West-centric bias of UN provisions on discrimination – only covering discrimination/exclusion associated with institutions of race, colour, national origin and its failure to extend other institutions of discrimination and exclusion typically found in countries of Asia and Africa covering a large section of population.

Discrimination and UN Framework

Before we present the central themes of the papers in the volume, we take a close look at the position of UN, particularly the CERD, on the issue of caste and similar forms of discrimination. Since 1948, the United Nations has been promoting and codifying human rights, with a common standard of achievement for all people and nations. Over a period of time, the concept of human rights has continuously expanded, from first-generation notion of political and civil rights to a range of economic, social and cultural rights, right to development and right of indigenous people. One of the important guiding concerns of this human rights framework relates to the principle of 'non-discrimination'. The Universal Declaration of Human Rights and other human rights instruments specifically refer to this principle.

Article 1 adopted by the United Nations on "Declaration on the Elimination of All Forms of Racial Discrimination" proclaimed: "Discrimination between human beings on the ground of race, colour or ethnic origin is an offence to human dignity." Article 2 adds: "No state, institution, group or individual shall make any discrimination whatsoever in matters of human rights and fundamental freedoms in the treatment of persons, on the ground of race, colour or ethnic origin." The International Convention on the Elimination of All Forms of Racial Discrimination, adopted in December 1965, defined the term 'racial discrimination' as "any distinction, exclusion, restriction or preference based on race, colour, descent, national or ethnic which has the purpose or effect of nullifying or impairing the recognition, enjoyment or exercise on an equal footing of human rights and fundamental freedoms in the political, economic, social, cultural or any other field of public life".

This provision of the International Convention is explicit and clear with respect to discrimination associated with race-colour-ethnicity-national and descent but not pointedly clear about the discrimination arising out of non race-colour-ethnic group identities. In other words, the discrimination emanating from institutions other than race and colour lacks clarity and therefore leaves considerable scope for interpretation.

Several groups from Asian and African countries which suffer from discrimination due to reasons other than race or colour (but quite similar to that of race or colour in nature of discrimination) have been advocating with the UN Commission on Human Rights (particularly, with the Committee on Elimination of Racial Discrimination) to bring them under its purview and treat them as 'discriminated groups' for the purpose of CERD. The untouchables (or Dalits) (from India, Nepal, Bangladesh, Sri Lanka, Pakistan) and Buraku from Japan, who suffer from discrimination based on social origin (such as caste or social status), have been advocating for over a decade to recognise and bring them under the purview of the UN Commission. Recently, some groups from African countries have presented the evidence of intense discrimination associated with caste and other forms of social stratification including occupations. These communities from Asia and Africa, highly diverse in geographical and historical origin, share to a greater or lesser extent several key characteristics that are inherently productive of discrimination and human rights violation.

UN's Response on Caste Discrimination (1948-2002)

As mentioned above, the Universal Declaration of Human Rights (UDHR), adopted in 1948 and signed by India just a year after independence, makes no mention of or reference to caste as a basis for discrimination, though it does make specific reference to race, colour, gender, ethnicity, religion, etc. Similarly, the International Convention on Elimination of All Forms of Discriminations (ICERD), adopted in 1965 and to which India was party, also did not refer to caste directly. In the absence of specific reference to caste-based discrimination, the issue had been raised under the alternative themes and forums. It is only in 1996 when the CERD made its first reference to caste discrimination, 'untouchability' and Scheduled Castes (although India had ratified ICERD in 1969), under the rubric of 'descent':

> "The Committee states that the term 'descent' mentioned in Article 1 of the Convention does not solely refer to race. The Committee affirms that the situation of the Scheduled Castes and Scheduled Tribes falls within the scope of the Convention".
>
> The CERD further observed:
>
> "It is noted that although constitutional provisions and legal texts exist to abolish untouchability and to protect the members of the Scheduled Castes and Tribes, and although social and educational policies have been adopted to improve the situation of members of Scheduled Castes and to protect them from abuses, widespread discrimination against them and the relative impunity of those who abuse them point to the limited effect of these measures. The Committee is particularly concerned at reports that people belonging to the Scheduled Castes and Tribes are often prevented from using public wells or from entering cafes or restaurants and that their children are sometimes separated from other children in school, in violation of Article 5 (f) of the Convention."

Likewise, though the Indian government ratified International Covenant on Civic and Political Rights (ICCPR) in 1979, it was almost twenty years later in 1997 the Committee first noted serious shortcomings in the performance of the government to guarantee basic human rights to Dalits:

> "Despite measures taken by the government, members of the Scheduled Castes and Scheduled Tribes, as well as the so-called backward classes and ethnic and national minorities continue to endure severe social discrimination and to suffer disproportionately from many violations of their rights under the Covenant, *inter alia*, inter-caste violence, bonded labour and discrimination of all kinds. It regrets that the *de facto* perpetuation of the caste system entrenches social differences and contributes to these violations. The Committee also recommended that further measures be adopted, including educational programmes at national and state levels to combat all forms of discrimination against these vulnerable groups, in accordance with Article 2."

In 1996 and 1997, the UN Special Rapporteur on Racism and Racial Discrimination enquired with the Indian government about the situation of 'untouchables' in the country, requesting the relevant information to be sent to him. The Special Rapporteur's report on the results of his enquiry speaks for itself:

> "The report recalls that communications concerning the situation of untouchables in India were sent to the government in December 1996 and August 1997. In its reply, the government rejected allegations that it tolerated untouchability, provided the Special Rapporteur with a list of the measures taken to curb discrimination between castes and maintained that a practice that is so old cannot be eliminated rapidly. The Special Rapporteur noted the discrepancy between the facts alleged and the government's reply and stated that a visit to India would permit him to evaluate the situation in cooperation with the government and the communities concerned."

When the Indian government submitted its first report to the Committee for Elimination of Discrimination Against Women (CEDAW) in 2000, the Committee raised many questions on the plight of Dalit women. Noting that Dalit women seem to be as yet an untouched sector, the Committee asked for various particular measures. In response, the Government of India provided details to say that various measures – legal and developmental – are being taken for the improvement of Dalit women. The final comments of the Committee included:

> "The Committee is concerned with the continuing discrimination, including violence, suffered by women of the Dalit community, despite the passage of the Scheduled Castes and Scheduled Tribes (Prevention of Atrocities) Act of 1989.The Committee considers that widespread poverty, such social practices as the caste system and son preference, as reflected in a high incidence of violence against women, significant gender disparities and an adverse sex ratio, present major obstacles to the implementation of the Convention."

The resolution of the Bellagio Consultation to the WCAR in Italy (January 2000), organised by the International Human Rights Law Group, was one such attempt which recommended that caste discrimination against Dalits be taken up at the WCAR and the Prep Com meetings. It also urged the need to address the concerns of similarly oppressed communities such as Buraku in Japan and Korea, Osu in Nigeria and Roma-Sinti peoples of Europe.

The First Prep Com of the World Conference, which was held four months later in Geneva (May 2000), adopted five broad themes of the Provisional Agenda for World Conference. Among other items, "sources, causes, forms and contemporary manifestations of racism, racial discrimination, xenophobia and related intolerance" received priority and were put on the agenda.

With input from the Bellagio resolution it was suggested at the First Prep Com that theme 1 includes caste under the theme of 'descent'.

During its 52nd session of the UN's Sub-Commission on the Promotion and Protection of Human Rights in Geneva in August 2000, Dalit bodies along with other groups like Buraku made several submissions. In response to these efforts, on 11 August 2000, the Sub-Commission unanimously passed a resolution to commission expert-member R.K.W. Goonesekere to prepare a working paper on "discrimination based on occupation and descent". The term 'discrimination' based on occupation and descent provides ample scope to highlight the issue of untouchability, caste-based discrimination and violence against Dalits in South Asia, as well as similar kinds of discrimination faced by the Buraku, Roma, and certain other communities in Senegal and Mauritania. The objectives of the working paper were to: (i) identify communities who continue to experience discrimination based on occupation and descent; (ii) examine existing constitutional, legislative and administrative measures for the abolition of such discrimination; and (iii) make any further concrete recommendations and proposals for the effective elimination of such discrimination.

Based on the findings of the working paper, the Sub-Commission stated that it would consider what course of action it should take to address this problem. A preliminary working paper was presented by R.K.W. Goonesekere during the Sub-Commission's 53rd session in 2001, in which he declared that:

> "Discrimination based on work and descent is a long-standing practice in many societies throughout the world and affects a large portion of the world's population. Discrimination based on descent manifests itself most notably in caste- (or tribe-) based distinctions. These distinctions, determined by birth, result in serious violations across the full spectrum of civil, cultural, economic, political and social rights. Likewise, the nature of a person's work or occupation is often the reason for, or a result of, discrimination against the person. Persons who perform the least desirable jobs in a society are often victims of double discrimination, suffering first from the nature of the work they must perform and suffering again by the denial of their rights because they perform work that is unacceptable. In most cases, a person's descent determines or is intimately connected with the type of work they are accorded in the society. Victims of discrimination based on descent are singled out, not because of a difference in physical appearance or race, but rather by their membership in an endogamous social group that has been isolated socially and occupationally from other groups in the society."

From 5 to 7 September, 2000, the governments of many Asian-Pacific countries held expert seminars to set an agenda of themes to be addressed at the WCAR. Various NGOs took this opportunity to raise the issue of caste discrimination against Dalits.

In Asia expert seminar in Bangkok (September 2000), there was a general support from the few members of CERD. R.V. Pillai (Indian member of CERD) stated that CERD had decided that the issue of caste is relevant on the basis of occupation and descent-based discrimination. Justice P.N. Bhagwati, chairperson of the seminar, closed the debate by stating that CERD has put the matter to rest by holding that caste is discrimination on the basis of occupation and descent. And, as result of this, the draft recommendations of the seminar made reference to caste discrimination in several places, associated with "descent and work occupation".

Asia expert seminar in Bangkok was followed by a preparatory conference in Teheran. The most startling development at the WCAR Asia-Pacific Regional Preparatory Committee meeting held in Tehran (February 2001) was the statement by Government of Nepal admitting the problem of caste discrimination against Dalits in its country and declaring that the issue should be squarely addressed in the WCAR. The forthrightness of the Nepalese government was a refreshing contrast to the Indian government which again refused to acknowledge that the issue of caste discrimination merits attention by the WCAR.

In a post-Durban development, however, the CERD in its 65th session held from 5 to 23 August, 2002, took fairly bold position and referred to caste as form of descent and work-based discrimination. One of the startling features of this session was the representation from a number of African countries, which brought out the discrimination based on caste and caste- like social institutions in their countries. The CERD general recommendation refers to caste in a number of contexts as under:

> "Reaffirmed that discrimination based on 'descent' includes discrimination against members of communities based on forms of social stratification such as caste and analogous system of inherited status which nullify or impair their equal enjoyment of human rights."

> "To take measures against any dissemination of ideas of caste superiority and inferiority or which attempt to justify violence, hatred or discrimination against descent-based communities."
>
> "To educate the general public on the importance of affirmative action programmes to address the situation of victims of descent-based discrimination."

The recommendations of the CERD are fairly comprehensive in nature and recognised the discrimination based on descent and work involved in caste and caste-like social stratification in Asia and Africa. This, in short, is the position of UN, which has evolved over a period of time.

Durban Conference and the Debate: Is Caste Race?

Thus the efforts by the Dalit organisations from India and Nepal and Buraku from Japan and others in securing the recognition to the discrimination based on caste, social origin and other bases could bring only limited gains in receiving approval of the respective governments either to include caste as an explicit category or extension of descent-based discrimination so as to include caste-based discrimination under its purview. The CERD merely responded to the demands of the groups like untouchables of India and Nepal and Buraku of Japan to examine the meaning and application of the existing provision of 'descent limb' of the definition of 'racial discrimination' in Article 1 (1) of the International Convention on the Elimination of All Forms of Racial Discrimination (ICERD) to include the other forms of discriminations. The CERD also explored the possibility of addressing the issue of caste and other forms of discrimination under other clauses, articles, charter bodies and instruments. From the historical efforts of groups from Asia since the mid-sixties, it emerged that the UN has been unable to bring the issue of discrimination associated with non-race-non-colour categories such as caste and social status/origin under its purview due to the limitations of its own framework.

However, the issue came into sharp focus during the Durban conference wherein the Dalits, particularly from India and Nepal, and Buraku from Japan, put forth their claim to either recognise the discrimination based on caste and social origin or alternatively extend the meaning and scope of descent-based discrimination to cover these two forms of discrimination. The efforts of Dalit groups on the eve of Durban conference brought the issue in open in public domain in India. The government, the civil society organisations, individual activists and academicians responded to the taking of caste issue in the UN conference.

The Government of India as we have seen, has been arguing in the UN human rights bodies that caste discrimination is not an issue relevant to the evaluation of its performance vis-à-vis the human rights conventions to which it is party. Thus, the official position has been quite clear. In one of the interventions, the government argued:

> "Article 1 of the International Convention on the Elimination of All Forms of Racial Discrimination (ICERD) includes in the definition of racial discrimination the term 'descent'. While castes and tribes are systems based on 'descent' since people are normally born into a particular caste or a particular tribe, it is obvious that the use of the term 'descent' in the Convention refers to 'racial descent'. Communities which fall under the definition of Scheduled Castes and Scheduled Tribes are unique to Indian society and to its historical process and do not come under the purview of Article 1 of the Convention. Caste-based discrimination should not, therefore, have been brought within the discussion in this Committee, which is charged solely with the responsibility of looking into racial discrimination."

In the context of Durban conference, the government took the position:

> "We are firmly of the view that the issue of caste is not an appropriate subject for discussion at this conference – it is neither legitimate nor feasible nor practical for this World Conference or, for that matter, even the UN to legislate, let alone police, individual behaviour in our societies. The battle has to be fought within our respective societies to change thoughts, processes and attitudes; indeed, the hearts and souls of our peoples."

The official position thus stated that caste is not race and that caste is an internal matter of India and any problem arising out of this should not be taken to any international forum. We have enough number of internal mechanisms and only these internal instruments or also internal forums should be used/approached for redressal of grievances, if there are any.

The responses and discussion by the academicians and civil society organisations before the Durban conference centred on these two issues, namely, Is caste race? and Should the caste-based discrimination be addressed in international forums, if Dalit and other organisations wish to do so? Most of papers included in this volume addressed these issues.

Drawing from the theoretical insights, some argued that caste cannot and should not be treated as race and therefore should not find a place in international bodies, which deal with racial discrimination. André Béteille, who in fact set the ball rolling, argued that "treating caste discrimination as a form of racial discrimination and, by implication, caste as a form of race, the UN is turning its back on established scientific opinion" and goes on to add that "it is sad but true that many forms of invidious discrimination do prevail in the contemporary world". But, to assimilate or even relate them all to "racial discrimination will be an act of political and moral irresponsibility". Dipankar Gupta cautions that "once we use the language of race to the caste situations, the emphasis shifts from removing the scourge of caste from Indian society to making one's caste identity a fixed political resource". D.L. Sheth observed: "To enter into a debate about whether or not to equate caste with race would be futile. For it is easy to show theoretically, sociologically and scientifically that the Asian phenomenon of caste is in some basic respect dissimilar to the western phenomenon of race and cautions that if the demand to see caste as race is accepted – and casteism is 'officially' viewed as a manifestation of racism – the social and democratic movements against caste in India will have to revise their ideological and organisational objections to the caste system that have been developed and effectively used to counter it."

However, others perceived the conceptual issue of interface between caste vis-à-vis race quite differently and argued that treating race as biological category and differencing it from other categories such as caste on that basis is to ignore the recent development in theoretical research on race. Gerald D. Berreman has argued elsewhere that anthropologists today overwhelmingly recognise that race is no more a biological or genetic fact than is caste. Both are social constructions: both arbitrarily separate and rank people according to culturally specific valued qualities (e.g., ritual purity in India; moral and psychological qualities in America) that are falsely regarded as innate. As race is socially constructed and acted upon in the form of racism, it is real and devastating – just as are caste and casteism. Berreman quotes André Béteille's article wherein Béteille wrote: "Treating caste as a form of racism is politically mischievous; what is worse, it is scientifically nonsensical." Berreman responded by saying that "what is in fact 'scientifically nonsensical' is Professor Béteille's misunderstanding of 'race'. What is 'mischievous' is his insistence that India's system of ascribed social inequality should be exempted from the provisions of a UN Convention whose sole purpose is the extension of human rights to include freedom from all forms of discrimination and intolerance – and to which India, along with most other nations, has committed itself."[1]

In a similar vein, T.K. Oommen observed that stony academic pronouncement that race is a biological category and caste is a social category and therefore there is no relationship between these two is unsustainable for two reasons. First, according to the latest research, race as a biological concept does not have any validity. So much so the American Anthropological Association has recommended to the US Government to eliminate the term 'race' in the 2010 Census because research in human genome shows that DNA of human beings is 99.9% alike irrespective of race. Therefore, what is relevant is not race, but racism, that is, the ranking of human beings based on their presumed biological origins and features. Similarly, caste as a social category is constructed on the basis of imagined attributes but casteism, that is preferential treatment to one's fellow castemen and caste discrimination based on the belief that some caste are inferior and others superior are of great significance. In contrast to racism, which is practised on the basis of physical differences, caste discrimination is anchored to values.

Gail Omvedt argued that while caste has nothing to do with race, the justifications of caste discrimination have a lot to do with the social phenomenon of racism. Teesta Setalvad also observed that, it is racism, and not the theory of race, that the Dalit movement as a whole seeks to link its condition and demands world understanding, international condemnation and support. Swami Agnivesh and Valson Thampu argued that the UN conference is not envisaged to be an academic exercise on race, but an initiative to address the evils of intolerance and discrimination in whichever form they exist. Else, the words 'xenophobia' and 'related intolerance' would not have found a place in the ambit of the conference. The basic question is not if caste is generically identical or related to race. It is if caste perpetuates intolerance and discrimination as race does. The mandate of the world body is not to shoot down race or caste, it is to rid the world of intolerance and discrimination in its myriad forms.

Should Dalits Use International Forums?

A related issue that a reasonably good number of papers have discussed is the efforts of Dalits to address the issue of caste-based discrimination in international forums like the UN. Should Dalits address the issue of caste in international forums or should it be dealt with only locally? The Indian government's official position was clear, since caste is not race and that it does not fall within the scope of Durban conference and so it should be treated as an internal matter. That country has enough number of internal mechanisms and only these internal instruments should be used/approached for redressal of grievances, observed Soli Sorabjee. Few variations in the positions figured in the discussion, one supporting the use of international forum by Dalits, another opposing the Dalit interventions and yet another one indicating that like others, the Dalits should have right to address the issue internationally but nothing much would be gained by international interventions. One of the most representative positions which opposed Dalits taking the issue to international forums is by P. Radhakrishnan. He observed that "India's pernicious caste practices have been part of the malignancy of Hindu society which can be extirpated only on Indian soil and only through social reforms and constitutional means, it can be gainsaid that in India's changed stature as a sovereign democratic republic Ambedkar himself would have found it ludicrous and even abhorrent to showcase caste, even as a tableaux, in an alien land and through a world body of which India is a member country – and added that even as an independent nation India should continue to be the "white man's burden", and also continue to have a big brother to clean up its augean stables. The UN summits and conferences, whether on racism or reptiles, should be non-issues to India "unwashed millions". He adds: "If they want to improve their lot and if the changes for it have to be substantive, the victim groups and those concerned about them should directly take on the might of the Indian state."

Others took different position and supported Dalits' right to use international forums but felt that it would not result in any gains and may even have adverse consequences locally. For instance, Dipankar Gupta observed: "When the government says that going to Durban will not help fight caste in India and that is why such a trip should not be allowed, it is being clearly unfair. It has never applied the same standards to other junkets involving other people. Of course, nothing tangible will come out of Durban conference, but with what face can the government use the same efficacy criteria in this case and not in others?" Seth argued on similar line and stated that the "internationalisation of caste-based injustice is in itself a worthwhile objective provided it strengthens rather than weakens the institutional and organised efforts against casteism. This is possible only if caste is presented as a caste and not forcibly fitted into the category of race, and at the same time, an attempt is made to promulgate an international charter against caste discrimination. This might yield new perspectives on those forms of discrimination in other societies of the world that have hitherto been seen only in the context of race".

Third view, however, deviates significantly from the above-mentioned positions. Some argued that by denying the use of international forums, in fact the government has been unfair to Dalits. It has never applied the same standards to other junkets involving other people – with what face then can the government use the same efficacy criteria in this case and not in others?" The Dalit activists argued that the issues related to women, labour, environment and the like have been discussed in international forums quite regularly. By singling out and opposing the democratic and lawful right of participation in international forums, including the WCAR, in fact the government revealed discriminatory attitude against a minority community. They also argued that there are no justifiable grounds to treat caste issue as an internal matter of India. Can anybody say that the apartheid regime in South Africa was an internal matter of that country? Did the apartheid regime come to an end merely because of internal movement of South Africans? They also raised question that, is it not that Indian government itself used the UN forum in addressing the issue of apartheid, Palestine and Roma community. Martin Macwan argued that the premise of the Government of India, that the problem of caste-based discrimination against Dalits is an internal matter, is based on weak grounds. He further argued that Dalits firmly believed that obviously the problem of Dalits has to be sorted out internally. But, the Indian government is a signatory to the charter of human rights since 1948. In addition, India has ratified the International Covenant on Economic, Social and Cultural Rights and the International Covenant on Civil and Political Rights in April 1979. Besides, India is a signatory to the resolution by the CERD on racial discrimination. The United Nations Covenants, including the one on the racial discrimination, are democratic and internalised external mechanisms to which the Indian government is a signatory. And that provision of descent-based discrimination, under which inclusion of the caste-based discrimination is sought by Dalit organisations, was introduced at the instances of Indian government, observed Martin Macwan. And, therefore, the World Conference Against Racism is an internal mechanism with respect to India, because India freely chose to ratify CERD in 1969, thus making it binding upon the nation.

Some argued that it is not true to say that Ambedkar would not have preferred such interventions. N. Paul Divakar and Ajai M. made reference to Ambedkar's efforts and interventions in Round Table Conferences held in London in the early 1930s. Thorat has provided elsewhere the direct evidence of Ambedkar's efforts to take the issue of untouchables in UN, right at the time of passing the Human Right Charter in 1947. As early as 1946, Ambedkar had represented the case of the untouchables to UN under the banner of slavery. In a letter to W.E.B. Du Bois in early 1946, Ambedkar had written:

> "There is so much similarity between the position of the Untouchables in India and of the position of the Blacks in America and that the study of the latter is not only natural but necessary" and further added that "I was very much interested to read that the Blacks of America have filed a petition to the UNO. The Untouchables of India are thinking of following suit".[2]

Thorat has also addressed elsewhere the question of omission of non-race-non-colour categories of discrimination and the pre-occupation of the UN with race and colour as only source of discrimination at the time of enactment of Human Rights Charter in 1948. The reasons for this exclusion of the caste and caste-like categories are not far to seek. The UDHR is partly a product of its times when racism and discrimination were primarily understood in the context of the decline and dismantling of European colonialism. The internal struggles of the discriminated groups of the peoples for freedom existing within the different colonies in Africa and Asia were overshadowed by the struggles of similar groups such as Blacks in USA and Europe. This resulted in certain priorities or emphases on certain communities of the former European colonies, in the process the claims of movements from within the former colonies of Asia such as the caste struggle against untouchability and discrimination in India were neglected. This neglect of historical claims of deprived people in South Asia is partly responsible for the omission of caste and other social categories identical to race and colour from UDHR. In fact, Du Bois, an African American academician and activist who was engaged in this process on behalf of African-American in USA prior to the passing of Human Rights Charter in 1946, expressed his concern about the narrow canvass of UN on Human Rights Charter and the geo-politics of its adoption. In one of his letters Du Bois wrote:

> "Other groups of people, notably the Indians of South Africa, the Jews of Palestine, the Indonesians and others are making similar petitions. I have on my desk a letter from Dr. B.R. Ambedkar, an

untouchable of India, in which he intimated that they may make appeal."[3]

Du Bois has also shared similar concerns in late 1944 about the American Jewish Committee's "Declaration of Human Rights" – a six-point statement that "greatly disappointed" by its failure to mention Africans and Asians "being deprived of rights". How appropriate was it, he asked, to call a document "very easily understood [as a] declaration of Jewish rights [having] apparently no thought of the rights of Blacks, Indians, and South Sea Islanders," a declaration of human rights?[4]

Renewed Discussion on Persistence of Discrimination

The debate and discussion that took place in the context of Durban conference also led to renewed discussion on the current status of Dalits. The campaign materials prepared by the NCDHR and other organisations were very extensive which highlight the continuing discrimination and deprivation and failure of the government and its machinery in providing justice to the Dalits. Some of the papers in this volume, including the one by N. Paul Divakar, and Ajai M. highlight the plight of Dalits. Due to the denial of rights to property, education, civil and political rights Dalits suffered from intense deprivation. The papers in this volume indicate that there has been only a marginal change in the situation of Dalits during the last fifty years.

In 2000, of the total SC households in rural area, only about 17% pursued cultivation as an independent (self-employed) occupation. About 12% were employed in some kind of non-farm self-employment activities (or business). In rural areas, thus, about 28% of SC households had acquired some access to fixed capital assets, (agricultural land and non-land assets) to which Dalits did not have access in the past. This was still a very low proportion compared with 56% for other households (non-SC/ST households). In urban area also, as compared to other households (35.5%), the access to capital assets to SCs was low (27%). Evidence shows that in 2000 the figures of landlessness and near-landlessness among the SCs in vicinity of 75%. Thus, since about three-fourths of the SC persons/households are either landless or near-landless, their main occupation turns out to be wage labour. Therefore exceptionally high percentage of the SC households depends on wage labour (casual and regular) – about 62% in rural area and urban area.

The SC workers also suffered from possible discrimination both in employment and wage earning in the labour market. Disparities between the SCs and others are reflected in the unemployment rate. Unemployment rate for SCs was about 5% as compared to about 3.5% for other workers in rural and urban areas. The data on the wage earning revealed disparities between SC wage labour and other labour; in 1999-2000, the average weekly wage earning of an SC worker (at 1993-94 prices) was Rs.174.50 compared to Rs.197.05 for other workers.

With lack of access to fixed sources of income and high incidence of wage labour associated with high rate of underemployment and low wage earning, the SC households suffer from low income, and high incidences of poverty. This is reflected in the proportion of persons falling below a critical minimum level of consumption expenditure, what is called the 'poverty line'. In 2000, about 36% of SC persons were below the poverty line in rural area as compared to only 20% for others (non-SC/ST); in urban areas, the gap was slightly larger 39% among SCs and only 15% among others, the poverty was particularly high among the wage labour in rural and urban areas – varying between 40 and 50% in rural and urban areas.

In addition to property rights, SCs have also suffered from exclusion and discrimination in education. There are large gaps in literacy rate and level of education between them and others. High dropouts in schools, poor quality of education and discrimination in education are some of the educational problems faced by SCs. In 1991, literacy rate among SCs was 37% compared to 58% among the non-SCs/STs. The literacy rate was particularly low among the females, (23%) – two times less compared with other women. School attendance was about 10% less among SC boys than other boys, while the difference is about 5% among the girls. Number of studies also observed discrimination in the school in various forms.

The Dalits perform quite badly on the situation of health. In 1998, at least 56% of SC women suffered from the anaemia. The incidence of morbidity among the children is high, more than three-fourths of SC children are anaemic, one-fifth to one-third suffered from fever, and another one-fourth from Acute Respiratory Infection (ARI) and diarrhoea. The extent of malnutrition and undernutrition among the SC children is high, as more than half of them suffered from this problem. High morbidity and child mortality among SCs is closely linked with poverty and low educational status, and with discrimination in access to health services. High incidence of illiteracy, poverty and discrimination reduces the capacity of SCs to demand and utilise the public health services.

There is also significant evidence on the economic discrimination against the SCs in labour and other markets. Violation of civil rights includes prohibition of SC to use public places and utilities such as wells, water tapes, temple, tea stall, restaurant, community bath, road, and other social services. Practice of untouchability and social discrimination continues to be of high magnitude. During the period between 1981 and 2000, a total of 3,57,945 cases of crimes and atrocities were committed against the SCs. Thus, annually, an average of about 22,371 cases of general crimes and atrocities were committed on the SCs during 1981-2000. The break-up of the atrocities and violence for the year 2000 includes 486 cases of murder, 3,298 of grievous hurt, 260 of arson and 1,034 of rape, and 18,664 cases of other offences.

Towards Consensus

Amidst the contentious issues, few papers also discussed the consequences of Dalit engagement at national and international levels in the post-Durban period. Dalit organisations and others who took the initiative to start a campaign succeeded up to a great extent in creating visibility at the national and international levels and evolved a common consensus on number of issues. Mari Marcel Thekaekara observed:

> "In spite of the world leaders buckling under pressure, the NCDHR had much to celebrate. Against all odds, it took the issue of caste discrimination to Durban and got the whole world to sit up and take notice. Just before the Durban conference, the National Human

Rights Commission admitted that the situation for Dalits was intolerable and lent its support to the NCDHR. The UN Human Rights Commissioner and heads of some countries publicly recognised the problem of Dalits. The declaration produced by the parallel NGO conference, affirmed the conclusions of the CERD and the United Nations Sub-Commission on the Promotion and Protection of Human Rights that untouchability, bonded labour, manual scavenging and other caste-based abuses are repugnant and insidious forms of racial discrimination. The conference was a movement builder and an organising tool that connected grassroots NGOs with international actors."

Smita Narula observed: "It also ensured that the governments of the countries where caste discrimination continues to be practised and condoned would no longer be able to escape scrutiny at home or abroad."

At its 53rd session, the Sub-Commission for the Promotion and Protection of Human Rights received and discussed the working paper submitted by R.K.W. Goonesekere, wherein it was pointed out that the focus of the paper was on Asia which studies the discrimination based on work and descent. It was also mentioned that the problem was not limited to Asia alone and that it existed in some parts of Africa and perhaps in South America too. In its decision, the Sub-Commission decided to entrust Goonesekere with the preparation of an expanded working paper on the topic of discrimination based on work and descent in other regions of the world. At its 54th session, in view of the fact that Goonesekere was not re-elected to the Sub-Commission and was therefore unable to fulfil the mandate entrusted to him, the Sub-Commission adopted a decision, in which it was decided to entrust Asbjorn Eide and Yozo Yokota with the preparation of the expanded working paper.

The successful participation of Dalits in WCAR is a pointer to the fact that Dalits from India and various groups of sympathizers within India along with Dalits from other South Asian countries and also discriminated groups from other countries have forged a national as well as global solidarity network to work unitedly for elimination of discrimination based on descent and work. It was because of the coordinated efforts of this national and global solidarity network that the CERD passed the general recommendation on descent-based discrimination on August 22, 2002, wherein it reconfirmed that the term 'descent' in Article 1, paragraph 1 of the Convention does not solely refers to 'race' and has a meaning and application which complements the other prohibited grounds of discrimination which would also include discrimination on the basis of caste and analogous systems of inherited status, as a violation of the Convention.

The expanded working paper, "Discrimination Based on Work and Descent" by Asbjorn Eide and Yozo Yokota, stated the fact that discrimination based on work and descent is prevalent in many African countries. The sources show that endogamous groups of musicians and artisans (blacksmiths, potters, musicians/bards or 'griots', leather workers, weavers, hairdressers/barbers and others) are found in over 15 ethnic groups and at least 14 modern states in West Africa. As a consequence of the endogamous and social isolation of these low caste-like ethnic groups, various kinds of human rights violation take place. As a matter of fact, segregation in housing/residence, bar on inter-marriage and commensality, and access to public places and services, poverty and wretchedness and large-scale violence whenever these communities have tried to alter the social norms, are some of the ways through which discriminatory practices are maintained in these traditional African societies. We can very well say that caste-like discrimination is not confined to South Asia alone. It is very much prevalent in other parts of the world, though the form and degree may vary from place to place.

In an important decision, the UN Sub-Commission on the Promotion and Protection of Human Rights, on 13 August 2003, adopted a resolution to entrust Eide and Yokota with the task of preparing another working paper on the topic of discrimination based on work and descent, with a view to fulfilling the mandate given in Sub-Commission's resolution, in order to examine legal, judicial, administrative and educational measures taken by the governments concerned; to identify additional communities affected by discrimination based on work and descent; and to prepare a draft set of principles and guidelines for all relevant actors, not only national or federal governments but also local governments as well as private sectors such as corporations, schools, in cooperation and collaboration with relevant international human rights treaty bodies and United Nations organs and agencies, taking full account of the contents of the Committee's general recommendation.

In the light of developments at the international level there seems to be at least a move towards some general consensus on the issue of caste discrimination against Dalits and similar groups from Asia and Africa. Some papers observed that "one thing seems to be in sight that the Dalit movement has now entered a new phase which would not only seek its own liberation by utilising all available channels/means – both national or international – but would also have close association with other discriminated groups from around the world as well as various groups inside the country to end discriminations on the basis of caste, social origin and other related forms of discriminations".

Notes

1. Berreman, Gerald D., "Caste and Race: Reservations and Affirmations", paper presented in an international seminar on "Beyond Durban: Caste and Race Dialogues", at South Asia Institute, Iowa State University, Ames, Iowa, USA, October 4-6, 2002.
2. Thorat, Sukhadeo, "Caste, Race and United Nation's Perspective on Discrimination: Coping with Challenges from Asia and Africa", paper presented at an international seminar on "Beyond Durban: Caste and Race Dialogues" at South Asia Institute, Iowa State University, Ames, Iowa, USA, October 4-6, 2002.
3. Letter by Ambedkar to DuBois and reply by DuBois to Ambedkar dated 31 July 1946, courtesy Dr. Gary M. Tartakov, Amrhest, USA.
4. Lewis, David Levering, *W.E.B. DuBois: Fight For Equality and the American Century (1919-1963)*, p. 503, Henry Holt and Company, New York, 2000.

UN and Dalit Intervention

Chapter 1

UN Bodies and the Dalits

A Historical Review of Interventions[1]

N. PAUL DIVAKAR AND AJAI M.

Several groups from Asian and African countries, which suffer from discrimination due to reasons other than race or colour, have been advocating with the UN Commission on Human Right (particularly, with the Committee on Elimination of Racial Discrimination CERD) to bring them under its purview and treat them as "Discriminated groups" for the purpose of CERD. The untouchables (or Dalits) from India, Nepal, Bangladesh, Sri-Lanka, Pakistan and Buraku from Japan who suffer from intense discrimination based on social origin (such as caste or social status) have been advocating for over a decade to recognise and bring them under the purview of the UN Commission. Several groups from African countries have also presented the evidences of intense discrimination associated with caste and other forms of social stratification. These communities from Asia and Africa highly diverse in geographical and historical origin share to a greater or lesser extent several key characteristics that are inherently productive of discrimination and human rights violation. A number of Dalit and other organisation from India have been raising the issue of caste-based discrimination in the international bodies, particularly the Human Right Commission and CERD.

This paper traces the historical evolution of the emergence of the caste related discrimination in the international discussion, discusses the interpretations of the caste related discrimination of major international covenants, examines the arguments for and against for inclusion of caste-based discrimination under the general rubric of exclusion and discrimination addressed by CERD, provides an account of the interventions made thus far towards their recognition by UN bodies and need of addressing the Dalit issues in the UN.

Who Are Dalits?[2]

The term evolved in South Asia out of the struggles of various movements to fight untouchability and caste-based discrimination. These movements chose the name because it could bring together all the affected 'untouchable' communities in South Asia under a common ideological appellation. Strictly speaking, then, the term Dalits refers to the people of South Asia who were outside the pale of the hierarchical caste system, and, therefore, deemed outcastes.[3] Regarded as the most marginalised of the castes in society, they were and are still considered polluted and assigned the occupations deemed too defiling for other castes to do, such as earth work, manual scavenging, sweeping, disposing of corpses, skinning and tanning of animal hides for leather making and sandal making, digging graves, etc. Born into her or his caste, a Dalit could not hope to escape her or his low social status or to employ himself in a more lucrative or socially respectable occupation. In this way, caste-based discrimination entrenched itself early on into the very structure of South Asian society based on descent and occupation.

Conceived more broadly, the term Dalit could be extended to communities, which suffers from discrimination on the basis of descent and occupation. This would include such communities as the Burakumin in Japan, Osu in Nigeria, Roma-Shinti (gypsies) in Europe and those that suffer similar discrimination in Senegal. Considered in this broad term, that is, those who suffer from discrimination based on descent and occupation, would constitute the single largest discriminated community on the globe today. In India alone, Dalits number 160 million, according to 1991 Government of India

Census. However, if the population of Dalit Sikhs, Dalit Christian and similar groups are included, this figure would sharply jump to 240 million. Without regard to religion, the total population of Dalits in the South Asia region may be in the range of 260 million. If we add the Burakumin in Japan, Osu in Nigeria, Roma-Shinti in Europe and other communities from ten countries who suffers from similar discrimination on the basis of descent and occupation, then rough estimate will put their population that equals to almost 500 million, or approximately 10% of the total world population.

The term Dalit, drawn from the Marathi language, literally means 'crushed' or 'broken', but more generally Dalits is translated into 'oppressed people'.

Historical Overview of the Emergence of Caste Discrimination Issue at International Level

Though Dalits, whether strictly or broadly conceived, constitute a vast section of the global population spread across numerous countries, the systemic discrimination they face has historically not been recognised by the United Nations and other international human rights bodies. It is only recently that the discrimination against Dalits has been receiving increasing recognition and concern in the UN and international human rights bodies. This section attempts to trace the history and evolution of the emergence of caste discrimination as a primary concern for these bodies. This evolution has four major phases as I see it.

I. Dr. B.R. Ambedkar's Interventions during the Movement for Independent India, 1930-1947.
II. Omission of Caste from UDHR, CERD: Causes and Consequences, 1947-1996.
III. Emerging Recognition of Caste Discrimination in UN Human Rights bodies, 1996-2000.
IV. Growing International Effort to Address Caste Discrimination in the UN WCAR, 2000-present.

Phase 1: Dr. Ambedkar's Interventions before the British Round Table Conference, 1930-1947

In the course of the movement for an Independent India, the problem of 'untouchability' and caste discrimination against Dalits became an international issue. It was due to the radical, bold stand that Dr. B.R. Ambedkar, a leading Dalit figure of the 20th century and architect of India's Constitution, made on behalf of the "Depressed Classes"[4] as the British prepared to transfer political power to the dominant castes who influenced the character of the Independence Movement.

He made one of his most brilliant stands on behalf of the "Depressed Classes", in 1930-1931 at the Round Table Conference in London, in which leading representatives of the various communities in Indian Sub-Continent met to discuss and come to an agreement on the main points that must be included in the Constitution for a self-governing India. Ambedkar plainly told the Conference that the "Depressed Classes" would not accept any Constitution for self-rule that did not guarantee them equal citizenship and fundamental rights and abolish the practice of untouchability.

> "The Depressed Classes cannot consent to subject themselves to majority rule in their present state of hereditary bondsmen. Before majority rule is established their emancipation from the system of untouchability must be an accomplished fact. It must not be left to the will of the majority. The Depressed Classes must be made free citizens entitled to all the rights of citizenship in common with other citizens of the State."

Ambedkar's bold, radical stance was strongly resented by many dominant-caste leaders of the Independence Movement, who accused him of dividing the Independence Movement and playing stooge to the British Raj. They lectured him that the situation of the 'untouchables' was an internal matter and urged him to wait until Independence was achieved and the British were gone to raise their concerns and demands.

Ambedkar, however, saw things quite differently. He knew that the majority dominant caste vision of *swaraj* had little in common with the Dalits vision of *swaraj.* Though a few reform movements emerged to address the practice of 'untouchability' and uplift the 'untouchables.' They relied too heavily on orthodox dominant-caste leaders and supporters to take any radical action to challenge the caste system and the practice of 'untouchability.' Religious orthodoxy and deep-rooted caste prejudice confined the nationalist movement to largely representing the aspirations of the dominant castes for political and economic power. Ambedkar was keenly aware of this.

> 'I am sorry to say, Sir, that I have been deluded. I find now that although some of our people would desire me and others to join them in their demand for Dominion Status, they do not join with us in demanding that the Government which will be set up under that Dominion Status shall be responsible to the people of India as a whole. I never thought there would be this division of opinion, and that I should have to stand up to defend the position we take. Now, Sir, speaking on behalf of the Depressed Classes I cannot honestly consent to responsible Government or to Dominion Status unless I can be sure that the people for whom I speak are to have a place in that constitution.

Ambedkar's intervention at the Round Table Conference articulated an authentic democratic vision of Swaraj based on equality, liberty and fraternity, principles alien to a social order based on caste division and hierarchy. It was largely as a result of Ambedkar's intervention at the Round Table Conference that the Indian Constitution guaranteed fundamental rights, established universal suffrage, abolished 'untouchability' and guaranteed reservation in legislature and government services for Dalits, Adivasis and minorities.

After Independence, to fulfill the Constitutional provisions, the Indian government has passed various legislations to enforce the abolishment of 'untouchability' and remove the barriers of caste discrimination impeding the socio-economic progress of the Dalits. This included the Protection of Civil Rights (Untouchability Offence) Act, 1955 and various land reform laws to redistribute land to the landless, a large and disproportionate percentage of whom were and still are Dalits. Later years saw the passage of the Bonded labour (Abolition) Act, 1976, Employment of Manual Scavengers and Construction of Dry Latrines (Prohibition) Act, 1993, Jogini Act No. 10, and the Scheduled Castes/Scheduled Tribes (Prevention of Atrocities) Act, 1989 and Rules, 1995. The central and state governments also established SC/ST Welfare Departments soon after Independence. In the early 1990s, the Central Government passed legislation establishing the National Commission for SC/ST and the National Human Rights Commission.

There is no doubt that none of these would have been possible without the interventions made by Dr. Ambedkar, to ensure that Independent India would be based on a democratic Constitution that guaranteed equality, fundamental rights and dignity to all regardless of caste. Had he succumbed to his contemporary dominant – caste nationalists who pressured him to settle these matters internally, Dalits would be much worse off than they are today.

Phase 2: Omission of Caste from UDHR, CERD: Causes and Consequences, 1948-1996

Though the dynamics of the movement for Independence in India gave a visibility to untouchability and caste discrimination in the international community, this severe form of discrimination, affecting, at that time, 43 million people, faded from international consciousness soon after India's Independence in 1947. The Universal Declaration of Human Rights (UDHR) adopted by the India and the other nations of the world in 1948, just a year after India's Independence, makes no mention of or reference to caste as a basis for discrimination, though it does make specific reference to race, colour, gender, ethnicity, religion, birth etc.

The UDHR itself is partly a product of its times when racism and discrimination were primarily understood in the context of the decline and dismantling of European colonialism. The internal contradictions of the peoples existing within the colonies were overshadowed by the their struggles against European colonial rule. This resulted in certain distortions of history favouring the elite communities of the former European colonies, while marginalising the subaltern movements from within these same former colonies, such as the Dalit struggle against untouchability in India. These distortions of history are partly to blame for the omission of caste from UDHR, CERD and other international human rights conventions.

This omission had serious negative repercussions on the ability of the UN to address discrimination against Dalits and on the ability of Dalits to raise their concerns at the UN. For many years, the UN treaty bodies such as ICCPR, ICESCR, CERD, CEDAW and ILO examined the problems affecting India – including illiteracy, wretched poverty, bonded labour, child labour, religious discrimination, human rights violations, gender discrimination-without realising that caste discrimination is a major factor contributing to these problems and that the majority of people who suffer from these problems are Dalits.[5] The primary determining factor of illiteracy, poverty, child labour, etc. in India was invisible to the UN bodies because none of the convention made specific reference to caste as a significant basis of discrimination on par with race, skin colour, gender and ethnicity.

The omission of any explicit reference to caste meant that the caste dimension of discrimination was often overshadowed by another dimension of discrimination more easily recognised outside South Asia. A case of rape against a Dalit woman, for example, would be raised under CEDAW, but the caste dimension of the case would be completely marginalised due to the dominance and wider recognition of the gender dimension. As a result, Dalits could only make use of limited spaces in the UN human rights bodies to raise the issue of discrimination based on caste. For example some human rights organisations raised the issue of discrimination based on untouchability under the theme of Contemporary Slavery in the World Conference on Human Rights in Vienna in 1993; in the working Group on Minorities under the Sub-Commission on the Promotion and Protection of Human Rights; and, in the Prevention of Discrimination and Protection of Minorities. Alternate reports were also submitted to some UN treaty bodies by various human rights organisations and NGOs.

Phase 3: Emerging Recognition of Caste Discrimination in UN, 1996-1999

Though India ratified CERD in 1969, it was not until 1996 that the CERD Committee made its first explicit reference to caste discrimination, 'untouchability' and Scheduled Castes:

> "The Committee states that the term 'descent' mentioned in Article 1 of the Convention does not solely refer to race. The Committee affirms that the situation of the Scheduled Caste and Scheduled Tribes fall within the scope of the Convention."

> "It is noted that although constitutional provisions and legal texts exist to abolish untouchability and to protect the members of the Scheduled Castes and Tribes, and although social and educational policies have been adopted to improve the situation of members of Scheduled Castes and Tribes and to protect them from abuses, widespread discrimination against them and the relative impunity of those who abuse them point to the limited effect of these measures. The Committee is particularly concerned at reports that people belonging to the Scheduled Castes and Tribes are often prevented from using public wells or from entering cafes or restaurants and that their children are sometimes separated from other children in school, in violation of Article 5 (f) of the Convention."

Likewise, though the Government of India ratified ICCPR in 1979, it was almost 20 years later in 1997 when the Committee first noted serious shortcomings in the performance of the Government to guarantee basic human rights to Dalits.

> "Despite measures taken by the government, members of the Scheduled Caste and Scheduled Tribes, as well as the so-called backward classes and ethnic and national minorities continue to endure severe social discrimination and to suffer disproportionately from many violations of their rights under the Covenant, inter alia, inter-caste violence, bonded labour and discrimination of all kinds. It regrets that the de facto perpetuation of the caste system entrenches social differences and contributes to these violations. The Committee also recommended that further measures be adopted, including education programmes at national and state levels to combat all forms of discrimination against these vulnerable groups, in accordance with Article 2, paragraph 1 and 26 of the Covenant's (*Consideration of Report by India to the Human Rights Committee, CCPR/C/79/Add. 81, August 4, 1997*).

In 1996 and 1997, the UN Special Rapporteur on Racism and Racial Discrimination enquired with the Indian Government about the situation of 'untouchables' in the country, requesting the relevant information to be sent to him. The Special Rapporteur's report on the result of his enquiry speaks for itself:

"The report recalls that communications concerning the situation of untouchables in India were sent to the government in December 1996 and August 1997. In its reply, the government rejected allegations that it tolerated untouchability, provided the Special Rapporteur (SR) with a list of the measures taken to curb discrimination between castes and maintained that a practice that is so old cannot be eliminated rapidly. The SR noted the discrepancy between the facts alleged and the government's reply and stated that a visit to India would permit him to evaluate the situation in cooperation with the government and the communities concerned." (E/CN.4/1998/79, paras, 53, 57-59)

Needless to say, the Indian Government has to date not permitted the Special Rapporteur to visit India as he requested.

When the Indian Government submitted its first report to the CEDAW Committee in 2000, the Committee raised many questions on the plight of Dalit women. Noting that Dalit women seem to be as yet an untouched sector, the Committee asked for various particulars on:

- The status of untouchability
- The impact of the caste system on the educational status of Dalit women
- Atrocities inflicted on Dalit women
- Bonded labour
- Women involved in manual scavenging
- Living standards of women in agriculture, and minimum wages
- Implementation of the SC/ST Prevention of Atrocities Act, 1989.

The Government of India provided details to say that various measures – legal and developmental – are being taken for the improvement of Dalit women. The final comments of the Committee were as follows:

"The Committee is concerned with the continuing discrimination, including violence, suffered by women of the Dalit community, despite the passage of the Scheduled Castes and Scheduled Tribes (Prevention of Atrocities) Act of 1989."

"...*The committee considers that widespread poverty, such social practices as the caste system and son preference, as reflected in high incidence of violence against women, significant gender disparities and an adverse sex ratio, present major obstacles to the implementation of the Convention (CEDAW/C/2000/1/CRP.3/Add, dt. 31.04.2000; emphasis added).*"

Phase 4: Emerging Recognition of Caste Discrimination in Preparation for the UN WCAR, 2000-2001

In the last two years various Dalit and pro-Dalit organisations have made a series of intense interventions in United Nations human rights bodies and in international meetings, which were organised in preparation for the forthcoming World Conference Against Racism (WCAR) to be held in South Africa in September 2001. Many of these interventions have been made in collaboration with other communities such as Burakumin and Roma Shinti who face similar discrimination based on descent and occupation. The main objective of these interventions has been to ensure the inclusion of caste discrimination related to occupation and descent against Dalits and other communities on the main agenda of the WCAR.

(a) Bellagio Consultation to World Conference - January 2000, Italy

The resolution of the Bellagio Consultation to the WCAR in Italy, organised by the International Human Rights Law Group, recommended that caste discrimination against Dalit be taken up at the WCAR and the Preparatory Committee (more popularly known as Prep Com) meetings. It also urged the need to address the concerns of similarly oppressed communities such as Buraku in Japan and Korea, Osu in Nigeria and Roma-Shinti peoples of Europe.

(b) 1st World Conference Preparatory Committee Meeting – May 2000, Geneva

The First Prep Com of the World Conference adopted the following five broad themes of the Provisional Agenda.

- Sources, causes, forms and contemporary manifestations of racism, racial discrimination, xenophobia and related intolerance;
- Victims of racism, racial discrimination, xenophobia and related intolerance;
- Measures of prevention, education and protection aimed at the eradication of racism, racial discrimination, xenophobia and

related intolerance, at the national, regional and international levels.

- Provision of effective remedies, recourse, redress, [compensatory] and other measures at the national, regional and international levels;
- Strategies to achieve full and effective equality, including international cooperation and enhancement of the United Nations and other international mechanisms in combating racism, racial discrimination, xenophobia and related intolerance, and follow-up.

With input from the Bellagio resolution as well as submissions by NCHDR and other IDSN members, it was suggested at the 1st Prep Com that Theme 1 include caste and Theme 2 include Dalits. The Government of India, however, adamantly opposed these submissions and stuck to its stand that the issue of caste discrimination has no relevance to race and therefore should not be an agenda item for the WCAR. It also stated that 'untouchability' practices no longer existed and that the government had taken adequate measures to end any further forms of discrimination against Dalits.

(c) UN Sub-Commission on the Promotion and Protection of Human Rights, 52nd Session – August 2000, Geneva

During its 52nd Session in Geneva in August 2000, NCDHR along with other members of the IDSN made several submissions to the Sub-Commission. On 11 August 2000, the Sub-Commission unanimously passed a resolution stating the following:

The resolution also commissioned Expert Member R.K.W. Goonesekere to prepare a working paper on "discrimination based on occupation and descent." The term discrimination based on occupation and descent provides ample scope to highlight the issue of "untouchability", caste-based discrimination and violence against Dalits in South Asia, as well as similar kinds of discrimination faced by the Buraku, Roma, and certain communities in Senegal and Mauritania. These communities will be the subjects of the working paper by Goonesekere. The three objectives of the paper are to:

- Identify communities who continue to experience discrimination based on occupation and descent.

- Examine existing constitutional, legislative and administrative measures for the abolition of such discrimination; and
- Make any further concrete recommendation and proposals for the effective elimination of such discrimination.

Based on the findings of the working paper, the Sub-Commission stated it would consider what course of action it should take to address this problem.

In its oral right of reply statement to the Sub-Commission, the Indian Government opposed these resolutions. It reiterated its standard position that caste is not race and, therefore, does not come under the purview of the World Conference. The government stated that "it is not persuaded that (caste) falls within the ambit of racism, racial discrimination and related intolerance...even though the caste system has been based on birth, it is obvious that the term 'descent' in the Convention (on the Elimination of All Forms of Racial Discrimination [CERD] clearly refers to racial descent.

(d) Asia-Pacific Experts Seminar: Asian NGOs lobby strongly for inclusion of caste discrimination in WCAR – September 2000, Bangkok

From 5-7 September 2000, the government of many Asian-Pacific countries held an Experts Seminar to set an agenda of themes to be addressed at the WCAR. Various NGOs took this opportunity to raise the issue of caste discrimination against Dalits. Asian Human Rights Commission and Asian Legal Resource Centre, both based in Hong Kong, along with 17 NGOs submitted a statement that caste discrimination against Dalits was one of the vital themes that need to be addressed by the WCAR.

As at the 1st Prep Com in May and the Sub-Commission Session in August, there was immediate opposition from the Indian Government on the familiar grounds that the issue of caste was not relevant to the issue of race and racism as caste is not race. However, as at the Sub-Commission, the Experts Seminar did not find the Indian Government's position convincing. R.V. Pillai, member of CERD, stated that CERD had decided that the issue of caste is relevant on the basis of occupation and descent-based discrimination. Justice Bhagwati, chairperson of the seminar, closed the debate by stating that

CERD has put the matter to rest by holding that caste is discrimination on the basis of occupation and descent.

Due to the strong stand made by the NGOs, the immediate outcome of this was that the draft recommendations of the Seminar made reference to caste discrimination in several places.

(e) World Conference Asia-Pacific Regional Preparatory Committee Meeting, Tehran, February 2001

The most startling and welcome development at the WCAR Asia-Pacific Regional Preparatory Committee Meeting held in Tehran was the statement by the Government of Nepal admitting the problem of caste discrimination against Dalits in its country and declaring that the issue should be squarely addressed in the WCAR. The forthrightness of the Nepalese Government was a refreshing contrast to the Indian Government, which again refused to acknowledge that the issue of caste discrimination merits attention by the WCAR.

The NGO Forum at Tehran came out very strongly in favour of including caste discrimination on the WCAR agenda. The Declaration of the Asia-Pacific NGO Forum stated that even though states have enacted laws to protect the rights of Dalits communities (broadly conceived), it is the states themselves who often violate these laws. It also recommended that the respective governments of countries home to Dalit populations create transparent monitoring mechanisms to ensure the implementation of legislation intended to ban caste-based discrimination.

Outcome: Visibility of Caste Discrimination in International Community Today

In the last five years, the UN human rights bodies have increasingly recognised the need to address the issue of descent and occupation based discrimination, including caste discrimination, against Dalit, Osu, Burakumin, Roma/Shinti and other communities spread across the globe. CERD, ICCPR, CEDAW, Special Rapporteur on Racism and the Sub-Commission have all explicitly recognised this kind of discrimination to be in violation of international human rights law and impressed upon the respective governments the urgent need for action to combat it, including utilising international human rights mechanisms.

At each and every intervention, national and international NGOs have also provided enormous solidarity to the affected communities, particularly supporting them in their efforts to ensure that this kind of discrimination finds a place on the agenda of the WCAR.

At the experts Seminar in Bangkok in September 2000, the governments of the Asia Pacific countries included references to caste in their (draft) recommendations to the WCAR. Closer to home in South Asia, the Government of Nepal just last month (February 2001) at the Asia Prep Com in Tehran, admitted the problem of caste discrimination against Dalits in its country and argued that the issue be squarely addressed in the WCAR.

Current Position of the Indian Government on Caste-based Discrimination

In light of these recent developments, the Indian Government sounds increasingly irrational as it shouts itself hoarse to deny a problem that everybody else can plainly see. Similar to its predecessors in the Nationalist Movement who opposed Ambedkar for raising the specific concerns of the Dalits with regard to Independence in the Round Table Conference, the Government of India today is also opposed to the efforts of Dalits who seek the support of the United Nations in the context of the World Conference Against Racism in strengthening India's own constitutional obligations to abolish 'untouchability' and caste-based discrimination.

The Government of India argues to the UN human rights bodies, including the WCAR, that caste discrimination is not an issue relevant to the evaluation of its performance via-a-vis the human rights conventions to which it is party. This argument is based on three main premises:

1. Caste is not Race: The term 'caste' does not denote race or racial grouping and even the term 'descent' in Article 1 of the CERD Convention refers solely to racial descent. Therefore, does not fall within the ambit of racism, racial discrimination or related intolerance.

2. Use Internal Mechanisms, not External ones: Numerous laws and government schemes exist already within the country to promote the welfare, rights and socio-economic conditions of the Scheduled Castes. These are adequate to protect the Dalits from discrimination and to promote their socio-economic advancement; therefore, there is no need to utilise international human rights mechanisms and bodies to strengthen these laws.
3. Change takes Time: Change is a slow process and respective countries are doing all they can to solve the problem.

Dalit Position

A. Caste may not be Race

Caste may not be Race, but it does not mean that there is no discrimination against Dalits. The first premise of the Indian Government's argument against inclusion of caste discrimination in the WCAR has already been dealt with and dismissed by the CERD Committee as mentioned above:

> "The Committee states that the term 'descent' mentioned in Article 1 of the Convention does not solely refer to race. The Committee affirm that the situation of the Scheduled Castes and Scheduled Tribes fall within the scope of the Convention."

The argument put forth by the Government of India that caste is not race has no relevance and is meaningless as it is based merely on semantics. Whether or not caste is the same as race, the reality is that caste is a basis of discrimination on par with racism and apartheid and severely reducing the quality of life of at least 160 million of its own citizens. To attempt to smoke screen this reality behind semantic gymnastics on the definitions of race and descent obviously never intended by CERD is nothing but sophistry.

B. Fallacy of the Internal – External Argument

The second premise of the Government of India's argument that the problem of caste-based discrimination against Dalits is an internal problem concerning India only sounds very familiar. Did not the dominant caste majority at the time of Ambedkar make the same argument to him when he used the Round Table Conference as a platform to ensure that Depressed Classes would not be second-class citizens in an Independent India? As Ambedkar already convincingly proved the hollowness of this premise 70 years ago, I do not need to do it again here, except to reiterate that it is largely because Ambedkar intervened on behalf of the Dalits before the Round Table Conference and other similar forums that India today has a democratic Constitution that guarantees fundamental rights such as universal suffrage and equality to all regardless of caste.

Ambedkar showed that boundaries for solutions to the problem of caste discrimination are not to be drawn around the village, district, state or nation. What is an internal solution or an external solution should not be determined by geographic borders or national boundaries. A solution is internal when it makes use of democratic, constitutional and legal space, bodies and mechanisms to which the state by its own volition is obligated. The United Nations World Conference Against Racism is an internal mechanism with respect to India, because India freely chose to ratify CERD in 1969, thus making it binding upon the nation. Terrorism or some other un-democratic methods are external solutions.

Therefore, to raise the problem of caste discrimination for attention and action by CERD and the WCAR is not to seek an external solution. It is rather a constitutional, lawful and democratic means to by which Dalits and other similarly discriminated communities hope to strengthen laws, which until now have failed to protect them from discrimination. Utilising international human rights mechanisms can only empower their respective governments to fulfill their own constitutional and legislative obligations, thus strengthening the national integrity and renewing the nation in its striving to approach the ideals conceived in its Constitution.

C. Laws have been reduced to mere paper tigers

The second premise also states that laws and legal mechanism exist within the country to protect them from discrimination and that Dalits should utilise these, instead of seeking solutions outside in the World Conference Against Racism or other UN human rights bodies. This is the only point in the Government of India arguments that we accept as valid, only to qualify it by emphatically stating that Dalits have every right to look for solutions at the international level when they have exhausted the national mechanisms to no or little positive effect. For more than 50 years since independence, Dalits have utilised the laws and mechanisms existing within the country to try to promote and protect their rights, only to find that dominant caste values, prejudice and vested interests prevalent across all levels of government and society so seriously debilitate the political will to implement and enforce these laws that they have been emasculated

Non-Performance of Government of India to Enforce Existing Laws

Below is presented a variety of the existing laws and policies which the GoI always is keen to mention in its reports to the UN human rights bodies in order to prove that it is doing all that it can do to combat untouchability and caste discrimination and that, therefore, there is no need for United Nation human rights bodies to intervene to strengthen the existing laws with international human rights mechanisms to which it is party. A quick overview of the outcomes of these policies will show that the government has failed to implement these laws effectively.

Manual Scavenging

The greatest scourge of untouchability is felt by manual scavengers whose job is to clear fasces from public and private latrines and dispose off dead animals. Deemed to be polluting and filthy as an occupation, this job is assigned exclusively to Dalits and that too to the Dalit women.

> This practice has long been outlawed. The passage in 1993 of the *Employment of Manual Scavengers and Construction of Dry Latrines (Prohibition) Act, 1993* which prohibited employment of scavengers and the construction of dry (non-flush) latrines. The *SC/ST (POA)* Act also made the act of employing manual scavengers a punishable offence. Despite these national laws,

- More than 800,00 Dalits are employed as manual scavengers today, according to the official statistics. The violators are

Municipal Corporations and the state governments themselves who employ manual scavengers.

- The Manual Scavengers Prohibition Act has not been adopted in 12 states.
- Though in 1992, the Government allocated a sum of Rs.4,640,000,000 (US$ 99.2 million) to a launch a national scheme to identify, train and rehabilitate manual scavengers throughout the country, the National Human Rights Commission and the Ministry of Social Justice and Empowerment have described the implementation of this scheme as poor.

Bonded Labour[6]

Article 23 of the Indian Constitution as well as *The Bonded Labour (Abolition) Act 1976* and the SC/ST (POA) Act prohibit bonded labour and mandate stiff punishments for bonded labour employees. The Bonded Labour (Abolition) Act aims to release all bonded labourers from bondage, cancel any outstanding debts, prohibit the creation of new bonded labour agreements and order the economic rehabilitation of freed bonded labourers by the state.

It is the most important to note that the evidence shows that the vast majority (87%) of bonded labourers in India come from Dalits and Adivasi communities.

A lack of reliable statistics regarding the numbers of bonded labour in India is a serious impediment to eliminating forced labour. Between 1976 and 1999, the Government of India identified a mere 280,340 bonded labourers. This figure is in stark contrast to the 1.25 million Bonded labourers in Tamil Nadu alone as estimated in 1995 by the Commission on Bonded Labour appointed by the Supreme Court. An accurate assessment of the number of people who are bonded, particularly at the local level, is essential if the government is to develop appropriate action plans to address the problem. This glaring, fundamental lacunae in the implementation of the Bonded Labour Act has been recognised by the ILO Committee of Experts, which recommended in its 2000 report that the

"[Indian] Government undertakes a comprehensive survey using valid statistical methodology to be broken down by gender. The Committee encourages the Government to utilise the services of an independent body to assist in developing the methodology and conducting the survey."

Even where official surveys have identified bonded labourers, action to release the bonded labourers in 'the shortest possible period' has not followed.

- An initial survey in 1997 by the Tamil Nadu State Government identified 25,000 bonded labourers. Of these only 2,444 had been released in the subsequent two and a quarter years, according to a High Court deposition filed by K. Chandrasekar on behalf of the organisation Development and Education for Worker.
- The deposition also stated that only 50% of those released (1,236) released had been given their full rehabilitation assistance of Rs.9,000 (US$197), to which they were entitled under the government regulations.

Failure to bring prosecutions against those using bonded labour is another flaw, which cripples the efficacy of the *Bonded Labour Act.*

- Only .32% of identified bonded labour cases lead to arrests and only 0.08% to imprisonment, according to human rights worker Vivek Pandit (*Prevention of Atrocities*, Vidhayak Sansad, Maharashtra, India, 1995).

With this kind of performance record of the government, the law, for all its good intentions, has no ability to empower bonded labourers to seek protection from the law or to deter offenders from continuing to employ bonded labour.

Economic Situation of Dalits

The caste involves exclusion of low caste untouchables (or scheduled castes) in multiple spheres, and high levels of economic deprivation and poverty. Based on official data, we present a brief sketch of the socio-economic condition of the SCs: with respect to occupation, ownership of agricultural land and non land capital assets access, education and health, employment and poverty.

Access to Agricultural Land and Capital

Data on occupation patterns capture the access of SC households to sources of income. The NSS provide data on economic activities or occupations in terms of proportion of self employed and wage labour households. While the former is a measure of access to capital assets like agricultural land and non-land capital assets (from which historically SCs have been debarred), the latter indicate continuing dependence on the traditional occupation of wage labour

In 2000 of the total SC household in rural area, about 17% pursued cultivation as an independent(self-employed) occupation. About 12% were employed in some kind of non-farm self-employment activities (or business). In rural areas thus, about 29% of SC households had acquired some access to fixed capital assets, (agricultural land and non-land asset). This was still a very low proportion compared with 56% for other households (non SC/ST households). In urban area also as compared to other households (35.5%) the access to capital assets to SC was low (27%).

Inadequate access to fixed capital assets, lead to exceptionally high dependence of the SC household on manual wage labour. In 2000, the wage labour household account for 61.40% of all SC households in rural area and 26% in urban area, compared to 25.50% and 7.45% for other households. In urban areas 38% of SC households also depend on regular wage and salaried jobs. Thus about 62% of the SC household in rural and 63% in urban area continue to depend on wage employment and only about 28% had acquired some access to fixed capital assets As we shall see latter although close to one-third has acquired access to fixed capital assets, most of them are small and marginal farmers and petty business holders.

Information on the ownership of agricultural land by the SC in rural area provides some insights for low proportion of self employed cultivators among the SC household in rural area. In 1991 about 13% of SC households were landless and 87% own some land. Among the latter (that is land owning household), about 56% owned less than one acre (of which 47.50% own less than half acre). Thus the landless and near landless (that is those owning less than one acre) account nearly 70% of the total SC household in 1991. Evidence for more recent year, 1999-2000 from alternative source namely NSS Employment survey put the figures of landless and near land less ness among the SCs in the vicinity of 75%.

Employment/Unemployment

Since more than 60% of the SC workers in rural and urban areas depend on wage employment, their earnings are determined by level of employment and wage earning, daily or regular. The SC worker seems to suffer from possible discrimination both in employment and wage earning in the labour market. The NSS data on employment for the year 2000 indicate that the SC worker suffered from low employment. The differences in the employment rate based on usual principal status (which capture open employment/unemployment) between the SC and others are not large. However differences emerge clearly for employment rate based on Current Daily Status (CDS), which capture the underemployment of the employed workers. In 2000 the CDS employment rate in rural area was 46% for SC male workers, compared with 48.40% for other male worker. Similarly the CDS employment rate for SC workers in urban area was 45.8%, compared to 49.9% for other households. Disparities between the SC and Others are reflected in the unemployment rate. Unemployment rates based on CDS for SC was about 5.0% as compared to about 3.5% for other worker in rural and urban area.

Poverty

With high incidence of wage labour associated with high rate of under-employment and low wage earning, the SCs household suffer from low income, and high incidences of poverty. This is reflected in the proportion of persons falling below a critical minimum level of consumption expenditure, what is called the poverty line. In 1999-2000, about 35.43% of SC person were below the poverty line in rural areas as compared to 21% among others; in urban areas the gap was slightly larger 39% of SC and only 15% among others.

The variation in poverty ratio across household types or occupational groups is striking. In 1993-94 the incidence of poverty was about 60% among agricultural labour followed by 41.44% among non-agricultural labour. The level was relatively low for persons engaged in self-employed activities in agriculture (37.71%) and in the non-agricultural sector (38.19%). Poor SC household were over-represented in these groups. In urban area the incidence was astonishingly high among the casual labour (69.48%). The poverty was also high among the self-employed households (54%). High incidence of poverty among those SC households engaged in self-employment in agriculture and in non agriculture indicate that they are normally concentrated in small farm and low income petty businesses. The recent data on monthly per capita expenditure (MPCE) for more recent year, 1999-2000 also bring out disparities between the two groups; practically for all household types the MPCE for the SC was lower than the other households.

Access to Education and Health

In addition to property rights SCs have been denied right to education. There are large gaps in literacy rate and level of education between them and others. High drop out in school, poor quality of education, discrimination in education, are some of the educational problems faced by SCs. In 1991 (latest census year for which data are available) literacy rate among SCs was 37% compared to 58% among the non SC/ST. The literacy rate was particularly low among the female (23%), two time less compared with other women. School attendance is about 10% point less among SC boys than other boys, while the difference is about 5% among the girls. Number of studies also observed discrimination in the school in various forms.

Evidence based on National Family Health Survey data for 1998-99 revealed wide gap between SC and others in health status and access to health services. Early marriage and high fertility characterised the SC population. The difference in the total fertility rate between them and others is by more than a year. The percentages of SC women using any method and their exposure to family planning messages or media are comparatively low. Infant (83%) and child mortality (39%) among the SCs is higher than others, 61% and 22% respectively.

In 1998-99 at least 56% of SC women suffered from the anaemia. More than 70% women's delivery took place at home and only one-fifth took place in institution and more than 40% of these are delivered by Traditional Birth Attendant (Village Dais).

The incidence of morbidity among the children is high, more than three-fourth of SC children are anaemic, one-fifth to one-third suffered from fever, and another one-fourth by ARI and diarrhoea. The extent of malnutrition and under nutrition among the SC children is high, as more than half of them suffered from this problem. High morbidity and child mortality among SCs is closely linked with poverty and low educational status, and with discrimination in access to health services. High incidence of illiteracy, poverty discrimination reduces the capacity of SCs to demand and utilise the public health services.

Untouchability and Atrocities

We now highlight SCs social disadvantages with particular reference to the practice of untouchability, and discrimination in public spheres and atrocities covered under the Protection of Civil Rights Act, 1955 and Prevention of Atrocities Act, 1989. Violation of civil rights include prohibition of SC to use public water bodies such as well, water taps, temple, tea stall, restaurant, community bath, road, and other social services. Practice of untouchability and social discrimination continue to be of high magnitude. During nineteen years period between 1981 to 2000, a total of 3,57,945 cases of crime and atrocities were committed against the SC. Thus annually an average of about 22,371 cases of general crimes and atrocities were committed on the SCs during 1981-2000. The break-up of the atrocities and violence for the year 2000 include 486 cases of murder, 3,298 grievous hurt, 260 of arson and 1,034 cases of rape, and 1,18,664 cases of other offences.

Economic Discrimination and Exclusion

Preceding sections show the disparities in ownership of capital assets, employment, education and access to health services between the SC and other households. Although there has been some improvement in the ownership of capital assets, still a large proportion of SC households continue to depend on the traditional occupation of wage labour. To what extent are the disparities and segregation into traditional occupations, the legacy of the past exclusion, and to what extent is it conditioned by continuing discrimination and exclusion in the market and non market transactions or both is an important question?

The issue of economic discrimination, particularly the market exclusion and discrimination has been almost neglected in the Indian social science research.

Very few studies have empirically examined the nature and magnitude of economic discrimination. Limited evidence points towards the presence of discrimination against the Scheduled Castes in labour and other factor markets. Studies observed that high landlessness could be due to weak resource position but also due to the discriminatory working of the land market which reduces the access of SCs to purchase and leasing of agricultural land (Nanchariah 1988). Studies also provide evidence that discriminatory working of the labour market may explain low employment rate and wage earning of the SC workers. Banerjee and Knight (1991) observed that: "there is indeed discrimination by caste, particularly job discrimination" and that "discrimination appears to operate at least in part through traditional mechanism, with untouchables disproportionately represented in poorly-paid dead-end jobs.." Even if discrimination is no longer practised, the effects of past discrimination could carry over to the present. This may help to explain why discrimination is greatest in operative jobs, in which contracts are more important for recruitment, and not in white-collar jobs in which recruitment involves formal methods. The economic function which the system performs for favoured castes suggests that taste for discrimination is based, consciously, or unconsciously, on economic interest, so making prejudice more difficult to eradicate".

Beside land and labour markets some studies also found discrimination in occupation, credit and other market transactions. An Andhra Pradesh study (Venketeswarlu 1990) observed social ostracism being used against SCs in changes of occupation. In Karnataka, Khan (1995) revealed that nearly 85% of the respondents continued with their traditional occupation and only 15% could make a switch over. In the urban areas, however, 56% had experienced a shift away from traditional occupation. An Orissa study (Tripathy 1994) observed discrimination in land lease, credit and labour markets in rural areas. Nearly 96% of untouchable respondents in one village and all untouchable respondents in the second village were discriminated against in wage payment; 28% in one village and 20% in the other faced discrimination in the share of rent; and discrimination in interest rate charged by moneylenders was found in both villages. A Coimbatore study (Harriss Kannan and Rodger 1990) observed that caste contact played a major role in sources of information and means of access to jobs.

Urgency in Addressing the Dalit Issue in the WCAR and the UN Level

- The severity of caste-based discrimination, related to descent and occupation, is on par with racism and apartheid, which the Indian Government, the UN, international community and human rights community actively addressed and intensely combated.
- The scope and enormity of caste-based discrimination encompasses 240 million Dalits in India alone, and almost 260 million in South Asia.
- Existing national legislations to prevent caste-based discrimination in South Asian countries have not been effective due to poor implementation, which itself is the result of a lack of political will of the governments involved. In spite of the various legislations, implementing agencies and monitoring bodies constituted, severe discrimination against Dalit persists. In fact, such discrimination has only intensified in recent years as evidenced by the alarming rise in violent atrocities and mass massacres against Dalits.
- Caste-based discrimination also afflicts a vast population of Dalits in other South Asian countries, namely Bangladesh, Nepal, Pakistan and Sri Lanka. Marginalised communities in Japan (Burakumin), Senegal, Nigeria (Osu), and Europe (Roma) also suffer from a similar kind of discrimination based on descent and occupation. All these communities, constituting an enormous section of the global population, also require an immediate attention and action.
- Despite completing more than 50 years of Universal Declaration of Human Rights, the international community and the UN bodies have failed to adequately address this major crime against humanity.

Conclusion

The situation today confirms Ambedkar's worst fears, that even with Constitutional guarantees and legislations in place, these would become mere paper tigers if they were not enforced by laws punishing their violation. Dr. Ambedkar could not have been more clairvoyant about the future of Independent India when he stated before the Round Table Conference:

> "It is one thing for the Constitution to say that no man shall be discriminated against, and that every man shall be guaranteed the free enjoyment, and so on: but I know as a matter of fact that we are hard up against facts, and that people will not allow us to enjoy the rights which are given to us by the Constitution. I am as certain of that as I am certain of my existence. I do not want merely a paper guarantee. The whole community will be against us, and we shall certainly never enjoy one-tenth of what is given to us... What is the use of those paper rights to me unless the Constitution provides that if anyone infringes my rights he is liable to certain penalties? ... What is important to an individual is not that his/her rights should be declared but that he/she should have the remedy in order to enforce those rights. That is the effective guarantee of the rights in the declaration, and therefore I want that the Constitution should give me some means whereby I can get redress. When I am wrong it is no use merely saying that there is no 'untouchability' and so on."

At every level, from the village to the Prime Minister's Office, the quest for justice is an uphill battle. When in the rural village Dalits attempt to register a criminal case against a non-Dalit, the local dominant caste leaders or the local village panchayat put tremendous pressure on the Dalits not to file a case, but, instead, to accept a compromise which is often partial to the non-Dalit accused.

When the informal 'judicial' institutions of the village fail to bring justice, the Dalit goes to the police, but they refuse to register the case and tell him/her to complain to the local village panchayat. If he/she succeeds in getting his/her case registered with police, the accused are not arrested and the investigation is neglected and eventually closed. If his/her case manages to make it to the courts, it is delayed for years, dropped on technicalities, or the accused acquitted on flimsy grounds.

The reality is that, wherever he/she goes, he/she will use what mechanisms are available to him/her to seek justice, but 99% of the time they fail to bring him/her justice. At every level, he or she is denied justice, forcing him/her to go one step beyond to a greater power. Eventually all mechanisms even at the national level are exhausted. He/she brings the case to the notice of the National Human Rights Commission, which has no legal power to arrest or prosecute the accused. There is only one place left to go – to the UN, international community and human rights bodies. When this happens, as it already has, we echo Dr. Ambedkar when he stated to the Round Table Conference:

> *I protest with all the emphasis I can that we will not stand this any longer. The settlement of our problem must be a part of the general political settlement and must not be left over to the shifting sands of the sympathy and goodwill of the rulers.*

Notes

1. The authors are thankful to colleagues in NCDHR and Sakshi.
2. There have been many words used to name the present "Dalits". In pre-independence days, the most popular word used was 'untouchables', which later in the political parlance was replaced with 'Depressed Classes'. After Independence, the official term of the Government of India for Dalits became Scheduled Castes. Gandhi popularised the word, 'Harijan', the children of 'Hari'-the Hindu god. As part of his political strategy, Gandhi fought tooth and nail every attempt to regard them as non-Hindu, but Ambedkar took the exact opposite stand. Before the Round Table Conference in 1930, he said, "The first observation that I will make is this-that we, the Depressed Classes, demand a complete partition between ourselves and the Hindus. That is the first thing. We have been called Hindus for political purposes, but we have never been acknowledged socially by the Hindus as their brethren. They have taken to themselves all the political advantage with our numbers, with our voting strengths, have given to them, but in return we have received nothing. All that we have received is a treatment, which is worse than the treatment that they themselves have accorded to other communities whom they do not call Hindus. That must be the first thing, therefore, that we want to be done"

(Round Table Conference, Sub-Committee No. III (Minorities), 2nd Sitting, 31-12-1930).

3. In the creation myth recorded in the Vedas, the four main Varnas, from which evolved the caste system, were born from the body of god Brahma. The Brahmins (priestly caste), the Vedas state, were born from Brahma's head, the Kshatriyas (the warrior caste, ruler) were born from his torso, the Vaisyas (artisan, merchant castes) were born from his legs, and the Shudras (manual labourers) were born from his feet. The most significant part of this myth is that it does not include the origins of the fifth 'Varna', the Untouchables. The exclusion of Dalits clearly implies that they are not even considered of human race nor do they share in any aspect of the divine as the other Varnas do.
4. Depressed Classes refers to Dalits and Adivasis (Tribals).
5. Dr. Ambedkar highlighted this directly proportional relationship between caste status of Dalits and their socio-economic condition in South Asia before the Round Table Conference in 1930: "The helpless, hapless and sapless condition of the Depressed Classes must be entirely attributed to the dogged and determined opposition of the whole mass of orthodox population which will not allow the Depressed Classes to have equality of status or equality of treatment. It is not enough to say of their economic condition that they are poverty –stricken or that they are a class of landless labourers, although both these statements are statements of fact. It has to be noted that the poverty of the Depressed Classes is due largely to the social prejudices in consequence of which many an occupation for earning a living is closed to them. This is a fact, which differentiates the position of the Depressed Classes from that of the ordinary caste labourers and is often a source of trouble between the two". ["A Scheme of the political safeguards for the protection of the Depressed Classes in the future constitution of a self-governing India", a memorandum submitted by Dr. B.R. Ambedkar and Rao Bahadur R. Srinivasan to the Round Table Conference, Sub Committee No. III (Minorities), 31-12-1930] (Emphasis added).
6. The statistics on bonded labour came from Anti-Slavery International's submission to the United Nations Economic and Social Council Commission on Human Rights, Sub-Commission on the Promotion and Protection of Human Rights, Working Group on Contemporary Forms of Slavery, 25th Session, Geneva, 14-23 June, 2000.

Chapter 2

(UN) Touchables in Durban

MARTIN MACWAN

The UN World Conference Against Racism, Racial Discrimination, Xenophobia and Related Intolerance (WCAR) held at Durban had three major agenda themes among others: identification of the sources and causes of discrimination, identification of victims of discrimination, and working out a programme of action including possible compensatory measures to combat racial discrimination.

Racial discrimination has been broadly defined as discrimination based on grounds such as race, colour, descent, and national or ethnic origin. With a special reference to India that declined to accept 'descent' as a ground of discrimination intrinsic to the caste system, maintaining that the term is system, maintaining that the term is applicable only in relation to racial discrimination, the ICERD, in 1996 observed that, 'The situation of Scheduled Castes and Scheduled Tribes falls within the scope of the convention' (ICERD).

It needs to be reiterated that the issue of caste-based discrimination has been raised by the National Campaign on Dalit Human Rights and others on the grounds of descent which, incidentally was incorporated in the convention on Indian insistence in 1964. The National Human Rights Commission of India has opined that all nations must respect treaty bodies, especially when they have signed and ratified international conventions.

For some in India, the Durban conference was a platform to voice opinion and debate ferociously whether caste is race and whether the issue of caste-based discrimination, howsoever important, needs to be internationalised. For millions of Dalits and their sympathizers, however, the event was more than a mere debate; it was an opportunity to voice the realities of discrimination born out of their own life experiences to a world in search for solidarity. The difference in both these positions has more to do with ones social origin and less with scientific or rational characteristics.

The discussion in India has, in fact been more than a debate. Some have attempted to link internationalisation of caste discrimination with *national interest* and further, to national integrity. Some have preferred to investigate the foreign, Christian and other possible motives behind such attempts. Such allegations are not foreign to the history of Dalit assertion movements in this country where caste, and not the national Constitution, continues to be the dominant factor. In my humble opinion, the issue at the core is: Do we as a nation wish to tolerate caste-based discrimination any more?

When we talk of Dalits, we refer to manual scavenging, a practice that according to official figures employs over a million people to sustain the system of manual handling of human waste; millions of those in rural areas whose existence faces constant threat; the *devdasis* who face the threat of everyday rape by the representatives of Hindu gods right in the temple premises; millions of innocent and bright children who are forced to drop out from primary education both due to poverty and humiliation by teachers and fellow students; millions of farm workers who do not enjoy uniform legal protection with respect to guaranteed minimum wages; and above all, the millions who are victims of caste prejudice of hardcore casteists, religious fundamentalists, 'defunct' sociologists, economists and politicians of various shades and colour who trace their social origin to the 'so-called' upper caste and class. And finally we talk of Dalits who, irrespective of the faith that they may profess, suffer from discrimination arising out of a caste mind as a national character and practice.

Let me share an experience. In 1995, Navsarjan, the organisation I work with, received a complaint about an assault on a Dalit in a small village in Surendranagar district. My colleague went to the village, met the victim and advised him to file a police complaint. The victim agreed and both set off for the village bus stand. Suddenly, the victim said to my colleagues, 'Can you wait here while I consult the "Durbar" (Khsatriya person) whether should I file the complaint or not? My colleague, a young man, burning with fire of bringing about social change, was speechless. The person whose advice was being sought was none other than the individual who had assaulted the victim.

But my colleague soon gathered himself and asked the man to do what he felt right (Such is the democratic society in which we live!). The man soon came back and reported, 'The Durbar is resting and his wife has asked me to come in the evening.' Since the Durbar has reportedly gone out of station in the evening, my Dalit brother decided not to file the complaint because he had not secured prior permission from the Durbar.

The irony is that Dalits, comprising 16% of India's population, suffer from a disease, even more pathetic than the practice of untouchability – the ideological dominance of the upper castes who control not only social, economic and political power in the country but even knowledge and opinion. Even the personal experience of being discriminated against does not become an issue unless 'permitted' by the experts and the state. To disbelieve them is a necessary precondition for Dalit assertion.

There is nothing surprising about the position of the Government of India in the context of the Durban Conference; it changes colours like a chameleon at the behest of its colonial masters of the past and their racist clan. In 1975, India voted in favour of the UN General Assembly resolution that equated Zionism with Racism. USA was not as aggressive then as it was during the Durban conference because of its own political interests. In Durban, India supported USA and the European nations on issues of both Zionism as well as the demand for reparations, probably as a tradeoff on the caste question. At the Tehran preparatory conference and elsewhere, India was the big philosophic brother arguing that the concerned conference was against racism and that any inclusion of other discrimination of a general nature in its ambit would dilute the focus of the conference.

We expected it to play a leading role in shaping world opinion against racism in Durban. What it did instead was to cowardly negotiate with other nations to drop paragraph 73, wherein discrimination based on caste found expression under the language popularised in the 53rd session of the Sub-Commission on Protection and Promotion of Human Rights and the subsequent preparatory meetings to the WCAR as, 'Discrimination based on work and descent.'

The essential question is whether discrimination based on race differs in terms of its intent and end results from discrimination based on caste? However, now, the Durban frenzy has been replaced by a global zeal to end terrorism. During Durban the Dalits managed to secure positive support, both within the country and outside. They achieved more than the Government of India could, and even more, with the NHRC having decided to stand by Dalit activists and not the GoI. In this context, it is now time, therefore, to shift our attention to the realities of caste discrimination and think of ways to end it without impotent ideological hang-ups.

Some of us activists, who have addressed issues of caste violence and discrimination at the grassroots for more than two decades, through an approach that is both humane and constitutional, have lots of experiences to share. We are not academics. We are grassroots activists and Dalits working with the sole objective of securing for our masses a life of dignity, freedom and equality, not as a favour but as a right. In our opinion the internationalisation of the caste discrimination issue has helped the cause, thanks to the Indian as well as international media, and especially the Government of India, which by thoughtlessly denying the problem, has ensured maximum publicity for the issue. In the aftermath of the Durban conference, which was another opportunity to highlight the issue on which we have worked for many years, new spaces have once again been created to articulate and mobilise public opinion as to the challenges that lie ahead to end caste discrimination in India.

I have attempted to briefly summarise the concerns as follows:

1. Caste discrimination is not an Indian problem: Caste discrimination exists in India, Nepal, Pakistan, Sri Lanka, Bangladesh, and in related forms in Japan and parts of the African continent. Though India has never denied the existence of caste practices domestically, it chooses not to admit it to the world outside. The Durban conference provided an opportunity for Dalits across countries to unite and portray the Dalit issue as South Asian concern.
2. Caste discrimination is a national concern: it is incorrect to argue that caste discrimination and its existence is a problem concerning only the Dalits. The Dalits are only the victims and the existence of such discrimination is a national problem, a reflection of the failure of our Parliament and judiciary.
3. Caste discrimination is not an academic issue: For activists, the situation demands more aggressive action at the grassroots. Priority attention is required to use law, advocacy and direct action to ensure the abolition of manual scavenging and rehabilitation of scavengers; implementation of land reforms; to ensure that no Dalit children drop out from schools and for action to be taken against teachers torturing such children; implementation of reservation and its extension to the judiciary and private sector, and: against violence and for ensuring gender equality.
4. Caste discrimination is a violation of human rights: there is a need to fight the 'monumentalisation' of caste-based discrimination, with its existence attributed to incomprehensible social system or prejudices and not to the failure of the Republic. It has to be established that there is a correlation between discrimination and the lack of political will of the nation and its people to change their irresponsible, inhuman and anti-national practices and behaviour. We, as a nation, had refused to tolerate the presence of apartheid and the backlash against the civil rights movement of the blacks. We need to show the same level of intolerance towards caste discrimination and invite global attention to the issue in the true spirit of vasudhaiv kutumbkam.
5. Caste discrimination cannot end without concrete social and economic change: Discrimination is not a mere ideational phenomenon. It manifests through a set of concrete practices

around economic, social and political issues. If I am an elected village sarpanch and continue to sit on the ground while other members occupy chairs, discrimination may not appear very obvious. But only by attacking such inhuman practices can we root out discrimination.

There are six major issues that need national attention:

(i) *Land reforms*: Gandhi, Nehru and others promised land reforms to control the violent actions of tenants, which led to movements such as land grabbing in the 1920s. Vinoba Bhave tried to play middleman through his famous Bhoodan movement, ensuring that the so-called high caste zamindars and their interests were not disturbed while simultaneously creating a perception that they were generous and poor-friendly. Even the most successful land reforms in the country benefited only a few caste communities like the Patels in middle Gujarat, even as they remained grossly unimplemented when it came to Dalits (outcastes) and tribals. The nexus between land reforms and political power is much too well known. The OBCs have risen as a political force not because of reservations. Land reforms need to be fully implemented in favour of Dalits and tribals.

(ii) *Abolition of manual scavenging*: Many argue that one reason why apartheid should not be compared with caste discrimination is because while the former is a state policy the latter is not. In my view, non implementation of legal and other measures against discrimination amounts to a hidden state policy. The best example of this is the system of manual scavenging. The government that has banned the system and made its practice a punishable offence under the employment of Manual Scavengers and Construction of Dry Latrines (Prohibition) Act, 1993, is the largest agency that employs and pays over a million scavengers in the country through its various organs to manually handle human waste. Scavenging has remained a caste-based occupation and become a source of their exclusion from other jobs. It needs to be noted that one does not hear about this crude form of human rights violation under the rubric of racial discrimination. The system needs to be abolished immediately and the scavengers rehabilitated. More significantly, the entire burden for the rehabilitation of the scavenging community has been passed on to commercial banks who take the ultimate decision as to whether or not it is viable to give credit to scavengers for rehabilitation.

(iii) *Primary education*: The correlation between quality education and emancipation is well established globally. How then can we justify that 50% of Dalit children (64% Dalit girl children) are pushed out of the school system before they can complete even primary education? How do we ensure a strong nation, assuming that Dalits are part of the nation, when we cannot even ensure basic education to 16% of our population? In Gujarat, like elsewhere, most of the education budget goes towards salaries for teachers. But the state budgets gives a mere Rs. 5 a month per teacher for extracurricular activities for the development of students.

To my way of thinking, an even more serious question is whether the state that represents a certain class and caste culture, can be entrusted with the responsibility of education, especially for Dalit children. Education, if perceived as a tool of empowerment, needless to add, cannot be trusted in the hands of state agencies.

(iv) *Comprehensive legislation to protect rights of unorganised workers*: Most Dalits are landless agricultural workers. Minimum wages, being a state subject, differ from state to state. Besides, in most cases, domestic legislation is not respected. Gujarat, until recently, perhaps had the lowest minimum wage at Rs 34 per day, but the workers were actually paid as little as Rs 12. A Navsarjan study suggested that the extent of underpayment to farm workers as a class, the gap between what is paid and what should be paid, amounts to Rs. 350 crore every years in the state of Gujarat alone.

(v) *Violence on Dalits*: The systematic elimination of six million Jews by Nazis hit us hard on the face because it took place in such a short span of time. In the case of Dalits, though the 'genocide' has been systemic, it has taken place at a slow pace. The current government statistics of murder, rape and assault that dalits are subjected to paint a horrible picture if extended to a history of 3000 years. We have reason to believe that approximately 21,90,000 Dalits have been murdered, 32,85,000 raped and over 7,50,00,000 assaulted. The violence perpetrated on Dalits cannot be rooted out until long term economic, social and political measures, such as land reforms, are firmly implemented.

(vi) *Equal opportunities for Dalit women*: Most scavengers are women. They are unaccounted bonded labourers. Dalit women continue to be dragged off as temple prostitutes and it is they who are increasingly the target of caste violence. Dalit women are excluded from the normal women's struggle, so far as their representation is concerned in the decision-making bodies.

6. *Globalisation*: International cooperation is an accepted modern day aspect of our political life. The areas of cooperation are not just economic and military or combating terrorism but also acting on the Universal Declaration of Human Rights. It is an undemocratic and discriminatory practice on the part of the state to deny any section of its society the right to international cooperation for human rights.
7. *Nationalism*: This has become a buzzword. However, for most in our country the notion of the nation is limited to their own caste and class. When their sectional interests are affected they propagate that national interests are affected. The situation is worse when narrow-minded patriarchs are in power. National interests of all citizens, determined on the basic principles of dignity, equality and equal opportunity. If certain sections therefore equate raising Dalit issues on an international platform as negatively affecting national interest, it is high time that they introspect whether Dalits are a legitimate part of the nation or not.

The continuing failure of the law and moral appeals to end caste-based discrimination has once again shown that the Dalits need to develop their own agenda for social change based on the facts of discrimination. Equality is a pre-condition for effective democratic participation and that is unlikely unless Dalits rise as a united political force. Our national tragedy is that the research and knowledge that we produce is susceptible to the influence of caste and class psyche and that is one reason why it has proved to be impotent in fuelling any worthwhile social change.

The Durban conference has once again provided an opportunity to all in the nation to introspect on these vital issues of human rights.

Is Caste Race?

Chapter 3

The Official Position

SOLI J. SORABJEE

I have listened with great interest and attention to the statements and interventions and the observations of my esteemed colleague, Goonesekere. I shall briefly refer to the working paper later. Additionally, let me state that I realise the arduous job he undertook and although I do not agree with some of his conclusions, I attribute no motives to him.

In reaching any decision the first essential point is that it should be an informed decision, base on facts, a rational, detached and objective decision unswayed by passion or prejudice.

Let me state a few facts. For centuries, Scheduled Castes and Scheduled Tribes, that is the Dalits, have suffered intense and extensive social and economic discrimination because of the caste system. They have been the victims of irrational prejudices. One account of this they have laboured under severe handicaps particularly in the field of education and public services.

In view of this position, the framers of the Indian Constitution incorporated in the Constitution itself provisions for affirmative action or compensatory discrimination as some people call it. This was done by providing for reservation of jobs for Dalits in government employment and reservation of seats for them in educational institutions [see Article 15 (4) and 16 (4)]

The Constitution of India provides for reservation of seats for Scheduled Castes and Scheduled Tribes (Dalits) in the Lower House of Parliament and in the state legislatures (Article 330 and 332 respectively). When the Constitution was enacted in 1950, the reservations were to cease after 10 years. However, having regard to the conditions of Scheduled Castes and Scheduled Tribes, the Constitution has been amended from time to time, and the period of 10 years has been extended to 20 years, then to 30 years, then to 40 years and then to 50 years. At present it provides that the reservation will cease after 60 years, i.e., after 2010 (see 79th Amendment Act, 1999 in Article 334).

Article 338 provides for the constitution of a National Commission for the Scheduled Castes and Scheduled Tribes. Article 388 (5) (b) makes it the duty of the commission to enquire into specific complaints with respect to deprivation of rights and safeguards of the Dalits. 1294 complaints were received in year 2000. After examining them, action has been taken by requiring competent authorities of the states to take cognizance under the penal acts. This has been done in a majority of cases. The Constitution further provides that the Union and every state government shall consult the commission on all major policy matters affecting Scheduled Castes and Scheduled Tribes.

With the increase in the quantum of reservations of jobs and seats there were court challenges. The Supreme Court of India ruled that as a general rule reservation should not exceed 50%. The court also held that whilst there can be reservation up to 50% in the case of initial recruitment there should be no reservation in respect of promotions.

In order to further protect and promote the fundamental rights of the Dalits, the Constitution has been amended to get over and neutralise these Supreme Court judgments. An act of the state of Tamil Nadu providing for reservation up to 69% has been the subject of a constitutional amendment (see 76th Amendment Act, 1994). Article 16(4A) and (4B) have been added to the Constitution by way of amendments in order to get over the aforesaid judgment (see 77th Amendment Act 1995 and 81st Amendment Act, 2000). These articles have escaped the attention of the author of the working paper.

Article 335 of the Constitution provides that in the making of appointment in public employment, 'the claims of the members of the Scheduled Castes and the Scheduled Tribes shall be taken into consideration, consistently with the maintenance of efficiency of administration.' In order to further advance the rights and claims of the Dalits there has been a constitutional amendment, viz. 82nd Amendment Act, 2000 which provides for 'relaxation in qualifying marks in any examination or lowering the standards of evaluation' for reservation in matters of promotion for Dalits. This significant constitutional amendment finds no mention in the working paper.

There have been protests from other sections of the society and complaints of reverse discrimination. There is lot of heart burning that a student who has secured 90% cannot get admission to a college whereas a Dalit student who has secured much lower marks can get admission. The government's view is that for century's Dalits have suffered worse and more severe discrimination and these measures are felt necessary at the present stage for their advancement. Is that apartheid? Is that racism or racial discrimination?

Untouchability, which is abhorrent, has been abolished by the Constitution. Its practice is made a penal offence and stringent punishment is provided, like mandatory minimum prison sentence and also forfeiture of property in some cases (see the Scheduled Castes and Scheduled Tribes – Prevention of Atrocities – Act, 1989). This Act also contemplates formation of special courts for trial of such offences, which are enumerated in the Act. Many district headquarters have a separate special court to try the offences under the 1989 Act. Eighty exclusive special courts have been set up in various states. Other states have conferred upon the existing sessions courts the powers of special courts for trial offences under the 1989 Act.

The rate of convictions is also growing. Of course, there could be and should be more convictions but remembered that Indian criminal jurisprudence is based on the presumption of innocence and proof beyond reasonable doubt in criminal cases. Partial or ineffective enforcement cannot amount to impunity, unless there is a deliberate official policy of non-enforcement. The number of people convicted in 1996 was 1827. For the year 1997 it was 2017.

The Parliament has also passed another law, Employment of Manual Scavengers and Construction of Dry Latrines (Prohibition) Act, 1993 whereby members of the disadvantaged section of society are to be prevented from doing manual scavenging. The government has formulated a scheme for liberation and rehabilitation of scavengers and their dependents. A National Safai Karamcharis Finance and Development Corporation is being constituted to provide credit at concessional rates to ameliorate the plight of the Scheduled Castes/Scheduled Tribes. From 1997-98, 1998-99, 1999-2000, over Rs 600 million have been spent for this purpose.

It is a fact that discriminatory practices against the Dalits do persist.

An absence of effective enforcement of the legal provision is one of the causes. Urgent action in this regard is necessary and the same is engaging attention of the authorities. But non-implementation of legal provisions is not confined to Dalits. In vast country like India beset with several problems, regrettably there is non-implementation in other cases also like labour legislation, legislation for protection of children and women, environmental laws and so on. India has a free and independent media, which also exposes and condemns discriminatory practices against Dalits. Articles by Dalit groups and those espousing their cause and which are severely critical of the government are widely published in several newspapers. There is no restriction or interference with the fundamental rights of the Dalits to organise conferences and seminars in which their grievances are ventilated and demands are made for further measures and initiatives.

In fact, a major conference lasting for four days was organised in New Delhi from 1 to 4 March 2001 by the National Campaign on Dalit Human Rights India, which our distinguished member from Sri Lanka, Goonesekere, attended as an invitee of the organisers of the conference. My regret is that during his stay in Delhi for four days, he did not contact me at all. Had he done so, I would have gladly forwarded to him all relevant information. A week back there was a national seminar-cum-consultation on racism organised by the National Human Rights Commission at the National Law School of India University in which issues relating to discrimination against the Dalits were freely and forcefully discussed.

The National Human Rights Commission, whose Chairman is required to be a retired chief justice of the Supreme Court, is also empowered to look into complaints of discrimination and atrocities committed against the Dalits. Many such complaints have been entertained. Moreover, wherever constitutional provisions and laws for the protection and promotion of the rights of the Dalits are not enforced, courts in the land can be approached for enforcement of their rights and reliefs have been granted. These are some of the fora which look into and take cognizance of the conditions and the current position of Dalits in government and in society.

Discrimination on the basis of caste cannot come within the concept of racism. The accepted definition of race is a group of people of common ancestry with distinguishing physical features and colour. Attention is invited to the passage appearing at page no 361 of *The New Encyclopaedia Britannica,* volume 15, 15th edition: 'On balance, the evidence that the Indian caste system is racial in origin and that India is or was a racist society is unconvincing. Race and caste are mentioned separately in the Indian Constitution as prohibited grounds of discrimination. They are not considered to be interchangeable or synonymous. The principal architect of the Indian Constitution was Dr. Ambedkar, a Dalit. He certainly knew the distinction between race and caste. If the concept of caste was included in race there was no reason to mention them separately.'

Article 1 of the International Convention on the Elimination of All Forms of Racial Discrimination (CERD) defines the term 'racial discrimination' to mean any distinction, exclusion, restriction or preference based on race, colour, descent, or national or ethnic origin which has the purpose or effect of nullifying or impairing the recognition, enjoyment or exercise, on an equal footing of human rights and fundamental freedoms. Thus the unmistakable characteristic of racism and racist regime are segregation and exclusion of persons because of their race from high public offices, educational institutions and from public employment.

In India, Dalits are not excluded from such offices and positions. The Indian Constitution provides for ample reservation for them in educational intuitions and in public employment [see Article 15(4); Article 16(4)]. There is no country in the world which has such extensive and positive affirmative action provisions as India. Dalits have been appointed as judges of the Supreme Court and the High Court. The President of India, the highest post under the Constitution, is graced by a Dalit. Ministers in the central and state cabinets have been and are Dalits. The future Chief Justice of India in the year 2004/5 will be a Dalit. Why is there no mention of these facts in the working paper?

It cannot be denied that more is certainly required to be done to improve the conditions of the Dalits and to curb and eliminate the discrimination practices do take time before they are rooted out. But it would not be correct to overlook the measures adopted and the efforts made in that direction, and some improvements effected in the conditions of the Dalits. As acknowledged by Goonesekere, given the continuing efforts by various bodies mentioned in para 23 of the working paper and to whom credit is given by him, there is bound to be substantial improvements. My plea is that we should take a balanced, not a one-sided view of the issue we are discussing.

Chapter 4

Race and Caste

ANDRÉ BÉTEILLE

As a student of anthropology in Calcutta in the 1950s, I was recommended a book written by the well-known physical anthropologist, M.F. Ashley Montagu, some of whose other works we also had to study. The book to which I now refer was entitled *Man's Most Dangerous Myth: The Fallacy of Race*. Ashley Montagu had overstated his case somewhat, but the basic point he was making, that the widely used concept of race was politically pernicious and scientifically anomalous, had come to be generally accepted among anthropologists by the middle of the 20th century.

Some anthropologists attended to the political mischief caused by the idea of race while other exposed its scientific ambiguities. The most notable among the latter was Franz Boas, widely regarded as the father of American anthropology. In his book, *Race, Language and Culture*, he established conclusively with a wealth of empirical material the distinction between race which is a biological category with physical markers and social groupings based on language, religion, nationality, style of life or status. Boas's conclusion may be regarded as the settled opinion on the subject among professional anthropologists the world over.

"Race, Language and Culture", published in 1940, was the culmination of systematic and painstaking research by two or three generations of anthropologist. In the 19th century, when anthropology was still largely an amateur pursuit, the concept of race was widely and loosely used to cover virtually every kind of social grouping. One read about the Aryan race, the Semitic race and the Irish race. The influential French writer Count Gobineau even proposed that the different social classes in France were made to link race with caste in India. Pseudo-scientific theories of race abounded in late 19th and early 20th century in Europe and America. They made no small contribution to Hitler's disastrous racial policies in Germany. Although the English, the French and the Americans adopted a self-consciously virtuous attitude after 1945, they too produced an abundance of pseudo-scientific theories of race before World War-II.

At about the same period of time, the Indian Civil Service counted a fair number of amateur anthropologists in its ranks. Some of them have left behind valuable accounts of the tribes and castes in India. Others took an interest in race that at times amounted to an obsession. The obsessive ones found evidence of race wherever they looked. Their main confusion was between race and language, and they wrote freely about the 'Aryan race' and the 'Dravidian race'. Some treated Hindus and Muslims as belonging to different races, and others expressed similar views about the upper and the lower castes. These views, based on a confusion of categories, are now regarded as worthless from the scientific point of view. It is not as if there was no serious scientific effort by the ICS anthropologists to study the racial composition of the Indian population. Several of them attended to the problem with patience and care, combining the study of physical features with that of social customs. The most notable was Sir Herbert Risley who produced a comprehensive classification of the races of India into seven types. But the principal 'racial types' in his classification – Aryan, Dravidian, Aryo-Dravidian and Mongolo-Dravidian – were linguistic or regional categories in disguise and not racial categories at all. The subsequent classification by B.S. Guha, made in connection with the census of 1931, was less ambitious, for it did not speak of 'racial types' but only of 'racial elements' in the population of the country.

In the mid-1950s when I was a student of anthropology, most anthropologists had lost interest in the racial classification of the Indian population. Although there were many different racial element in it, it was difficult, if not impossible, to sort them out into distinct racial groups. In the 1970s, I took some initiative on behalf of Oxford University Press to update Guha's work on racial element. I approached a number of physical anthropologists, but they either declined or said that they would do it but failed to deliver. I am now convinced that identifying the races in the population of India will be an exercise in futility. Despite all the hard work done by anthropologists from Boas onward, the idea of race dies hard in the popular imagination. That is understandable. What is neither understandable nor excusable is the attempt by the United Nations to revive and expand the idea of race, ostensibly to combat the many forms of social and political discrimination prevalent in the world. It is sad but true that many forms of invidious discrimination do prevail in the contemporary world. But to assimilate or even relate them all to 'racial discrimination' will be act of political and moral irresponsibility.

Not content with condemning racism and racial discrimination, the UN now wants to take on 'racism, racial discrimination, xenophobia and related intolerance'. It has in its wisdom decided to expand the meaning of racial discrimination to accommodate exclusion or preference 'based on race, colour, descent, or national or ethnic origin'. In doing so it is bound to give a new lease of life to the old and discredited notion of race current a hundred years ago. By flying in the face of the distinctions between race, language and culture, it is seeking to undo the conclusions reached by the researches of several generation of anthropologists.

Interested parties within and outside the UN would like to bring caste discrimination in general and the practice of untouchability in particular within the purview of racial discrimination. The practice of untouchability is indeed reprehensible and must be condemned by one and all; but that does not mean that we should now begin to regard it as a form of racial discrimination. The Scheduled Castes of India taken together are no more a race than are the Brahmins taken together. Every social group cannot be regarded as a race simply because we want to protect it against prejudice and discrimination.

In the past, some groups claimed superior rights on the ground that they belonged to the Aryan race or the Teutonic race. The anthropologists rejected such claims on two grounds. First, on the ground that within the same human species no race is superior to any other, but also on the ground that there is no such thing as an Aryan race or a Teutonic race. We cannot throw out the concept of race by the front door when it is misused for asserting social superiority and bring it in again through the back door to misuse it in the cause of the oppressed. The metaphor of race is a dangerous weapon whether it is used for asserting white supremacy or for making demands on behalf of disadvantaged groups.

If discrimination against disadvantaged castes can be defined as a form of racial discrimination, there is no reason why discrimination, real or alleged, against religious or linguistic minorities cannot be phrased in exactly the same terms. The Muslims and other religious minorities will claim that they too, and not just backward castes, are victims of racial discrimination. The initiative taken by the UN is bound to encourage precisely that kind of claim.

The UN initiative will open up a Pandora's box of allegations or racial discrimination throughout the world. The latitudinarian attitude of the UN will encourage religious and other 'ethnic' minorities to make allegations of racial discrimination not only in India, but everywhere. The Catholics in Northern Ireland can claim that they too are victims of racial discrimination. The French Canadians, whose grievances are real enough, can also make the same claim. One can multiply examples from every corner of the world. By treating caste discrimination as a form of racial discrimination and, by implication, caste as a form of race, the UN is turning its back on established scientific opinion. One can only guess under what kind of pressure it is doing so. Treating caste as a form of race is politically mischievous; what is worse, it is scientifically nonsensical.

Chapter 5

Caste Is Not Race

But, Let's Go to the UN Forum Anyway

DIPANKAR GUPTA

The mindset created by our liberalisation drive has not become self-generating. Beginning with our dependence on foreign expertise to fight industrial downturn and depleting foreign exchange, we are now looking for foreign help to fight everything, including the caste system. Surely, when liberalisation began nobody could have forecast the ground that it would eventually cover. It is now to Washington or Geneva that one must turn for help in every matter.

At a recent seminar organised in New Delhi by the National Human Rights Commission (NHRC) on whether caste should be included in the forthcoming UN conference on race in Durban, it was interesting to observe many notables were of the strong opinion that caste cannot be fought with national resources alone. It was repeatedly asserted that the might of international agencies needs urgently to be recruited to fight the caste system. So to Durban we shall go was the rallying call, and there the UN committee against racism would be pressured to include caste within its purview and only then would consciousness be raised in this country and the government be forced to deliver.

That the temperament of liberalisation should have gone this far should not come as a surprise. We have ceded knowledge advantage to the West on one front after another – beginning with the economic, then flowing on to the political, and now we need tips on how to handle cultural discrimination as well. It is not as if one must not learn from western experience, that would indeed be stupid. The issue really is that we are increasingly giving up intellectual and political expertise. How do the enthusiasts who want to go to the Durban conference imagine that international agencies will help fight caste in India? Have they thought this matter through? Will the UN sanction a bombing raid on Delhi? An economic embargo? Or, as the preliminary documents of the Durban conference suggest, the best that the UN can do in this matter is to provide intellectual and strategic direction, as if we haven't had enough of that already.

Of course, our government officials have got off on the wrong foot as usual. They argue that as caste is an internal matter there is no point in talking about it in front of strangers in Durban. But this does not sound convincing especially as this government, and past ones, have sent off missions all over the world to attend conferences on poverty, which is also an internal matter. Many of our problems are so well known, and have been internationalised for so long, that it is indeed ridiculous suddenly to get possessive about caste. We have a whole lot of dirty linen that has piled up on issues such as poverty and leprosy to AIDS and Kashmir. All of these have been taken to the public realm, but on each occasion we have come back without giving them a wash. Whether or not these causes have profited from such foreign exposure is debatable, but there is no doubt that those who have championed them have benefited enormously in their individual capacities.

Nor can the government say with a straight face that haring off to the Durban conference will not help fight the caste situation one bit. This is a correct assessment, but it loses its meaning as it is coming from a non-credible source. Our governments have never used the efficacy criterion in sanctioning foreign trips. Huge delegations have attended various Olympiads at enormous public expense, and there has been no improvement as far as India's athletic abilities are concerned. Only recently there was another major jaunt for officials to the Cannes film festival even though there was not a single entry from

India at this event. Therefore, when the government says that going to Durban will not help fight caste in India and that is why such a trip should not be allowed, it is being clearly unfair. It has never applied the same standards to other junkets involving other people. Of course, nothing tangible will come out of the Durban conference, but with what face can the government use the efficacy criterion in this case and not in others?

Liberalisation has also meant that all so-called grassroots activists must now have updated passports if they want to add mileage to their portfolios. An activist at the NHRC seminar complained that he had faced state persecution in the past as his passport had once been impounded and he could not go abroad for six months. Liberalisation has clearly ushered in a new perspective on popular activism in India. Obviously we have internalised the mantras of liberalisation quite comprehensively.

In liberalised times again it is almost bad manners to argue that at the base of social discrimination is grinding poverty. To say this is like going back to the 1960s. The flavour of the new millennium is cultural rights. As if people live and die for culture alone. But such a position to a convenient one to take as politicians of all stripes are now let off the hook and do not have to take tough decisions that would inevitably hurt their sectional interests.

The truth is that Dalit women who are brutalised by policemen and political heavyweights are without exception, most vulnerable because they are poor. In India today, over 12% of Grade A services in the government bureaucracy are occupied by members of the scheduled castes. Nobody dare do anything to them, or to their dependents, and hope to get away with it. This is because these families are now economically secure and this makes them politically confident. To fight casteism it is important to economically uplift members of the scheduled castes and empower them to fight their own battles.

Nowhere have prejudices been eradicated by government fiat or by goodwill. Consciousness raising is a project that only flabby minds and failed philosophers will find attractive. Caste prejudices can be fought effectively only by the scheduled castes themselves, which is why the policy of reservations for SCs is such a good idea. There should be more of that and greater vigilance needs to be exercised to make sure that more avenues are opened for the economic betterment of the most underprivileged communities in India. This Durban cannot do, but Delhi can.

Chapter 6

Dalits and Durban

P. RADHAKRISHNAN

> It maybe your interest to be our masters, but how can it be ours to be your slaves?
>
> Thucydides

This quote with which Dr. B.R. Ambedkar, who exposed the numerous Hindu myths, mysticisms and mumbo-jumbo justifying the injustices of Indian society, and tried to instill in the vast masses of India's out castes a sense of confidence, defiance, dignity, freedom, and hope, began his controversial work, 'What Congress and Gandhi have done to 'the Untouchables' is as relevant today as in 1945 when he wrote it.

However, convinced as he was that India's pernicious caste practices have been part of the malignancy of Hindu society which can be extirpated only on Indian soil and only through social reforms and Constitutional means, it cannot be gainsaid that in India's changed stature as a sovereign democratic republic, Ambedkar himself would have found it ludicrous and even abhorrent to showcase caste, even a tableaux, in an alien land and through a world body of which India is a member country. More so, as it was mainly because of Ambedkar's initiative as the chief architect of the Indian Constitution that the numerous safeguards for the untouchables and the other weaker sections were enshrined in the Constitution.

The reference is to the United Nations World Conference Against Racism, Racial Discrimination, Xenophobia, and Related Intolerance, to be held in Durban, South Africa, from August 31 to September 7, the confusion and controversy about caste and race as discriminatory categories, and the furore in India and abroad on inclusion of caste in the conference.

Understanding the fallacies underlying this confusion and controversy, and their fallout for India calls for understanding the widely varying postures on caste and race by the proponents and opponents for inclusion of caste in the conference, and the role of the UN as a global "do-gooder".

Going by press reports, there has been widespread support through social mobilisation, meetings, conferences, and writings in the press for inclusion of caste in the conference. The most prominent and vociferous proponents are the "Dalit activists", who are a heterogeneous ensemble. The organisations purportedly representing them include the National Campaign on Dalit Human Rights, the Republican Party of India, People's Watch, the National Council of Churches in India the highest body in the country representing different denominations of the protestants and so on. Whether the "Dalit activists" are leaders from among the Dalits, or non Dalits feigning to be self appointed Dalit leaders of pressure groups, or both is a moot issue. This issue is, however, very important for at least two reasons. One, if the Dalits could spawn such aggressive, articulate, globetrotting and internationally acclaimed and influential leaders, they would have overcome long ago their precarious plight as the despised and the damned, the depressed and the downtrodden of the caste ridden Indian society. Two, if evidence and experience are any indication, the "Dalit cause" is hard currency for "Dalit activists" operating in developed countries, though it is questionable how far the Dalits themselves have been beneficiaries of the western dole.

Sources would have it that in Geneva several NGOs in special consultative status with the UN have been spearheading the movement for inclusion of caste on the agenda for the conference, and a number of organisations have joined forces to form the International Dalit Solidarity Network.

As notable among them are the World Council of Churches, the Lutheran World Federation, and similar organisations from Europe and the US their involvement and vociferous claims are certainly grist to the Hindutva mill. While the initiative of the church-related organisations is laudable and hopefully indicative of the revival of the long dormant liberation theology, ignoring for the time being the Hindutva monster, one might ask what the Church related organisations have been doing to overcome the discriminatory practices among the Indian Christians, in particular Christian converts of Scheduled Caste origin, the persistence of whose disabilities and plight as "twice alienated" have necessitated their organised demands for at least the last ten years for treatment as Scheduled Castes so as to enable them to take advantage of the State's affirmative action and special treatment programmes, though here again the imitative of the Church-related organisations has been commendable.

Whether by the Church Council or other organisations, the claims for inclusion of caste in the conference are of two broad streams. The first would have caste as race, caste as worse than race, caste discrimination as racism and more and so on. The second would have Dalit oppression as worse than racial discrimination; Dalits as victims of centuries old polluting and stigmatising occupations such as scavenging, persistent discrimination and atrocities, untouchability, social segregation and denial of access to public place and spaces forcing them to live at the margins of society; the history of Dalits as a genealogy of pain captured in the very etymology of the word, and so on.

While all this is true, the claim that the justification for inclusion of caste in the UN Conference is to "internationalise" Dalit discrimination raises several issues. One, equating caste with race. As Dipankar Gupta observed in his work *Interrogating Caste: Understanding Hierarchy and Difference in Indian Society*, despite some commonalities between caste and race, particularly between the bottom end of the caste system and the segregationist racism, caste and race are vastly different, for which reason they should not be collapsed into a single analytical category. Important among the differences are the caste system is about 300 years old, extremely complex based on multiple hierarchies, characterised by the pervasive purity pollution dichotomy, and graded discrimination. In contrast, racism is of recent origin, and as race is based on phenotypic criteria there can be no dispute about where one belongs in the race hierarchy.

Caste has been under extensive debate and in-depth research for several decades now and the literature on it is probably much more burgeoning than on race though race has also been under extensive debate and in-depth research and Gunnar Myrdal's *American Dilemma*, followed by Oliver Cromwell Cox's *Race: A Study in Social Dynamics* are still probably the most important works on racism, racism is predominantly an American and South African problem, and even here race relations have undergone tremendous changes during the last three decades. So, a UN Conference on caste or race or both may not add up.

Two, equating the caste system with Dalits, as if it comprises only Dalits and none else. This is political appropriation of the caste system by "Dalit activists". Though Dalits are certainly the worst victims of discrimination, and account for about one fourth of India's population, their existential problem cannot be isolated from that of the rest of society.

Other traditional caste groups barring Brahmins and probably a few other upper castes have also been victims of the caste system. It is recognising this pervasive nature of discrimination, disparities, and disabilities, that the first All India Backward Classes (Kaka Kalelkar) Commission of the 1950s recommended reservation for a separate category just above the Scheduled Castes; and it is in keeping with this recommendation that some states such as Tamil Nadu have created the Most Backward Classes category for reservation purposes.

II

If these lower castes (whom some States have classified under the most backward classes category) have not been included among the Scheduled Castes it is for the reason that they were not identified as untouchables – a requirement for inclusion in the Constitutional category of Scheduled Castes. However it is officially recognised that most of them have been as backward as Dalits and are also victims of most of the same disabilities. The only difference is compared to Dalits most of them are minuscule, disparate groups, such as washer men and barbers, and certain nomadic groups known in colonial officials as "criminal tribes". In Tamil Nadu, these groups together account for about one third of the population eligible for 20% of the state's 69% reservation. It is in recognition of these groups apart form Dalits, and also other disabled groups in the traditional caste hierarchy, that the Supreme Court ruling of November 16, 1992, approved, with modifications, the Government of India's notifications for reservation for the backward classes.

A third issue which can be raised about the justification for inclusion of caste in the Durban conference of racism is: as no other social institution in India has been so much internationalised as the caste system along with its attendant evils, first by the Christian Missionaries form the West (for example, William Ward in the early 19th century, observed that "like all other attempts to cramp the human intellect, and forcibly to restrain men within bounds which nature scorns to keep, this system, however specious in theory, has operated like the Chinese national shoe; it has rendered the whole nation cripples"), then by the British administration, then by the nationalist leaders in particular Ambedkar himself, then by western (followed by Indian) scholars, will UN Conference add any new perspective to the issue and transform possible solutions and the progressive provisions of the Indian Constitution form rhetoric to reality? As the UN does not have a magic wand for this dramatic change, is it not for the victims themselves, their political leaders, the "Dalit activists" and the central and state government to tackle the problem?

Closely related to the justification of the "Dalit activists" for internationalising caste discrimination is that of sections of the intelligentsia that bringing up caste at an international forum like the UN will increase global pressure (read pressure from the master world) on the Indian government to protect the lower castes. This claim is tacit admission that even as an independent nation India should continue to the "white man's burden", and continue to have a big brother to clean up its augean stables. If the Government of India is insensitive and irresponsible to the problems of Indian society, which it is supposed to be governing, no external power on earth can make sensitive and responsible to these problems. It may introduce cosmetic changes to appear civil in the comity of the master world, but going by the fate of the welfare commissions not much can be expected from such changes.

Among the opponents to the inclusion of caste in the conference are also NGOs. An example of this is a letter from Teheran purportedly by 35 NGOs, addressed to the chairman of the Asian Preparatory Meeting on the Conference. The letter vehemently opposed the inclusion of caste in the conference, gave as many as 12 reasons for doing so, and conveyed "the firm view" that since caste and race are different, caste is beyond the domain of the conference theme and caste discrimination can not be treated as racial discrimination.

The most important opponent, however, has been the Government of India itself, whose posture is hamstrung. The views of André Béteille, who, stung by criticism by the pro inclusion camp, resigned form the committee set up by Prime Minister, A.B. Vajpayee, to draft India's posture, are eloquent on the committee's claim that equating caste and race is harmful to national interest.

Béteille would have it that race is a biological category having distinctive physical markers whereas caste is social category; treating caste as a form of race is politically mischievous and scientifically nonsensical, the consequences of which will be fabricating or inventing more divisions in Indian society.

While both the arguments may be valid in theory, they sound hallucinatory. For, caste has been discussed in any number of international conferences, and no debate has so far caused, and no debate in future is likely to cause, any harm to national interest unless of course it is understood as interest of the upper castes. While the government could have certainly seen the UN Conference as an important opportunity to sensitise itself and sensitise all those concerned with the caste problem, in the event of its reluctance to do so, it could have at least come out with a detailed well informed document on caste vis-à-vis race, the Constitutional provisions for redress of historical wrongs and traditional social distortions, presenting a self appraisal of its own performance, and what it proposes to place the provisions on fast track ensuring effectiveness and continuity in future implementation.

In this context, it is relevant to note that India has had a well-conceived pragmatic programmatic for at least the last 50 years to tackle caste discrimination. In fact, India is probably the first country in the world to devise reservation policies, and as Marc Galanter wrote in his book, *Competing Equalities: Law and the Backward Classes in India*, "India's system of preferential treatment for historically disadvantaged sections of the population is unprecedented in scope and extent".

In contrast to the gradual dismantling of affirmative action in the US, and weakening of Black policies and caste politics have been gaining in strength and popular support. This is only to be expected considering that American society is fundamentally and foundationally individualistic and even the socially neglected and victimised Blacks would prefer to be "achievers" instead of the stigmatising beneficiaries of Affirmative Action: Whereas in India caste continues to shadow the individual, so much so that despite the Constitutional provisions on fundamental rights of the individual, group is still subsumed under it.

If Dalits and other dis-privileged castes have not benefited much from the Constitutional provisions and are still victims of discrimination, it is not so much the inclusion of caste in the UN Conference but identifying the fault lines in India's governance that needs emphasis. In this sense, the pressure should be on the Government of India to convene a summit to take stock of what the state has done hitherto with the Constitution in relation to the dis-privileged groups.

Turning to the UN, which Christian Gauss in an Introduction to The Prince by Machiavelli characterised as "a more determined attempt to create a 'super-state' which to succeed must have at least some power in the interest of peace and human welfare", its role as a "global do-gooder", especially in the context of its recently-invented exclusion – integration rhetoric and the related summit humanitarianism, is farcical. Given its track record as an active (or passive if you wish!) agent of the US and its allies, which have been active in their attempts to exterminate countries such as Iraq, the UN cannot be seen as working for the well-being of the victims of various forms of discrimination and disparities, and the UN summits and conferences are too routine and ritualistic often ending up in glossy reports released with much fanfare and distributed in select circuits with hardly any follow up action.

So, the UN summits and conferences, whether on racism or reptiles, should be non-issues to India's "unwashed millions". If they want to improve their lot and if the changes for it have to be substantive the victim groups and those concerned about them should directly take on the might of the Indian state and make it work, transparent, and accountable to the public. How they will do it is a larger issue.

Chapter 7

Caste Consciousness

Initiate an Open Discussion in Durban

ANDRÉ BÉTEILLE

Dalit activists and human rights gurus have joined hands to press for the inclusion of caste discrimination and the practice of untouchability on the agenda of the UN conference at Durban on racism and racial discrimination. This is wrong because caste is not a form of race and untouchability, no matter how reprehensible, is not a form of racial discrimination. The Indian government is determined to prevent this, presumably because it does not want its dirty linen to be aired outside. This is futile because in a democracy there is no effective way of preventing the discussion outside the country of social evils that are known to exist within it.

There is no harm in discussing, whether inside or outside India, the discriminatory practices of caste, including untouchability, and I have done so myself in papers and articles published in India and abroad. But the discussion should be in good faith and not under false pretences. Some of those who wish to include caste discrimination in the agenda at Durban know very well that caste is not a form of race, but they are not averse to stretching the point somewhat in the service of a good cause.

One must not misuse the metaphor of race even in a good cause – and who will deny that the abolition of untouchability is a good cause?

Extensive misuse of the metaphor of race has had tragic consequences in Europe. Once it is conceded that caste discrimination is a form of racial discrimination, there will be nothing to prevent religious – or linguistic – minorities from saying that they too are victims of racial discrimination. It is well to remember what the noted geneticist and biometrician, J.B.S. Haldane had said: "As for the word race, it has so many different meanings as to be useless in scientific discussion, though very useful for getting members of the same nation to hate one another".

I am convinced that the Government of India is not in favour of caste discrimination or the practice of untouchability. They are not in its own interest. To represent the government as being opposed, or even indifferent to the abolition of untouchability is to act in bad faith whether one does it in Delhi or in Durban.

I do not wish to suggest that the Government of India itself acts in good faith in all matters, because it does not. Its basic instinct is to brush all unpleasant things under the carpet, and to filter out every hint of dissent – no arguments please, we are all Indians. Bureaucracy can be particularly obdurate. Some 30 years ago, I was briefly involved, along with the late Professor V.M. Dandekar, in a project sponsored by a UN agency to study the economic and social implication of the Green Revolution. The project required clearance from two government ministries. At the first meeting, there were two joint secretaries who told us they had no objection to the economic side of the project because India was doing well economically but that they were worried about the social side since it was bound to deal with caste and other practices, which would show India in a bad light. I was appalled. But I need not have worried, because Professor Dandekar, who did not suffer fools gladly, wiped the floor with the two joint secretaries.

It is the same obstructive mindset that leads the government to issue *fatwas* from time to time to restrict the entry of foreign scholars into India or their participation in seminars and conferences. I am not talking now about restrictions imposed on particular individuals whose bona fides may be in question, but a blanket ban on foreign scholars on the ground that they may hear or say things that could damage India's reputation abroad. This is bizarre for the simple reason that Indian academics are, in general, better equipped than Indian bureaucrats to deal with foreign critics of India. And they are no less patriotic.

The government has been caught on the wrong foot by a combination of elements that seems to have no hesitation in embarrassing it. When it comes to media attention, the NGOs can beat the government hands down, nationally as well as internationally. The NGO explosion is a phenomenon of the last ten or 15 years, and nobody really understands how the NGOs have grown or what role they will play in the society of the future. At one level, one can say that they have expanded in response to the failure of the government on the social front, just as the market has expanded in response to its failures on the economic front.

The ascendancy of NGOs like the ascendancy of the market is a worldwide phenomenon, driven in some respects by the same forces. The NGOs are not only a worldwide phenomenon; there is a strong international presence in them though this may be less visible in India than in smaller countries such as Nepal, Bangladesh and Sri Lanka. Again this is not necessarily a bad thing and certainly in a large and self-confident country such as ours there is no need to be paranoid about it.

At the same time, there must be wider public scrutiny of what the NGOs are actually doing. The getting together of Dalit activists and human rights gurus may have a lesson to offer, but it is doubtful that the Government of India will learn it. Such an alliance might not have been possible or effective without the abundant presence of NGOs ready to take on the government in the cause of social justice. The activists provide the youth, the energy and the dynamism, and the gurus the wisdom often gathered in the corridors of power in national and international agencies.

Personally speaking, I have some sympathy for the Dalit activists even when I find their approach wrong. Their movement is driven by a genuine passion to break free from monstrously oppressive social system. I cannot say the same for the human rights gurus. Their social and occupational background is very different. They are usually much older persons often with successful careers in the civil service, in diplomacy or in the judiciary behind them. I do not envy them their frequent visits abroad at public expense. What I deeply regret is that there is so little of intellectual worth in what they say or write about the creation of a more just and humane society. And as to their passion, it is often a simulated passion.

Chapter 8

Caste, Race, Politics

DIPANKAR GUPTA

The arguments in this paper are set out in two stages. I will first point out why caste should not be seen as another variant of race. If this position is sustained then it follows that casteism is not racism under a different name. In the second section I hope to demonstrate the political consequences, some quite damaging, if caste were to be equated with race.

For a long time anthropologists and sociologists felt that the 'caste-is-race' thesis was dead and buried. Obviously, it was not given a decent enough burial for it surfaced again in the context of the United Nations conference on racism held in Durban in August 2001. The heat and dust raised during the Durban conference necessitates a return to some of the points made much earlier in scholarly contributions on caste. Though, on occasion, the professional academic might get a sense of déjà vu while going through this paper, the fact that the parallelisms between caste and race are still compelling enough for many political activists demonstrates that something was obviously missing in previous presentations. In my view, the best way to nail down the caste-is-race thesis is to logically show how this equation is politically misleading if not, in fact, dangerous. To do so it is ineluctable that the distinction between caste and race be made more fulsomely than before, keeping in mind all the while that this exercise has clear political implications.

Why is caste so often mistaken to be another kind of racism? There are two reasons for this. One is a misreading of Vedic texts inspired by the distinction made by early indologists between fair Aryans and dark Dravidians. The other reason for equating caste with race comes about because there are some similarities between the ways blacks were treated in southern United States, or in apartheid Africa, and the treatment meted out to so-called 'untouchables' in caste Hindu society.

There is no doubt that people known as the Aryans came to India around 1,500 B.C. in successive waves and settled down in the Indo-Gangetic plains. But there is no unambiguous evidence to suggest that these in-migrating Aryans were physically of a different sort from those who were already living in this region. What is clear, however, is that the Aryans who came across the mountains brought in a different language that was quite distinct from the families of languages spoken by the people who were earlier inhabitants in the land mass which we now identify as India.

There also appears to be good reason to believe that Aryans met with some resistance from autochthonous peoples of this region. It is, however, far from clear whether Aryans over came such opposition by superior military might, or by ideological warfare, or by hard-nosed diplomacy. The evidence seems to suggest a combination of all three.

Early European Indologists took a shine to the notion that fair Aryans conquered dark Dravidians in remote history probably because it justified such a re-enactment in colonial India. But what is more surprising is the alacrity with which some Indian intellectuals internalised this position and began to draw racial lines of distinction within Hindu society.

There is a well-worn sociological cliché, which says that the dominated people often appropriate aesthetic standards of the superior community. This seems to have happened in India as well. Thus, those from Punjab and the northern regions proudly took on the mantle of being Aryans and distanced themselves from the darker people of the southern provinces of India as they considered them to be Dravidians. Even a staunch Hindu nationalist like Bankim Chandra felt a sense of pride in the belief that superior Aryan blood coursed through his veins.

Those from the South, not to be undone by all this, began demonising Aryans and all those who claimed ancestry from them. This was how the Dravida Kazhagam and later Dravid Munnetra Kazhagam rationalised their demands for secession from the Indian union several decades ago. So the caste is race thesis played a politically divisive role during the years of our nationalist struggle against colonialism. If left unattended it will continue to be divisive, though 'racial' opponents may be arraigned differently at different times. But we are already jumping ahead of our presentation.

In terms of empirical detail a lot more is required than has been provided so far if the theory of the racial origin of caste is to be made convincing. The factual evidence given in favour of this point of view is exceedingly exiguous. In fact, the manner in which dark skin and fair skin have been read into Vedic texts is itself highly disputable. What is interpreted as 'fair skin' in the *Vedas* could easily mean, and most probably did mean, 'light', in which case it was not a matter of skin complexion but of knowledge? The Aryans then distinguished themselves from others not by their complexion, but by their belief that they were in possession of superior knowledge and wisdom. They were the carriers of light, and that is how they dispelled the *darkness* and ignorance that reigned during pre-Aryan times.

Further, there is only one passage in the Vedas that purportedly depicts the Dravidians as being 'noseless and bull-lipped'. The Sanskritist, Hans Hock has convincingly demonstrated that this particular sentence in the Vedas has been translated and interpreted in a highly dubious fashion. The same word, viz., anas, can also mean a person of poor speech and not someone who is nose less.

If the Aryans indeed brought in a new language then it is only natural that they should emphasise proper speech and pronunciation *(uccharan)* to differentiate themselves from those others over whom they ruled, or with whom they had an uneasy relationship. The term bull-lipped can also have a variety of meanings. Remember, the bull is not really looked down upon in India as it is in many European metaphors (see Hock 2000). The bull in Indian tradition is not seen as dumb and obdurate but strong and determined. So the evidence from the Vedas is far from conclusive. Moreover, what is most striking is that this description of the autochthonous original inhabitants is to be found in only a single passage in the Vedas, and yet so much has been made of it.

It should also be noted in this connection that the term *Varna* in the Vedas need not necessarily mean skin colour. Varna can also refer to order. Therefore, if there were four Varnas, or two (as in the early Rig Veda), then it signified that the society was stratified along four orders, or two orders, as the case may be. Each order was supposed to have a colour pennant of its own as they represented different phases of the sun's journey around the earth.

The rising sun, the grandest of all, was red, and this was the colour given to the ruling kshatriyas. Brahmans were signified by the colour white because that was supposed to be the colour of the sun at noon. Vasishyas were yellow because that is the colour the sun took in the East, and finally sudras were blue, for that was the hue of the setting sun. To extrapolate racial segregation from factual material of this order is indeed far-fetched.

It will then have to be admitted that even the Vedas concede that kshatriyas are superior to brahmans as they represent the rising sun. Further, from where does the colour yellow get any material substantiation? Why have yellow or red not received any attention from those who argue in favour of the racial origins of caste? Why are many of us committed to a two-race theory and not a four race one? Quite clearly the thesis that caste originated from race is flawed as it is based on flimsy evidence.

The race argument takes a further beating when we study gene distribution and racial measurements along caste lines. Once again no clear pattern emerges between different castes on the basis of the distribution of heavy gamma chains and light kappa chains in their genetic makeup. It has also been pointed out in this context that the presence of African haplotype among some people of North India obviously means that the term 'African' is a misnomer (see Field, Surje and Ray 1988:34)

Much earlier in 1960, Majumdar and Rao conducted a statistical study of so-called race elements in Bengal and came to the interesting conclusion that there were overwhelming physical similarities between high and low castes within the same geographical region. But the story was different between different regions. Upper castes in one area differed a great degree from upper castes in a different geographical locale. The same held true between lower castes in different regions of the country (Majumdar and Rao 1960).

In an influential paper published in 1990 in *Current Anthropology*, an international team of scholars undertook anthropometric exercises and found no differences between different castes. They took three important measurements, viz., head length, head breadth, and bizygomatic breadth. After examining a wide range of material they came to the conclusion that all efforts 'at typological/"racial" classification should be abandoned' (Majumder, Shanker, et al.).

Interestingly enough the various *smritis,* like the *Yagnavalkyasmriti* and the *Manusmriti* strongly disapprove of marrying outside one's caste. Out of such cases of miscegenation, the smritis argue, that new and despicable castes are formed. Thus the chamars were born out of the union of a vaideha and a nishada. In the case of the lowliest of the low caste, the chandals, something much, much worse is said to have happened. A Brahman woman had sexual relations with a sudra man and, not surprisingly, therefore, monster in the shape of a chandal was born (see Gupta 2000:71-2).

Note, no matter how fanciful and spiteful such origin tales might be, nowhere is it said that the child of such unions is half a vaideha and half a nishada, or half a brahman and half a sudra. The miscegenes of such highly despised unions belonged to a different breed altogether, to a completely different caste. Mixed marriages, in such cases, do not result in mixed off-springs but in dangerous and impure outcastes.

This situation changes when we move from caste to race. Children born out of inter-racial unions, however, are socially recognised to carry the strains of both parents and are thus classified as hybrid, mulattos, octoroon, quadroons, and so on. In many racist societies, mulattos and mestizos have greater privileges and occupy a higher rank than other blacks. We will have occasion to return to this when we discuss the differences between the politics of caste and race.

It needs also to be mentioned that it was common place to have a black cook or wet nurse in white homes in racially segregated ante bellum southern United States. While blacks were despised they were not considered polluting. Imagine the horror that would be aroused in the home of a traditional privileged caste in India at the very suggestion of an untouchable cook in the kitchen. Thus, while racism at its height might consider blacks to be despicable, it did not regard them as polluting.

Additionally, in a racially segregated society one's sense of identity gets stronger as one moves from the particular to the more general level. In other words, it does not matter if the person is from Belgium, Germany or Holland, as long as the person is white. Any further sub-classification is not necessary and may indeed take away from the power of racial consciousness. Likewise, to be considered black it is not at all important, or relevant, to know whether the person is from Botswana or from Nigeria. If the person is black then that is enough regardless of where the person comes from.

Caste identity works in a reverse direction. Caste loyalties gain in commitment the more localised and particularised they get. It is not enough to be a Brahman but to be a Brahman of a certain endogamous jati, such as the kanyakubja Brahman or chitpavan Brahman or barendra Brahman. In many cases this may not be enough either, and further sub-divisions are necessary. The same holds true for rajputs, jats and kayasthas, and indeed for all other caste clusters as well.

This brings us to the crucial analytical difference between caste and race. Strata based on race are arranged along a continuum of colour. Whites occupy one end and blacks the other of this hierarchical ladder. The colours in between are positioned accordingly along this scale. This is why those who are one-eighth black are superior to those who are one-fourth black and so forth.

In Washington, light-skinned blacks set up an organisation called the Bon-Ton Society in the 1930s. To be a member of this society was fairly prestigious for mulattos of various degrees, but they had to pass two qualification tests. Their skin colour had to be lighter than the standard brown paper bag, and when a comb was run through the prospective candidate's hair it was not supposed to meet with any resistance. In Nashville around the same time there existed the Blue Vein Society. This too was formed by light-skinned blacks, and they too wanted it to be quite an exclusive affair. The criterion in this case was that the fine blue criss-cross of veins on the applicant's should be easily discernible (see Gupta 2000: 91-2).

In the Caribbean, in Latin America, and in the United States there are ranges of terms to encompass those who are not black but not quite white either. Harry Hutchinson found eight terms in Brazil distinguishing different shades of black (Hutchinson 1957: 12). Charles H. Parrish listed 145 different terms to denote fine shades of colour distinction in the United States (Russel, Wilson, Hall 1992:60). Malcolm X, the famous Black Muslim leader, confessed in his autobiography that he was favoured over his siblings by his mother because he was lighter skinned than them. Melville Herskovitz studied successful black couples in Harlem and found that as many as 56.5% black men married light-skinned women (ibid: 116). The really successful black men like Quincy Jones, Justice Clarence Thomas, O.J. Simpson, James Earl Jones, and even the revered Frederick Douglas, all had white trophy wives.

The colour continuum is in many senses objective and demonstrable. There is little point in a black person claiming to be white if the person's skin colour and features do not help to back this claim. On the other hand there are a large number of light skinned blacks who want to be taken for whites and often succeed in 'passing' off as one. This phenomenon of 'passing' has been widely noticed and commented upon in the United States. Journals such as *Ebony, Jet and Essence,* which have a predominantly black readership, devote pages to help black women solve their 'hair problem'. Straightening one's hair and cosmetically changing the colour of one's eyes are quite well known among black people in America (see ibid: 47). In other words, blacks accept white aesthetics and would like to be like them if it was possible. The only way this could happen is through inter marriage.

This is probably why blacks in America have a low sense of self-esteem, nor have they much use for their heritage. This is also evident in the politics of Louis Farrakan. Farrakan urges blacks to reform themselves, to be caring parents, and to be hard working and diligent bread winners. If blacks are in bad way, Farrakan would argue, the prevailing black way of life is certainly not going to help them come out of their misery. The 'black is beautiful' phases is now more or less over in the United States. As many as 72% blacks prefer to be called blacks and not Afro-Americans (ibid: 71; see also Gutman 1976:309).

Caste-based stratification displays very different characteristics. To being with, it is impossible to construct a uniform hierarchy of caste based on the notion of purity and pollution. No caste would acquiesce to its placement among the so-called 'untouchables'. No caste would agree that members of other castes are made up of substances better than theirs (Gupta 2000: 72-85; see also Appadurai 1974). No caste would like its people to marry outside the community. No caste would like to merge its identity with any other caste. No caste accepts that it has originated from a shameful act of miscegenation. Any suggestion of being half-breed is dismissed haughtily across the board by all castes (see Gupta ibid).

It is true that castes try to elevate their social status through a process known as Sanskritisation. This term should be handled carefully for it can give rise to certain misinterpretations. It is not at all true that those castes that emulate the lifestyle of powerful brahmans, or kshatriyas, or baniyas want to merge their identity with these castes. The viswakarma brahmans have Sanskritised much of their lifestyle but do not want to marry chitpavan or saraswat or any other kind of Brahman. They want to stay separate but would claim equality with, if not superiority over, other brahmans and prosperous castes.

Sanskritisation does not mean merger with other castes. On the contrary it is a show of defiance and an extraversion of what the caste always believed in an introverted fashion all along. In the past, members of such Sanskritising castes dare not work out their ambitions, or express them in any way, for fear of being punished by wealthier and powerful castes. But now with democracy and an open market economy such displays of self-assertion are gaining prominence. In Rajasthan till a few decades ago, jats could not wear a turban, carry arms, or ride a horse (see Sharma 1998:83). Jats today flout all these restrictions against them, but in the 1930s they encountered stiff resistance from rajputs. Now that jats lead a lifestyle similar to rajputs it does not mean that jats want to merge with rajputs, or 'pass' off as them.

While Sanskritisation may involve some amount of emulation of the powerful caste of the region, it is not as if the upwardly mobile

Sanskritising caste is ready to jettison all its earlier beliefs and practices. Castes always differentiate themselves from other castes on multiple fronts: on how they get married, how they conduct their funerary ceremonies, the cuisines they cook and prefer, and even on the basis of gods that they each castes considers to be special to its members (Gupta 2000: 77-85). Each caste has a clear idea of which caste it considers to be below it and which ones roughly equal.

Endogamy, or marrying within one's jati, is a strict rule that all castes hold dear. It is not at all true that poorer castes are less punctilious in observing their caste norms. Each caste inspires its own variety of caste patriotism for which reason jati puranas, or origin tales, are such an important aspect of their cultural legacy and heritage. All dominated castes explain their subjugation, not on the basis of purity and pollution, but on the basis of lost wars, chicanery and deceit by kinsmen and fair weather friends. Some times the gods too are blamed for being fickle, inconstant and temperamental in bestowing their favours (ibid: 73-78, 116-129).

Unlike the distinctions used to demarcate racial separation, there is no objective indication of which category is to be placed where in the caste hierarchy. As no caste accepts that it is less pure than other castes, though it would easily grant that brahmans are ritual specialists, there are probably as many hierarchies in practice as there are castes. In the past when the economy was controlled by rural oligarchs and petty potentates, the hierarchy on the ground was the one that was ordained by the superior caste of the region.

Other castes had to acquiesce to this or face brutal consequences. They dared not express their version of the 'true' hierarchy. With the growth in commercialisation, urbanisation and democracy, poorer castes are becoming bolder and now have the courage to openly express what they have always held dear but dared not manifest in any form in the past.

The distinguishing characteristic of the caste order is the discrete character of its constituent units that resist being forced into a single hierarchical frame. As these castes are discrete and semaphore their separation on multiple fronts, caste competition is built in at various levels. It is only by accepting the reality of multiple hierarchies that we can conceptually make room for the existence of caste politics. If one were to go by the traditional understanding of a single hierarchy of purity/pollution, with brahmans at the top, then any evidence of caste conflict should have meant the dissolution of the caste order.

Nor is it true that caste politics is a recent phenomenon. All through traditional and medieval India castes have fought and slaughtered each other to gain worldly preeminence. Once a caste is politically and economically powerful it can then live out its own believed-in hierarchy. This is as true of the Gujara Partihara and Rajput kingdoms in medieval India (Chattopadhyaya 1979: 59-82), as it is of jat supremacy in Punjab several centuries later, and of baniya ascendance in Rajasthan and Gujarat today (See Babb 1998; Shah and Shroff 1975).

The difference between traditional and modern displays of caste politics is not that there were no power struggles between communities in the past, but that the format for such competition and strife has now changed. Democracy and commerce have created new avenues that were not available to caste antagonists even in early colonial India.

If one is to understand caste politics in its vivacity and depth it is necessary to appreciate that in the caste situation there are multiple nodes. Jats are against gujars, together they are against urban caste; kolis are against patidars; thevars oppress pallars of the devendrakula vellalas; the vanniyars torment adi dravidas, even as many of them may be against, or for, brahmans in their local settings (see Radha Krishnan 2001).

Caste alliances such as the KHAM (Kshatriya, Harijan and Muslim) and AJGAR (Ahir, Jat, Gujar and Rajput) are made and then caste aside. New alliances come into being with quite different caste friends and enemies. Even as castes may enter into political alliances, however aphemeral, they do not drop barriers of endogamy, though they may occasionally ease up on inter-dining restrictions.

Race politics gets its charge from the bipolar antagonism between blacks and whites. Half breeds, mestizos or quadroons are of no consequence. They have to align themselves with one side or the other. They cannot form an independent front of their own. In America till about fifty years ago the 'one drop rule' applied. This meant that if a person had as low as one-sixty fourth black blood, then the person was considered black. This is why many who would like to 'pass' as whites cannot easily pull it off. As the Black Panthers put it in America: 'You are either part of the problem or part of the solution.' There is no other alternative.

As castes operate on the basis of separation into discrete categories, which then fashions multiple hierarchies, the single hierarchy principle of race would be quite alien to it. Consequently, caste politics would be imbued with a logic quite different from what obtains in racist politics. It is because many members of India's literati did not quite appreciate this and, perhaps unconsciously, applied the race model to caste politics that they let the Mandal recommendations pass without too much opposition.

In the view of these pro-Mandalites, caste politics in India is really between powerful brahmans and the oppressed rest, just as in race politics it is whites versus blacks. In fact, brahmans do not always occupy the top spot in most hierarchies. And whenever brahmans hold such a position it is because they have economic and political power to match. But this would still be a very small and atypical part of the entire caste and politics scenario. If caste politics is seen only in terms of superior Brahman versus the suffering rest then the atrocities that yadavas inflict on ex-untouchables, what thevars do to pallars, and what rajputs did to the jats, would be unnoticed and brushed aside. This would impoverish and distort our understanding of caste politics in India and would allow for the intellectual acceptance of dangerous and retrograde policies such as those recommended by the Mandal Commission.

The distinctions between the politics of caste and race can and should be made if one is interested in fighting casteism in a concrete and meaningful way. While a radical advocacy of some form of inverted racism may seem feasible to some in the United States, such a stance would make no sense in terms of caste politics in India. In caste politics there is casteism at multiple levels and inversions at one level would leave the rest quite untouched.

This is why B.R. Ambedkar saw no future in politics of this sort. He anticipated the limitations of using caste as a perennial political resource and fought instead to extirpate this cultural blot from our society. As there are multiple castes in India, and as many of these castes also occupy, statistically at least, different positions in the economic structure, caste politics often passes off as democratic politics. I have heard it being said that in India we have caste democracy.

It is possible to overlook the inherent drawbacks of caste democracy as there are so many castes occupying different occupational and income positions in society. There is no caste that is dominant in numerical terms, and if the plain game of numbers were to apply then a semblance of democracy may well be arrived at. But at what cost? Caste would be a permanent feature of mobilisation, dividing the country on the basis of birth and ascription without giving citizenship a chance to establish itself. Caste then becomes an immutable category.

The reality of caste is, however, very different. Not every harijan is a leather worker, and not every Brahman is a pandit. There are more harijans employed as agricultural labourers than any other single caste group in Uttar Pradesh. Today many of them are also moving to cities and have jobs far removed from what their predecessors were forced to commit themselves to just a few generations back.

When an equation is made between caste and race the suggestion often is that these caste categories are fixed and immutable. But many once upon a time low castes have become kshatriyas, sudras have become elite pen pushers and, if the tales of doms and mochis are to be believed, then those who were once in positions of power have now fallen into really bad days. If the ignominies heaped on certain castes arise from the occupations they were forced to follow by tradition, then it can be safely said that such a state of affairs no longer holds everywhere with the same degree of consistency. It is very rarely that one can correlate caste and occupation in contemporary India.

Race politics accepts that blacks and whites are immutable categories. In this situation there are two options: inverted racism, or racial representation. In either case one has to work within the framework of race. Black Panthers advocated inverted racism and it did not work. A small minority cannot overturn a majority. What remains problematic, however, is that in inverted racism it is racism that is still triumphant, albeit of another kind.

Race representation, the other alternative, accepts that races are here to stay as it is not possible to change the colour of one's skin. Hence, even when there is a question of fairness, the tendency among liberal democrats is to push for a policy that would ensure some kind of proportionate representation in the job market and in educational institutions. In caste order, how a caste is perceived depends to a very significant extent on what occupation members of that caste follow.

In India it is possible and, indeed, feasible to move from one kind of job to another in one's lifetime, and with greater facility over two to three generations. Over 13% of Grade A services in the Government of India are today occupied by those whose predecessors were once considered untouchables. This percentage is bound to increase in the years to come. In that sense those who are descendents of so-called untouchables are no longer untouchables today. For them, at least, their caste position has changed significantly.

Caste is, therefore, not as immutable a category as race is. This is why the provisions for reservations in the Constitution could think in terms of extirpating caste altogether in the not too distant future. Reservations for Scheduled Castes and Tribes in India were never envisaged in terms of either compensation or retribution, as is the case with affirmative action in America. In racism a person continues to be black no matter what position that person may occupy in terms of status and wealth. But history has shown that though caste mobility may be much more pronounced today, it was not unknown in ancient and medieval India.

The reservation policy for Scheduled Castes is based on giving this latent dynamic a greater fillip by unearthing and releasing talents that were hitherto hidden in these communities. In this process it is not just that these historically dis-privilege castes would improve their status, but that society as a whole would benefit from a wider pool of talent that would now be available to it. As the question is not of compensation but of a dynamic transformation of the caste order itself, the system of reservation eventually looks towards a state of affairs when it would make itself redundant.

In race the scenario is quite different. Once a black, always a black. This fixity cannot be transposed to caste politics, without doing a lot of damage to empirical reality. Once a chamar is not always a chamar, once a scavenger is not always a scavenger, and so forth. The vahivanca barots of Gujarat earlier called themselves kshatriyas but now prefer to be known as baniyas (Shah and Shroff 1975). Further, as we mentioned earlier, ex-untouchables have never ideologically acquiesced to their own degradation. This is why whenever they are able to improve their economic situation they successfully shed their earlier caste status and moved on.

Once we use the language of race to the caste situation the emphasis shifts from removing the scourge of caste from Indian society to making one's caste identity a fixed political resource. In which case, quite understandably, castes would tend to be viewed as permanent fixtures and caste identities as political assets. The task would then be not so much to eradicate caste but to give proportionate representation to different castes in educational institutions, in jobs, housing, and so on.

This again closely resembles the Mandal formula. The current Raj Nath Singh government in Uttar Pradesh is making an even finer distinction among the Other Backward Castes (OBCs). According to his formulation from the 27% reserved seats for OBCs, 5% should go to yadavas, 9% to eight Most Backward Castes such as lodhs, kurmis and jats (sic), and the remaining 13% or so to the 70 other OBCs that remain (Bhambri 2001).

Mandalism encourages this game of numbers and proportionate representation. It does not employ reservations to uproot caste identities in public life, but rather to perpetuate it. Those Scheduled Castes activists who want to see caste as a form of race should then be prepared for this eventuality. Caste identities, in this case, would always be an important mainstay of public life in India, a self-defeating project for any self-respecting activist.

To sum up, if caste were race then caste politics would be salient only when brahmans are pitted against the rest. Ahirs, kurmis, thevars, vanniyars, vokkaligas, rajputs and jats, then do not matter as full bodied entities. If caste were race then the reality and brutality of yadavas marauding in the fields of Bihar would be a bloodless reality and would not have any symbolic energy at all. It has to be a Brahman plot, or a Brahman inspired one, nothing else is of any significance. Those who have felt the full wrath of non-Brahman superior castes, either in the North or in the South, will never accept such a characterisation of caste atrocities. Further, if caste were race, then one's caste identity is fixed, both internally and externally.

There is one similarity, however, between the fight against caste and the fight against race. Ultimately the battle has to be fought and won by those who are victims of such stratified social orders. It is only by empowering the Scheduled Castes and blacks that casteist and racist prejudice, respectively, are not given the scope to manifest themselves in practice in everyday relations. No amount of consciousness raising can do this job adequately. Only when those that have been hitherto disprivileged have the power and the wherewithal to fight back will sectarian prejudices be halted in their tracks.

References

Appadurai, Arjun (1974); 'Right and Left Hand Castes in South India', *Indian Social and Economic History Review*, Vol. 11, pp. 216-260.

Babb, L.A. (1998), 'Rejecting Violence: Sacrifice and the Social Identity of Trading Communities', *Contributions to Indian Sociology* (N.S.), Vol. 32. pp 387-407.

Bhambri, C.P. (2001), 'Caste Aside', *Pioneer*, 3 October 2001.

Chattopadhyaya, B.D. (1976), 'The Origin of Rajputs: The Political, Economic and Social Processes in Early Medieval India', *Indian Historical Review*, Vol. 3, pp. 59-82.

Field, Leigh, Sira Surje and Ajit K. Ray (1988), 'Immunoglobin (GM and KM) Allotypes in the Sikh Population of India', *American Journal of Physical Anthropology*, Vol. 75, pp. 31-35.

Gupta, Dipankar (2000), *Interrogating Caste: Understanding Hierarchy and Difference in Indian Society*, Penguin Books, New Delhi.

Gutman, Herberg G. (1976). *The Black Family in Slavery and Freedom*, 1750-1925, Pantheon Press, New York.

Hock, Hans Henrich (2000), Philology and Historical Interpretation of the Vedic Texts. Paper presented at a meeting of the World Association for Vedic Studies, Hoboken, New Jersey, U.S.A. July 2000.

Hutchinson, Harry (1957), *Village and Plantation Life*, University of Washington Press, Seattle.

Majumdar, D.N. and C.R. Rao (1960), *Race Elements in Bengal: A Quantitative Study*, Asia Publishing House and Statistical Publishing Society, Calcutta.

Majumdar, Partha N. and B. Uma Shanker et al., (1990), 'Anthropometric Variation in India: A Statistical Appraisal', *Current Anthropology*, vol. 31, pp. 94-103.

Radhakrishnan, P. (2001), 'The Politics of Perdition', *The Hindu*, 21 September 2001.

Russel, Kathy, Midge Wilson and Ronald Hall (1992), *The Colour Complex: The Politics of Skin Colour Among African Americans*, Anchor Books, Doubleday, New York.

Shah, A.M. and G. Shroff (1975), The Vahivanca Barots of Gujarat: A Caste of Genealogists and Mythographers', in Milton Singer (ed.), *Traditional India: Structure and Change*, Rawat, Jaipur.

Sharma, K.L. (1998), *Caste, Feudalism and Peasantry: Social Formation of Shekhawati*, Manohar Books, Delhi.

Chapter 9

Caste in the Mirror of Race

D.L. SHETH

The demand to equate caste oppression with racial discrimination has triggered a new debate in the Dalit movement. A section of Dalit activists have initiated a global campaign for incorporating the issue of untouchability in India within the wider western discourse on racism. This campaign gained visibility at the Geneva conference attended by several Dalit intellectuals and activists as well as some government representatives and was further strengthened at the World Conference against Racism and Xenophobia (WCAR) held recently in Durban. Among other objectives, it aims at making the United Nation accept that caste oppression be officially treated as a form of racial discrimination and, as such, an international campaign be launched against it under the aegis of the world organisation.

Notably, political parties like the BSP and the Republican Party who claim to represent Dalit interests did not join the debate and the campaign remained more or less confined to the NGOs. Particularly active were the organisations attached to the World Council of Churches. Indeed, some of the organisation leading this movement even hoped to assume political leadership of Dalits, replacing those whose primary political preoccupation, in their view, has only been with electoral calculus. This new, aggressive politics of NGOs has contributed to a situation where anyone even in slight disagreement with these organisations is labelled a supporter of untouchability and Brahmanism.

As for the attitude of the government, it was, as ever, a knee-jerk reaction. Whether it is an issue of violation of human rights by its own institutional agencies, of child labour or the demand for declaring tribes as indigenous peoples, we witness a similar conditioned response from the government. If those opposing a particular policy do not achieve a degree of coherence about the terms in which to oppose the policy, it gives the government an additional excuse to ignore the opposition.

Yet, I believe, the political implications of perspective of race could be quite serious and should, therefore, be examined as dispassionately as possible. I would, however, like to make it clear at the very outset that I see nothing wrong in the internationalisation of caste. First, caste discrimination is by no means confined to Indian society alone. It is found in several countries of South Asia and East Asia, even though its nature and extent may vary. Even untouchability is not an exclusively Indian practice. For example, because of their long association with leatherwork in the past, the Buraku of Japan suffer a predicament comparable to that of the chamars of India. The case of the Peekchongas of Korea and Ragyappas of Tibet may also be cited in this context.

Second, if untouchability is a crime against humanity, which it indeed is, how on earth can we assume that all of humanity is exhausted in the Indian nation state? The question of untouchability should not be seen as one of nationalism; it is about the right to be human. As such the question must be raised in all available and appropriate fora so that a powerful politics against its ideology and practice can be built up, both nationally and globally. It is necessary to construct a universal moral discourse against all types of social and cultural practices leading to different forms of sub-humanisation of the excluded 'others'. This, however, should not compel us to mix metaphors/categories in a manner that might prove counter productive in devising a politics to counter the process of sub-humanisation of specific population groups in society.

To enter into the debate about whether or not to equate caste with race would be futile. For, it is easy to show theoretically, sociologically and scientifically that the Asian phenomenon of caste is in some basic respects dissimilar to the western phenomenon of race. Race has a biological connotation whereas caste is a socio-cultural construct. It is obvious that like any other caste conglomeration, the Dalits of different regions of India cannot be seen as of one race.

To be sure, both caste and race are hereditary. Unlike race, however, a caste formation is not determined by biological characteristics such as the colour of one's skin. It is function of a complex socio-historical structure within which a social group is assigned a ritual status specifying a degree of purity or pollution attached to it, an occupation, and a specific range, within which its members can forge matrimonial alliances. Racism on the other hand is a form of social and political discrimination based on biologically manifest inter-group differences. In any case, the European claims regarding the inherent superiority of one social group over the other have been thoroughly discredited.

While the fact that caste is different from race cannot be disputed, several aspects of injustice on account of racial discrimination in Europe, America and Africa appear similar to those perpetrated in the name of caste in India. The earlier generation of Dalit leaders even started a Dalit Panther movement drawing inspiration from the Black Panther movement in the US. A number of established Dalit litterateurs have fruitfully used the idiom and imagery of the anti-apartheid movement to analyse and articulate Dalit awareness and aspirations.

II

The fact of the matter is that the issue of caste vs. race is primarily political rather than academic, and must be understood as such. While it is true that no national society can objectively be divided into racial groups, for the idea of racial purity has been proved to be nonexistent, discrimination on the basis of a perceived notion of race is a reality. It is, therefore, irrelevant whether the notion of race is scientific or not. It is a socially, culturally and politically operative construct on the basis of which a section of the population is seen as the lesser and inferior 'other'. A racial division of 'us' and 'them' has thus become a prevalent classificatory scheme, even when the idea of race is scientifically rejected.

This scheme is informed by a culturally constructed belief that certain communities are lacking in specific bio-physiological virtues because of the colour of their skin, a particular shape of nose or a specific type of hair texture. This bio cultural belief, however, is sought to be presented as a 'scientific truth'. Even after the legitimacy of such beliefs is conclusively repudiated, the structures of associated ideas and prejudices continue to affect inter-community relations. The racial discourse is thus designed to marginalise certain groups and deprive them of normal individual and group rights. That is why, despite its scientific invalidation, racism not only survives but continues to grow. It finds its expression in the inter-community relations within a national society as also in relations between nation states. Indeed, racism today is more prevalent in international relations than in inter-community relations in non-western societies.

Having lost its scientific basis, race, like caste, has become a cultural and political means of marginalising disempowered groups in society. In spite of this obvious similarity, thus seen, the Dalit problem is fundamentally different in its constitution from the problem of the blacks.

But what if the demand to see caste as race is accepted by the United Nations, and casteism is 'officially' viewed as a manifestation of racism? If this happens, the social and democratic movements against caste in India will have to revise their ideological and organisational objections to the caste system that have been developed and effectively used to counter it. This would be unacceptable to the leaders of the Dalit movement, when they begin to confront such objections on the ground, in everyday politics.

True, the 'international community' understands racial discrimination more easily than casteism. Yet, if the vocabulary of race is given currency merely to make caste as an understandable, palatable category to the international community, many significant achievements of the movements against caste and untouchability would be lost to the anti-caste movement in India.

At one level, the discourse issuing from the Durban conference is welcome. It has drawn the world's attention towards the inhuman oppression and human rights violations of the Dalits. But the more important question is: How will the conceptual and ideological consequences of viewing caste as race affect the Dalit movement?

A possible consequence might be that the readymade conceptual categories developed by the anti-racist movement would replace those developed by the long experience of Dalit struggle. Today the ideology of casteism and untouchability finds expression in the context of perceived higher/lower status of communities, not in the vocabulary of biophysical discrimination. Casteist ideology uses a moral and religious language. Categories determined by a religiously sanctioned social hierarchy fix the limits of purity and impurity within which social groups are assigned different status. The entire system helps legitimise the association of social hierarchy with ritual purity. Racism does not operate in this manner. The language of racial discrimination is about fixing stable and total alienation of communities, whereas that of caste-discrimination leaves the scope for appropriating social and cultural spaces for caste-communities and thus expands their communal and secular interests simultaneously.

Because of their position at the bottom of a hierarchy-based system, Dalits are the most deprived among the lower castes. Even today most of them are condemned to live more or less in a subjugated condition. Yet, they are not outside the system. Rather, they may even be kept forcibly 'within' the system. On the other hand, the ideology of racism totally alienates those who are biosocially demarcated as the 'other'. The 'ruling races' can accomplish such domination through a blatant exercise of power. Moral or religious arguments have little scope in racial discourse. To put it differently, democratic politics can obviate caste status but not do the same thing so easily for a race. In a racial system, non-whites continue to exist outside the moral-ideological universe of the whites. In the case of caste-based discrimination, however, moral language can be deployed to ensure and elicit co-operation even of the subjugated. In the racial context this can be achieved only through power.

Racism is thus practiced through use of coercive power, whereas caste-based discrimination depends to a significant extent on the consent of the oppressed (which could conceivably be withdrawn in democratic politics). Accordingly, casteist society imposes certain definitions on communities as if they represent their own self-image as communities so that they accept their state of being as 'natural'.

At the root of caste oppression is the notion of purity/impurity. Untouchability should, therefore, be understood as an ideology that goes far deeper and has much more complex meaning systems than any form of racial discrimination that is primarily a relationship of power between two or more biologically demarcated.

Another important difference between race and caste is that the Indian caste society allows an opportunity for upward mobility to the 'lower' castes under certain condition, although such opportunities were in practice rarely available to castes in the fifth *varna* (pancham). Significantly, however, large number of such castes claims that historically they were the upper castes, but were pushed down in the hierarchy for practicing a 'polluting' occupation for survival – as an *apad dharma.*

Today's powerful community of Nadars in Tamilnadu, for example, were considered untouchable in the past. The Ezhavas of Kerala, who today have a decisive voice in the politics of the state, were once 'untouchables'. Within a span of 50 years, greater occupational diversification has been witnessed in these two communities than even the agricultural and artisan caste groups otherwise higher in traditional social hierarchy. Many members of these erstwhile untouchable communities have not only broken out of traditional caste occupations but have succeeded in registering socio-economic progress through employment in the industrial and other sectors of the modern economy.

There are other examples of those in the hereditary occupation of cleaning who, at least individually, have succeeded in acquiring a better social status. Obviously, it is inconceivable to even theoretically establish claims of upward mobility for a subjugated race, unless, of course, it succeeds in changing the power relationship as was done by the South African blacks who also happened to be a majority. It would sound baseless and illogical, for instance, to talk about two races being the same in the past or becoming so in the future.

But two hierarchically differently located castes can plausibly lay claim to have enjoyed similar and equal status in the past and can visualise attaining equality vis-à-vis each other in the future. This makes it possible for members of such unequal castes to claim equal opportunity. It is for this reason perhaps that the Dalits have been able to utilise the constitutional provision of reservation in India far more effectively than the blacks have done in USA. We, therefore, cannot rule out the possibility that the progress registered by the Nadars and Ezhavas will not be replicated by other Dalit castes in other parts of India in the new century.

In brief, if the modes of caste and racial oppression are different, the movements against them must also adopt different strategies. To put it differently, the process of democratisation and modernisation affords far greater possibilities of uprooting caste oppression than of doing away with racism. Victims of caste oppression can subvert the system from within, using ideas from without. The victims of racial discrimination can only locate themselves in a position of permanent opposition, but cannot subvert the system while acting as insiders.

It is not that those appealing to the United Nations to consider caste discrimination as identical to racial discrimination are devoid of this basic understanding. If nevertheless they continue to raise this demand, it is because they hope to derive certain advantages that are not available through the current political and constitutional provisions.

Perhaps the first significant gain that they see in adopting such a position is that caste-based injustice would be globally understood almost instantly within the given categories of racial discrimination, making it easier to raise the problem at international fora. To fit one's case in readymade, given categories does save one the trouble of thinking through and communicating the specificities of one's own situation. The protagonists of the campaign are, however, not prepared to face the question as to what impact this international recognition of caste as race might have on the more than a century old anti-caste movement of the Dalits. Would the promise of a few short-term advantages deprive the Dalits of benefits gained through a long movement?

Even more serious is the apprehension that in the anxiety of fitting the purely Asian category of caste into the western template of race, the Dalits might allow the socially emancipatory perspective of the movement into accepting for itself an identity of permanent victim-hood. Those searching for arguments in favour of equating caste with race should, therefore, first try to foresee the possible problems they may create for themselves and the Dalit movement.

If caste-based discrimination can be construed as racial discrimination, will not the brahmans of Tamilnadu, pundits of Kashmir, Buddhists of Ladakh and the religious and linguistic minorities in various states avail of the opportunity to portray themselves as victims of racial discrimination? Once castes other than the Dalits are also considered a race, casteism would begin to be understood in a bland and generic international idiom rather than in its distinctively Indian character that hurts Dalits in a different and deeper way than racism does the black. Racism casts the 'other' away; casteism draws the 'other' nearer. The former creates an adversary, the latter a 'willing' victim.

Another aspect that needs to be considered is the impact this move would have on the caste structures in communities outside the Hindu fold. Every religious minority in India has its own Dalits – the discriminated 'other'. Claims and reassurances to the contrary notwithstanding, the Christians, Sikhs, Muslims and even the Dalits themselves have failed to break free of the scourge of caste.

One immediate consequence might be that the constitutionally guaranteed provisions for reservations could come under question. The opponents of reservation would get another chance to reopen the policy and place it at the centre of the newly revived political and constitutional debates. Even worse, the moral passion against untouchability in the wider public sphere may lose its political edge. The non-Dalit radical consciousness, seeds of which were sown by the rich egalitarian traditions of anti-caste movements, may also be blunted by the new, exclusionary politics of Dalits discourse epitomised in the Durban debates.

Ambedkar's message to get educated organised and agitated itself a product of anti-caste discourse – might appear pale in the midst of a new discourse which celebrates victim hood of the Dalits rather than cultivate their social and political power to overthrow the structure of caste dominance. Indeed, the whole range of Baba Saheb's ideas might face a big question mark as there was no scope in his scheme of things for viewing caste through the prism of race.

To put it in his words: 'The purpose of the caste system cannot be considered to be prevention of racial intermixing, nor can this system be understood as a means of preserving purity of blood. The truth is that even before the caste system came into being, the various races had already go intermixed in India as far as culture and blood is concerned. To consider different castes as if they are different races would be to completely distort the facts. What racial similarity can there be between a Brahman of Punjab and a Brahman of Madras? What racial similarity can there be between an untouchable of Bengal and an untouchable of Madras? What racial similarity can there be between a Brahman of Punjab and a chamar of Punjab? What racial similarity can there be between a Brahman of Madras and a paria of Madras? Caste system does not divide races; it is the name of social division within a race' (Bhim Rao Ambedkar, *Annihilation of Caste,* Anand Sahitya Sadan, Aligarh, 1989, p.40).

III

The campaign to equate caste with race might have the following possible consequences for the Dalit movement: The culture of voluntary organisations would make inroads into the Dalit movement leading to its NGOisation. As a result, the movement might distance itself from the mainstream of electoral and party politics, and thus reduce for itself the possibility of sharing governmental power and may construct its role in terms of a permanent confrontation between the establishment and its victims.

This new tendency might – on the basis of the exigencies associated with the apolitical, developmental and foreign funds – subvert the original and abiding thrust of the movement as a socially emancipatory and politically participative process.

A politics of a permanent 'minoritisation' of the Dalits might be initiated. If this happens, the prospects of Dalits-bahujan unity would vastly diminish.

By framing caste in the racial discourse, Dalit politics will be trapped in the situation of opposing the immediate, rather than the distant but real oppressor. More specifically, it would lead to a Dalit verses OBC polarisation. The first signs of this have already appeared in the form of attempts by some academics to project Mandalites and Dalit politics as two separate and antagonistic models of politics.

It is likely that the upper castes may eventually support the position that the government opposed at Durban, i.e., of equating caste with race because it might give them another opportunity to re-open the issue of caste-based reservations.

This may result in a total communalisation of the politics of religious minorities as that would help hide caste discrimination within minority groupings and present themselves as racially discriminated essentialised entities.

The process of incorporation of Dalits into the middle classes – part of the current thrust of anti-caste movements – might give way to ethnicisation of Dalit politics.

The debate that is currently conducted in terms of Manuvad vs. the bhujan might be converted into one between the state and Dalits.

The Dalit movement might witness a new factionalisation between the governmental *(sarkari)* and 'radical' Dalits, leading to a further fracturing of the movement.

Symbolic politics might begin to overshadow the real politics of power sharing in the government. There is a danger that Dalit politics might be caught in the whirlpool of that brand of 'twice-born' politics that attempts to render the state powerless and empower market forces. This when the Dalit and other backward communities are getting closer to political power and the upper castes are being pushed away from it because of Mandalite politics.

IV

The crucial question in the whole debate is: When will we shed our colonial mentality and give up attempts to understand Indian reality through western categories of analysis? In this context, the usually invisible process of globalisation of ideas and concepts must also be taken into account. Caste is a South Asian reality, most densely manifested in India. Instead of trying to trim it to fit into the readymade western category of race, can we not try to understand social discriminations in US, Canada, other western countries and Japan through the category of caste? Such an exercise would surely strengthen the positive aspect of comparative sociology.

So far, we have been taught to ignore and reject the experience of our own society. We have attempted to see images of caste in the mirror of class and look for a purely hierarchy-based social system in the mirror of the West. Instead of trying to see caste through the mirror of race, let us now also try to see race in the mirror of caste. It is understandable if the victims of racial discrimination were to develop an elementary understanding of caste through race, but we have no such compulsion. In fact, after losing its scientific – ideological basis, the nature of racial discrimination has in practice largely approximated caste discrimination.

South African apartheid is a case in point. At the root of apartheid is an ideology of white superiority, very similar to the brahmanic ideology that legitimises caste. Even after being legally removed, this ideology persists in social behaviour and seeks to project the majority of the population as sub-human. It is also essential to note the predicament of gypsies in Europe, probably the most oppressed community in the whole world. While they do not suffer from untouchability, they have no rights and are totally ostracised and expelled. They are not allowed to stay at one place and their oppression is not even talked about. They are truly the international Dalits.

The origin of the Buraku of Japan is also similar to that of the untouchables of India. Even after giving up their traditional occupation of leatherwork, they have been unable, in practice, to obtain any social-civil rights in Japanese society. If these examples of discrimination are seen from a caste instead of race perspective, it will surely enrich the understanding of their condition and the way of overcoming them. The international community too will then be able to take more effective initiatives against such discrimination. From the same perspective, appropriate categories of analysis might evolve to understand the problem of American blacks and the indigenous peoples of North America.

The internationalisation of caste-based injustice is in itself a worthwhile objective provided it strengthens rather than weakens the institutional and organised efforts against casteism. This is possible only if caste is presented as caste and not forcibly fitted into the category of race, and at the same time an attempt is made to promulgate an international charter against caste discrimination. This mighty yields new perspectives on those forms of discrimination in other societies of the world that have hitherto been seen only in the context of race.

Chapter 10

Race and Caste

Anthropological and Sociological Perspectives

T.K. OOMMEN

The stony academic pronouncement that race is a biological category, and caste is a social category and therefore there is no relationship between these two is unsustainable for two reasons. First, according to the latest research race as a biological concept does not have any validity. So much so the American Anthropological Association has recommended to the US Government to eliminate the term race in the 2010 census because research in human genome shows that DNA of human beings is 99.9% alike irrespective of race. Therefore, what is relevant is not race, but racism, that is, the ranking beings based on their presumed biological origins and features. Similarly, caste as a social category is constructed on the basis of imagined attributes but casteism, that is preferential treatment to one's fellow caste men and caste discrimination based on the belief that some castes are inferior and others superior are of great significance. Secondly, terms and concepts rarely retain their precise meanings and pristine purity. They are manipulated by ideologues, politicians and even scholars to meet the needs of vested interests. Therefore, we need to look at the career of the concepts of race and caste.

The concept of the race had passed through at least four phases. In the beginning race was defined as a biological category by biologists and physical anthropologists who divided human race based on physical characteristics; a widely endorsed categorisation being the division into Caucasoid, Mongoloids and Negritos. But now we know those phenotypical differences between these categories is negligible. And yet, discrimination occurs when inter-racial interaction takes place because the races are categorised into a hierarchy – the top one is believed to be not only physically beautiful but also mentally and intellectually superior. The problem of racism could have been overcome through scientific education if matters stopped here. But that was not to be as the philologist entered the scene launching the second phase when race came to be defined as a linguistic category. Categorisations such as the Aryan, the Dravidian, and the Nordic races had become common. This was indeed a stupid idea. Max Muller said that to refer to Aryan race is as absurd as talking about dolicocephalic grammer.

To complicate matters further race came to be viewed as an ethnological that is cultural category in the third phase of its career. Language is often taken to be the core of culture. If race can be viewed as a linguistic category it may as well be viewed as a cultural, that is, ethnic category, went the argument. Thus the biological, linguistic and cultural came to be co-terminus. From here the distance to the fourth phase, the political one, was rather short. In West Europe nations are conceived as linguistic cultural entities with a geographical anchorage. Understandably races came to be considered as nations. This four-in-one phenomenon gave birth to the idea of unity in blood, language, culture and nation (see Oommen 1997). The most notorious products of this conceptualisation were fascism and Nazism with their abominable consequences – extermination of inferior races. The career of the concept of caste is not exactly similar but not entirely dissimilar either, to the account of which I shall turn subsequently. But before that it is necessary to understand the historicity of the issue.

There is a body of scholars who view that caste is "invented" by the orientalists who aided colonisers to subjugate India. That is, orientalism is viewed as an instrument of colonialism. But the nationalist scholarship, which attacks orientalism, is not different methodologically; the scientificity of both orientalists and nationalists is suspect. Both are biased, although their biases lie in different directions. If the orientalists aided and abetted colonialism by external agent, nationalists often facilitated internal colonialism.

The attack against oriental scholarship was first articulated by Edward Said in his famous book *Orientalism* (1953). And more recently Ronald Inden in his *Imagining India* (1990) reinforced this line of argument with special reference to India. I want to enter a couple of caveats here, before proceeding any further. First, there are at least three Orients – Far, Middle and Near – but Said refers mainly to the Near Orient given his biography and interest. Inden talks about sub-continental India, which is vast and varied with too many internal differences. That is orientalism is constructed by its critics as a master narrative. But much of the internal variations is concealed in this master narrative. We need to have several micro narratives to unfold the diversity and richness of reality in the orient. Second, there is no consensus among the colonial scholars about the nature of Indian social reality; it is not a master narrative to them. The difference among them is not a matter of their ideological or methodological differences but largely conditioned by the "fields" they have studied – the property of the situation, which they investigated.

Now, let me answer the following question: (1) Is caste an invention of the orientalists? (2) How far is it corrects to say that caste has nothing to do with race? Oriental scholarship is an instrument and a product of colonialism as I hinted above. But even a cursory understanding of the two ancient texts of India – Mahabharata and Ramayana – unfold the following: (1) The Hindu Society was hierarchical and it had a racial basis as the distinction between fair-skinned Aryans and dark Dasyus existed; (2) The Hindu Doctrine of Creation refers to the Chatur Varna (four-colour) scheme which orders the four categories into a hierarchy. In this scheme white denoted Brahmins, red Kshatriyas, yellow Vaishyas and black Shudras. These categories emerged respectively from the mouth, arms, thighs and feet of the Primordial Man; (3) The possibility of varnasankara (confusion and/or mixture) was conceded through two sources. First a theory of mobility according to which originally.

> "... Brahma created just Brahmins but those who were short-tempered and violent left their Varna, turned red and became Kshatriyas, those who took to cattle rearing and agriculture turned yellow and became Vaisyas, and those who in their delusion took to

injury and untruth turned black and became Sudras; those who diverged still further from the proper norms and did not recognize them became Pisacas, Raksasas, Pretas and various sorts of Mlecchas (foreigners, barbarians)" (Brockington 1997: 99).

Second, through inter-varna marriages, both anuloma (hypergamus) and pratiloma (hypogamous), mixed varnas emerged (4). There are references to the Pahlvas, Sakas, Yavanas and Kambojas of North West, Tamils and Sinhalese of South as well as to Mlechas and Barbaras-the foreign elements. These were referred to as racially distinct elements.

The point of interest here is that the orientalists could not have invented the racial-cum-caste categories in Ramayana and Mahabharata, although of course, they seem to have interpreted the bases of categorisation facilitating colonial domination. However, it could be argued, and many have, that these books-views are at variance from the field-views. It is well known that the varna scheme is vague and ambiguous and particular varnas may be absent in given regions (for examples, the Vaishyas are absent in the caste structure of Kerala). But, this does not nullify the fact that the varna scheme is essentially a scheme, which hierarchically ordered population based on a colour scheme. Secondly, each varna had several, sometimes numerous, castes (jatis) under its rubric. At any rate, co-terminality between text view and field-view seldom exists particularly in theological matters such as the Doctrine of Creation. Therefore, one is driven to the conclusions that (a) the race-caste link is alluded to in the ancient Hindu texts, and (b) it is wrong to assert that the phenomenon of caste is an invention of orientalism.

II

Having said this I must address the differences among colonial scholar-administrators regarding their understanding of Indian social reality. James Forbes published his *Oriental Memoirs* (4 vols) in 1813. He uses the terms caste, tribe, nation and race imprecisely and interchangeably. He categorised the "Hindu race" into 84 classes or castes each separated by rigid laws of endogamy, each differing in physical features, dress and appearance. Forbes points to the distinction based on skin colour: "...the inferior castes are of darker complexion than superior Hindoos" (vol. 1 p. 172.) Admittedly caste and colour (read race) was connected in the analysis of Forbes.

William Ward in a view of the *History, Literature and Religions of the Hindus* (4 vols) published between 1817-20 also uses the terms race, caste and race loosely and imprecisely. He attested the primacy of Brahmins and accepted the ideology of varna as axiomatic. Ward concluded that the caste system degraded the victims.

Caste and race had been conflated not only by colonial scholar-administrators but also by Indians. One Kashi Nath wrote in 1873 in Indian Antiquary that the Khattris are "descendents of a war-like race", next to Kashmiris, "the fairest race in Hindustan", of "pure Aryan blood" and "next to Brahmin are the most religious class, reading much of the Hindu scriptures". He was offended by an article published in *Indian Antiquary* a year earlier, by J. White, the Asst. Collector of Fatehpur in the North Western Province, who referred to Rajputs, Khattris and Jats as races who shared a common descent. The fury with which Kashi Nath responded asserting the racial superiority of Khattris clearly shows the ease with which race and caste were conflated in 19th century India, not only by colonisers but also by Indians. In fact Brahmins, Rajputs, Kattris, Santals, Tamils, Bengalis and many other were referred to as 'races'.

However, it is important to recall here that the race – caste conflation was partly determined by the field situation studied by the scholar-administrators of colonial India. Thus Walter Elliot in his article entitled "On the Characteristics of the Population of Central and Southern India", published in the *Journal of the Ethnological Society of London*, in 1868-69, took the position that South India consisted primarily of "races", who had been oppressed by Brahmanical notions of caste on the pre-Aryan and non-Brahmin people who lived there.

As against the above view W.W. Hunter in his *Annals of Rural Bengal* 1897 (7th edn.) maintained that caste was adverse and regionally specific phenomenon connected with the relatively recent race history which took two forms: (1) Caste was a creation of the Aryan race in Gangetic upper India; (2) Caste in Bengal represented the opposition of high and low races, the conquerors and the conquered. The high castes and high races were co-terminus as was the low castes and low races. Hunter's ideas reincarnated in Risley's racial theories of caste expounded in 1901 Census of India. Risley categorised Indian population into Aryan (upper caste), Dravidian (low caste) and Mongoloid (tribes) races.

In contrast to the views of Elliot and Hunter, Denzil Ibbetson in his *Punjab Castes* (1916) argued that caste distinction was based on occupation and political power and he designated Rajputs, Jats, Gujjars, Meos etc. as castes and not races. His field study compelled him to conclude that the community of blood has been de-linked from the community of occupation when caste demography created imbalances. However, Ibbetson endorsed the distinction between Aryan and non-Aryan racial stocks but scarcely invoked the term race in its biological/evolutionary sense. But yet, the separation of occupation (caste) and descent (race) did not stop. Further, caste as a Brahmanical vision of society based on rank, purity and life-style was not characteristic of the Punjab. This was reinforced by the presence of Muslims and Sikhs in large numbers. Thus Ibbetson concluded: (1) Caste could be viewed as a bond of blood association; (2) As a designation for immigrants irrespective of their internal variations; (3) Caste as a ritual ranking and status affirming mechanism, and (4) Caste as an occupational or trades-guild system. Thus caste may stand for different things – race, occupation, outsiders, ritual status – singly or in combination in different parts of India.

To conclude, there is a bewildering complexity and astonishing diversity regarding the literature on 'castes' 'tribes', 'race' and 'nations' and it cannot be unequivocally said that these writing played second fiddle to the colonial regime. I am inclined to agree with Susan Bayley who concludes after an excellent and elaborate discussion on colonial ethnography thus. "...concepts of caste, race, and national identity interacted in complex and dynamic ways with the changing orthodoxies of evolutionary race theory" (1997:215).

III

It is time that I turn to the nationalist discourse on race and caste. Swami Dayanand Saraswati, the founder of Arya Samaj, in his Satyartha Prakash (Light of Truth) contends that Vedic Aryans are the primordial and elect people of humanity to whom Vedas has been revealed by God, their Language, Sanskrit, is the mother of all languages. He prescribed varna endogamy to maintain the purity of castes. Common racial origins of Europeans and Aryan Hindus has been endorsed by Lokamanya Tilak too. However, the two most important Hindu nationalist ideologues for the present purpose are Golwalkar and Savarkar.

M.S. Golwalkar, in his *We or Our Nationhood Defined*, consider Hindus as a race. But according to him the Hindu race encapsulated both Aryans and non-Aryans, i.e., Dravidians and tribes. This implies (a) there was an Aryan invasion, and (b) Aryans are outsiders. Therefore, Savarkar rejects this view and emphasised culture that is sanskriti and territory, which should be viewed as Fatherland and Holy land. For him the fusion of common blood and similar culture makes the Hindu race (Savarkar 1969). However, even Golwalkar's definition of race is more cuturological. That is what he could see the possibility of Dravidians and tribes being accommodated under the rubric of Hindu race. He writes:

> Race is a hereditary society having common customs, common language, common customs, common language, and common memories of glory or disaster; in short it is a population with a common origin under one culture. Such a race is by far the most important ingredient of a Nation (1947:26).

Both Savarkar and Golwalkar translate race into jati, meaning species, a biological category. There has to be several species in a society. The hierarchical view of the caste system with the Brahmin at the top fits in with this perspective. The Aryan Hindu nationalist ideologues were interested in sustaining the hierarchical unity rather than racial purity; their version of racism was an instrument of domination and not extermination. This is a qualitative difference from Nazism and fascism. In the Hindu nationalist rendition the inferior was not excluded but accommodated but in a subordinate rank. This is what caste hierarchy is all about "*upper caste racism*" as Gyanendra Pandey would designate it (1993:252). It is here that the Aryan-Dravidian wedge deepens.

The Aryan-Dravidian difference, although is a linguistic one, has caste connotations as the archetypical Aryan Hindu was the Brahmin.

The dichotomy also had historical implication as in this view Aryans were outsiders and Dravidians were natives. The notion of Adi-Dravidas brought in the caste element in that they were usually untouchables. "Dravidian had always been more a linguistic and geographical term until Europeans made it into a 'racial' distinction" (Hellman-Rajanayagan 1997:135). The Dravidian movement was based on the belief that Dravidians constituted a race (inam) and in so far as they are non-Aryan, that is lower castes, subjugated by the conquering Aryans the link between caste and race comes alive. Ramaswamy Naicker, known as Periyar, posited a dichotomy between jati and inam, as the proud Dravidian inam has in Aryan perception become the shudra jati. "The Dravidian in Periyar's account has been subjugated to racial, not cultural, suppression by the Aryans" (Ibid: 137). According to him Brahmins had tried to foist their language and social system on Dravidians to erase their race consciousness and therefore, Periyar constantly prodded the Dravidians to uphold their 'race consciousness'. However, he did not advocate the superiority of one race over the other but insisted on equality for all. Thus the fundamental difference between the two is crucial; Aryan Hinduism is hegemonic Dravidian Hinduism is emancipatory.

Periyar not only accepted the Brahmins as Aryan but also their superiority. But this for a tactical reason, to keep Brahmins outside the Dravidian race and nation. In this perspective the Brahmin could inhabit Tamil Nadu, speak Tamil language and thus nationalise herself but cannot become a member of Tamil inam (race). After independence the Dravidian parties shifted the emphasis from inam (race) to language and territory, that is, to Tamil nation. The feared imposition of Hindi was seen as a racial and religious suppression of the Dravidian by the Aryan race. To the extent Dravidians are constituted by non-Brahmin castes and the Aryans are dominated by Brahmin, the caste element is implicated in the Aryan Dravidian conflict.

From what I have said so far it is clear that the career of caste is not very different from that of race. It is widely acknowledged that the institution of caste has emanated Varna Vyavastha (system) an Aryan gift. And the adjective race is frequently invoked to qualify both Aryans and Dravidians, although these are linguistic categories.

Further, Aryans consisting of the twice-born varnas are believed to be fairer as compared with the darker Dasas, consisting of Dravidians and Adivasis. Thus race is implicated in the distinction between the Aryan upper castes and the non-Aryan Dalit bahujans, consisting of the other backward classes, the Scheduled Castes and Scheduled Tribes of India today. Aryan Hindu nationalists conceptualised Hindus and Dravidian nationalists conceptualised Tamils as races. Thus, like the orientalists, the nationalists too have interchangeably used castes, races and nations; both indulged in master narratives ignoring empirical realities on the ground. Insistence on semantic purity will be at the cost of intimidating substantive reality.

IV

It is necessary to note here that the tendency to equate caste with race in a neat and tidy vein is not also sustainable. The idea of racial superiority was initially propounded by the French writer, Count Joseph Arthur de Gobineau (1816-82). To prove racial superiority a new science or discipline was established – Anthropometry. But the foundational flaws of this discipline were two: (1) The physical characteristics of the Caucasians (Whites) were taken to be desirable and ideal, and (2) an unsustainable correlation was assumed between these characteristics and institutional, mental and moral superiority. Skin colour, cephalic index (worked out on the basis of ratio of head's greatest breath and length), nasal index, blood group, across section of the heir were the major anthropometric measures. The discipline of Anthropometry reinforced racism.

The 'science' of Anthropometry flourished everywhere, including India, for sometime. The Indian data showed that the upper and lower castes of the same linguistic regions – Tamil Nadu, Maharashtra, Punjab, the Hindi belt shared more of these characteristics than say Brahmin or other upper caste samples drawn on an all-India basis. Which is to say to look for isomorphism between the racial characteristics of upper or lower castes was wild goose chase. But yet racism and caste discrimination shared several common features. For example, exclusion manifesting in physical segregation. The extreme instances of exclusion in the case of racism was apartheid in South Africa and residential segregation of 'untouchables' which persists even to day in Indian villages. In turn this resulted in avoidance of commensality (inter-dining) and endogamy (inter-marriages).

If racism and caste discrimination share certain features it is also true that they differ with regard to two fundamental characteristics – physical and ideological. As racial characteristics are physically visible, racism can be practiced everywhere. That is why, in spite of the fact that racism is constitutionally abolished by all states, everyday racism persists with vehemence. Everyday Racism manifests even in impersonal and anonymous encounters in the context of traveling, shopping, and dining in hotels etc. but everyday racism changes as particular physical types achieve great success and development. Now the 'yellow race' is perceived as a threat by the white race; the new yellow peril is fast emerging. It is also possible to celebrate and uplift one's thus far stigmatised racial identity. This is precisely what is communicated through the phrases 'Black is beautiful'. Therefore, one can legitimately distinguish between racism that is negative and rarity, which is positive (Oommen 1997).

In contrast to racism, which is practiced on the basis of physical differences, caste discrimination is anchored to values. Caste discrimination cannot be practiced in situations of anonymity as castes do not have clear-cut physical differences. That is why caste discrimination is relatively absent in big urban centres. But the moment the veil of anonymity is lifted caste discrimination comes alive. The phenomenon of caste discrimination is rendered extremely complex because the values involved pull in opposite directions. The State Legal System (SLS) of independent India has made the most loathsome caste discrimination, namely the practice of untouchability, a punishable offence. But the Hindu Religious Legal System (RLS) prescribes that the believer should practice untouchability. For example, Apastamba Dharamasutra warns:

> Pollution will occur if these people (read untouchables) are touched, conversed with, or even looked upon.... If the Chandala was touched, you must bathe submerging the entire body, if conversed with exchange of words with a Brahmin; if looked upon, observe the lights (Sun, Moon, Stars).

The rationale of caste inferiority and superiority is legitimised through the doctrine of Karma and Reincarnation. The religious sanction provided for practicing caste discrimination make it extremely difficult to delegitimise it. To complicate matters, as noted above, the SLS and the RLS pull in opposite directions.

It goes to the credit of Indian State to have abolished untouchability and its practice is made a punishable offence through the Untouchability (Offences) Act of 1955. The Protection of Civil Rights Act 1976 was passed to plug the loopholes in the 1955 Act. In the meantime the Scheduled Caste gradually came out of their traditional passivity and started interrogating the privileged in the system. This led to the unleashing of atrocities against them particularly by the newly prosperous OBC's as well as those who are experiencing downward mobility among the upper castes. To meet this new exigency the Scheduled Caste and Scheduled Tribe (Prevention of Atrocities) Act 1989 was passed. The need for enunciating these new legal instruments is ample proof of the persisting discrimination against the Scheduled Castes.

As in many other contexts the Indian State is well fortified with legal provisions but its ambivalence to implement the laws is proverbial. It is further complicated in the present case because of the conflict between SLS and RLS. From 1955, the year in which the practice of untouchability was legally banned, and 1995, two lakh seventy four thousand four hundred and thirty eight offences have registered. This works out to be 6,693 cases per year, that is 18 cases per day. It is well known that large number of cases remain unreported because of the dependency and intimidation syndromes which persists particularly in rural India in the relationship between Scheduled Castes and others. But even the reported cases provide eloquent proof to establish unequivocally the prevalence of widespread caste discrimination.

V

One more comment and I am done. It is necessary to remind ourselves that the manner in which a phenomenon surfaces or practiced in a local is not entirely conditioned by all the attributes of that phenomenon. But both space and time would mould it. For example, racism in anti-bellum South of the US in 17-18th centuries steeped in slavery was qualitatively different from racism which prevailed in 19-20th centuries in Brazil, where racial democracy was the proud motto. The racism in both these sites varied from the abominable apartheid in 20th century South Africa. In India we will look in vain for a mechanical replication of the practice of racism from any of these places, and yet as I have noted at the very outset the Hindu Doctrine of Creation, the chaturvarna scheme of hierarchy and the notion of varanasankara connote discrimination based on colour and caste; colour indeed is one of the most visible marks of race. And, what is more, the chaturvarna scheme does not even recognise the panchamas, those of the Fifth Order, the contemporary Scheduled Castes or Dalits. This is not a slip but a deliberate omission because they are below the pollution line and invested with congenital inferiority.

That there is no neat and tidy co-terminality between the physical types (races) and the social types (castes) is understandable because all the castes, high and low, lived in the same climatic conditions for millennia. Further, the possibility of miscegenation, often surreptitious and illegitimate always existed. To complicate matters the legitimisation provided by religion to the caste system through the theory of Karma and Reincarnation reinforced caste discrimination. Which is to say, in the Indian situation it was and continues to be a coupling of racial and caste discrimination. And, in spite of the legislative measurers discrimination continues unabated particularly in rural areas as noted above.

Finally, facticity alone is inadequate to understand social phenomena. Perceptions are equally important. As the Thomas theorem in sociology upholds, if human beings define a situation as real it is real in its consequences. Earlier we recognise this theorem the better it is for understanding and solving social problems in a humane manner.

References

Bayley, Susan (1997) 'Caste and "Race" in the Colonial Ethnography of India'. In Peter Race (ed.), *The Concept of Race in South Asia*, Delhi, pp. 165-218.

Brockington, John (1997). 'Concepts of Race in Mahabharata and Ramayana', in Peter Robb(ed) pp. 97-108.

Dayananda, Swami (1981), *The Light of Truth*, Allahabad (translated and introduced by G.P. Upadhyaya).

Elliot, Walter (1968-9) 'On the Characteristics of the Population of Central and Southern India', *Journal of the Ethnological Society of London*, pp. 94-128.

Forbes, James (1813) *Oriental Memoirs* (4 vols), London.

Golwalkar, M.S. (1947) *We or Our Nationhood Defined*, Nagpur.

Hellman-Rajanayagam, D. (1997) Is there a Tamil Race, in Peter Robb (ed), op.cit, pp. 109-145.

Hunter. W.W. 1897, *Annals of Rural Bengal*, (7th edn), London.

Ibbetson, Denzil 91916), *Punjab Castes*, Lahore.

Inden, Ronald (1990) *Imagining India*, Oxford.

Kashi Nath, (1873), "Khattris", *Indian Antiquary*, pp. 26-8.

Oommen, T.K. (1997) *Citizenship, Nationality and Ethnicity: Reconciling Competing Identities*, Cambridge.

Pandey, Gyanendra (1993) 'Which of Us are Hindus? In Pandey G. (ed), *Hindus and Others: The Question of Identity in India today*, New Delhi.

Said, E.A. (1991), *Orientalism: Western Conceptions of the Orient*, London (first published in 1978).

Savarkar, V.D. (1969) *Hindutva-Who is a Hindu?* Bombay.

Ward, William (1817-20) *A View of the History, Literature and Religion the Hindus*, (4 vols), London.

White, John (1872) "Khattris", *Indian Antiquary*, p. 289.

Chapter 11

Silence of the Lambs

Durban and the Indian Elite

SUBHASH GATADE

> Untouchability is abolished now and its practice under any form is prohibited – Indian Constitution, Article 17. Despite the Constitutional mandate, untouchability is prevalent in 12 States – Andhra Pradesh, Bihar, Karnataka, Gujarat, Kerala, Madhya Pradesh, Maharashtra, Orissa, Rajasthan, Tamil Nadu, Uttar Pradesh and Pondicherry.
> It is prevalent in a mild form in six states – Jammu and Kashmir, Punjab, Haryana, Himachal Pradesh, Goa and Delhi – and in the Union Territories.
>
> (Maneka Gandhi in Parliament, *Deccan Herald*, July 29, 1998)

This statement by Maneka Gandhi as a Minister on the floor of the House certainly sounds out of tune with the spirit of the new millennium. However, it is not so shocking as it seems at first sight to anyone who is aware of the scourge of untouchability in India. There is no denying the fact that despite half-a-century of Constitutional measures the system continues in myriad ways and forms. The Dalits till date are denied entry into temples or served tea in different glasses in hotels and restaurants or are not allowed to draw water from government wells which are situated in dominant caste areas or Dalit women are driven to prostitution through religious customs like Devadasi or are forced to do menial and polluting jobs like scavenging. And it is a sign of the longevity of this system that despite many a superficial change due to the compulsions of modernity, it has maintained the core of purity and pollution intact.

Of course, you have every right to ask why the need has arisen to recapitulate all these details about a system which can be said to be a characteristic feature of Indian polity and society and which, in the words of Dr. Babasaheb Ambedkar, acted not as a "division of labour but as a division of labourers."

To put the facts straight, the issue of caste apartheid or caste discrimination, especially Dalit oppression, has become a new focal point as far as the proposed Durban World Conference Against Racism, Racial Discrimination, Xenophobia and Related Intolerance is concerned. Debate has arisen among the broad spectrum of Indian society, especially among the intellectuals, activist groups, political formations/organisations and many a concerned individual, about the inclusion or exclusion of the issue of caste oppression, especially Dalit oppression, at the Durban Conference. As you might be aware, the proposed conclave (August-September 2001), to be held under the auspices of United Nations, has been timed to mark humanity's successful victory over apartheid a decade ago and also to chalk out a strategy to do away with the vestiges or remnants of similar nature.

The multi-layered debate has raised quite a few questions, the first and foremost being defining the agenda of the Conference itself. Whereas a significant majority would like to move beyond formal proclamations on racism and would certainly like to discuss discrimination based on 'occupation' and 'descent' as well which are part of the agenda of the Conference, India has taken an intransigent position as far as the question of Dalit oppression is concerned. Although it is ready to discuss the Romas of Europe or the Burakus of Japan, it has strong reservations about the inclusion of Dalit oppression in the agenda. It thus stands at variance with it South Asian neighbours, especially Nepal and Sri Lanka, who are ready to include caste oppression in the agenda of the meet. It may be noted that in Nepal the Dalits constitute 22% of the population. It is interesting that India, which is an early signatory to the Convention on Elimination of all sorts of Racial Discrimination (CERD), had at one time taken an initiative for inclusion of discrimination based on 'descent' in one of earliest CERD conferences but is today apparently back-tracking on this earlier commitment.

The second pertinent question which has arisen concerns what constitutes an 'internal' issue of any country and what constitutes an 'external' issue. The position taken by the Indian Government is that caste oppression is an 'internal' issue of India. People are rightly asking; on what basis could racist apartheid be interpreted as an external issue and caste apartheid (nee discrimination) as an internal one?

A third point of debate is what constitutes a nation and what is its relationship with the people living there? To put in other words, does national interest mean the interests of the broad masses of the people or is there some dissonance in it?

A fourth point of debate is on the similarities and dissimilarities in race and caste. Although this point is completely irrelevant at the present juncture, it has been raised by many ill informed or motivated people to divert attention from the focal point of discussion.

Even a cursory glance at the draft documents of the Conference makes it quite clear that the issue is not that complex as it has been made out to be. It is, therefore, disturbing to note that a majority of the Indian elite has adopted an ostrich-like attitude towards it. In doing so most of them by their silence have unashamedly become tacit supporters of the government stand which says that caste oppression (nee Dalit oppression) is an 'internal' matter of India and should not be raised in an international forum of this nature.

One also notices a strange convergence of views from the far Right to the Centrist forces to the mainstream Left as far as this issue is concerned. They have, by and large, maintained silence and are not ready to take a clear-cut position about an issue which is linked to the real empowerment and humanisation of around a fifth of the Indian population who have been denied even the most basic right to be human since thousands of years.

Apart from a significant minority comprising of a few Dalit organisations and concerned NGOs, few radical political formations and independent intellectuals, nobody has the audacity of questioning the rational behind this stand by the Indian Government and demand the inclusion of the issue of Dalit oppression in the proposed Conference. The motley combination has also questioned the modus operandi adopted by the government to reach this decision keeping the representative organisations of people, the Parliament in the dark and even not consulting the NHRC (the National Human Rights Commission), the prime human rights organisation constituted by an Act of Parliament.

One can gauge the turmoil which the issue has engendered from the fact that in the last leg of May 2001, André Béteille, a leading sociologist from India, resigned from the committee constituted by the Prime Minister for drafting India's response at the UN Conference (NDTV, May 21, 2001). According to him,

"Race is a biological category having distinctive physical markers whereas caste is a social category. The consequences of this will be to add more divisions in Indian society. We have enough divisions based on language, religion and caste, which we have to address. So we don't need to fabricate or invent yet another based on race".

His opinion matches the posture that India wants to take at the UN. It is another matter that while his academic opinion that caste is not race may be debatable; but it overlooks the simple fact that both racism and casteism are social categories with political ramifications. His stand vis-à-vis the UN Conference also completely neglects the ambit of the Conference which in its draft document, specifically takes into consideration 'discrimination' based on 'occupation' and 'descent'. Another leading political scientist, Dheerubhai Sheth, while noting the benefits accruing to the Dalits if the issue comes up for discussion, concludes by raising the spectre of the abolition of affirmative action if caste is equated with race (*Jansatta*, June 12, 2001). A leading columnist Rajkishore has also echoed a similar position (*Amar Ujala*, June 19, 2001).

At the other end of the spectrum stand the Dalit activists who have denounced the 'narrow definition of caste which is inherent in this discourse'. They sincerely believe that bringing up caste bias at an international forum like the UN will increase global pressure on the Indian Government to protect the lower castes, who even today continue to be victims of severe oppression. Apparently the whole debate about inclusion/exclusion of caste/Dalit oppression in the agenda of UN Conference has boiled down to a debate around the sameness/differences or the race/caste scenario.

As far as the Government of India is concerned, it approach is quite clear. Savitri Kunadi, the Permanent Representative of India at the United Nations, clearly stated the government's stand at the 57th session of the Commission on Human Rights that the caste system does not fall within the purview of racial discrimination. It was not surprising that the organisers of a Global Conference against Racist Oppression and Caste Oppression (Delhi, March 2001) had to face the wrath for this approach; the Indian Government refused permission for many a delegate from outside. Doubts are also being raised in many a quarter whether the Indian Government will permit at all those formations, organisations and individuals who have been championing this cause for quite some time and who wish to attend the Durban Conference.

Referring to the note *Perspective of UN Treaty Bodies on Caste* one notices that in recent years the United Nations Human Rights bodies have in their documents underlined the existence and persistence of caste-based oppressions in India and many a South Asian country. It is also noteworthy that they have also emphasised the fact that various existing national level legislations have failed to protect the Dalits from discrimination.

> ...Though India has ratified the Convention on the Elimination of all forms of Racial Discrimination (CERD) in 1969, it was not until 1996 that the CERD Committee made its first explicit reference to caste-based discrimination, 'untouchability' and Scheduled Castes. In its 1996 state report to CERD the Government of India took the position that caste discrimination did not fall under the purview of CERD, because caste was not the same as race and the term 'descent' in concluding observations on the Government of India's 1996 state report, CERD opposed this position stating that though caste may not be equivalent to race, caste, nevertheless, fell within its purview under Article 1 of the Convention.

> According to CERD doc A/51/18 Donas 339-73, The Committee states that the term 'decent' mentioned in Article 1 of the Convention does not solely refer to race. The Committee affirms that the situation of the Scheduled Caste and Scheduled Tribes fall within the scope of the Convention.

If one refers to the history of CERD itself then one comes across the interesting fact that when the draft of the CERD did not include the term 'descent' in Article 1, it was the Indian Government itself which insisted on including it. Today, the same government is opposing the inclusion of caste-based discrimination in CERD and the WCAR under the term 'descent' (Ref: *Perspective of UN Treaty Bodies on Caste*).

A statement released by academic, jurists and civil society groups at the end of a Delhi Conference demanding inclusion of the caste issue in the Durban agenda makes it quite clear how the Indian Constitution itself looks at the whole issue of caste vis-à-vis race. According to the statement,

> Article 15 of the Constitution of India which outlaws discrimination based on grounds of religion, race, caste, sex or place of birth, treats caste at par with race as a prohibited ground of discrimination...Article 17 while declaring the abolition of untouchability has in effect accepted the existence of caste-based discrimination and its effect of untouchability as racial discrimination.

> Article 341 of the Constitution states that

> The President may with respect to any State or Union Territory and where it is a state after consultation with the Governor thereof, by public notification, specify the castes, races or tribes or parts of groups within castes, races or tribes which shall for the purpose of this Constitution be deemed to be Scheduled Castes in relation to the State or Union Territory, as the case may be.

> From the statement it can be construed that "according to the Indian Constitution the concept of SCs is inclusive of the concept of race..."

The Delhi conference also looked at a few of the judgment relating to discrimination against Dalit and inferred that many of these judicial decisions recognise caste "as a prohibited ground of discrimination not only at par with race but also as a form of racial discrimination". The different definitions of caste, adopted by the several decisions of the Supreme Court of India, show that for the purposes of treating caste as a prohibited ground of discrimination, caste is race in the Indian context. [K.C. Vasant Kumar versus State of Karnataka 1985 (supp.) 1 SCR 352] The nine-judge Constitution Bench in the case of Indira Sawhney versus Union of India [1992 (supp) 3 SCC 217 at 714] defines caste in the following terms:

> A caste is noting but a social class – a socially homogeneous class. It is also an occupational grouping, with this difference that its membership is hereditary. One is born into it. Its membership is involuntary.

In another judgment the same Supreme Court described "caste discrimination to be more atrocious than racial oppression".

The National Human Rights Commission has rightly observed in the case of a Dalit oppression from Devaliya, district Ameli, Gujarat (No. 14/6/99-2000).

> (D)evaliya is only a tip of the iceberg of the atrocities flagrantly committed with impunity on the Dalits in the country. Their total dependence on daily earnings is the root cause of their being subjugated to indignities. Due to education and marginal cultural development, when some youths either assert the right to equal treatment or attempt to protect the dignity of their person or of their women or resist the perpetration of the practice of untouchability or atrocities being committed on Dalits, they are often branded as Naxalites and extremists, they are implicated in false crimes and killed in false encounters...

Of course, the observations of the NHRC very much converge with the conclusions of various commissions and committees formed by the government itself from time to time to look into the cases of atrocities against the Dalits. Definitely the plight of the more than 16 crore Dalit population despite more than 50 years of promulgation of the Indian Constitution demands urgent attention and action on part of the government and civil society organisations.

The approach of the judiciary towards matters of Dalit oppression and exploitation also does not seem satisfactory. One is reminded of the judgment in the Killevanamani massacre (Tamil Nadu 1969) wherein more than 35 Dalit women and children were killed in cold blood by the local dominant castes as retaliation for demanding better wages. One is shocked to read the final judgment by the courts in this first organised massacre of this kind in post-independence India. All the accused were allowed to go scot free with a spacious argument that – since they are upper caste people it appears impossible that they would have gone walking to the hamlets of the Dalits.

Any pro-people government or progressive civil society atmosphere would have definitely taken the lead in putting the issue before the world and would have had no qualms in sharing the experiences of other countries in elimination of discrimination of similar/different nature. But it is not less than ironic that the same government which keeps tomtomming its 'progressive' image for its moral and other support to the fight against apartheid or the Palestinians' struggle for national liberation, has no qualms in saying that caste discrimination, especially Dalit discrimination, is an 'internal matter' of India. It become quite clear that the government is employing double standards as far as cases of its own commission and omission are concerned. How can the sufferings of more than 2% of the world population be construed as an 'internal' matter of any country?

The 52nd session of the UN Subcommission for the Promotion and Protection Human Rights, which was held in preparation of the agenda of the Durban Conference, adopted a unanimous resolution recommending that (Ref: *Perspective of UN Treaty Bodies on Caste)* the world conference focus inter alias on the situation of racism, racial discrimination, xenophobia, related intolerance and ethnic conflict and other patterns of discrimination such as contemporary forms of slavery that are based on race, colour, social class, minority status, descent, national or ethnic origin or gender, including topics such as:

(a) The link between forms of slavery and racial and other discrimination based on descent.
(b) The implications of multiple identities (race, colour, descent, minority status, national or ethnic origin, gender) (Ref. E/CN4/Sub2/2000/1/rev, 1-01 August 2000).

It is interesting that India was also a party to the unanimous decision in that conference. The same meeting entrusted as expert member, Goonesekere of Sri Lanka, to prepare a working paper on forms of discrimination based on occupation and descent with special reference to South Asia to identify those communities wherein such discrimination is practiced, know the judicial and legislative measures adopted to ameliorate their conditions and make future recommendations. The 53rd session of the UN Sub Commission will be held in August 2001 to discuss the paper. What stand the Indian representative takes at the proposed meeting is being watched with bated breath.

It is possible that India would try to transcend its supposedly 'national' interests and be ready to discuss its 'internal' matter in the world fora with an open heart or will it stick to its incongruous position that no one has a right to comment on the fate of 2% of the world population even if a majority of them are denied a minimum human existence at the beginning of the new millennium and would continue to remain there if some drastic steps are not taken.

It is not true that any such discussion would enhance the principles of equity enunciated in the Indian Constitution and would strengthen the commitment made by the broad masses of the Indian people towards values of pluralism, tolerance, diversity in their 'tryst with destiny'?

Time has presented us with a golden opportunity to show our readiness to rid us of our past mistakes and present incongruities. It has been more than 200 years ago that in the name of fighting a larger evil, namely, imperialism, colonialism or capitalism, problems of deprivation, injustice and social insult faced by the marginalised sections of Indian society, namely, Dalits, women and other exploited and oppressed sections, have been put on backburner. History, it seems, is repeating itself when the powers-that-be are unashamedly saying that commenting on the plight of the Dalits would be an affront to their sovereignty.

Would a saner advice help the powers-that-be to wriggle out of their incongruities? It seems the famous Hindi poet of the sixties Sarveshewar had all such situations in his mind when he wrote: "A nation is not just a map made on a piece of paper".

Chapter 12

UN Conference Against Racism

Is Caste Race?

AMBROSE PINTO

The United Nations third World Conference Against Racism, Racial discrimination, Xenophobia and Related Intolerance popularly known as World Conference Against Racism (WCAR) will be held from August 31 to September 7, 2001 in Durban, South Africa. The earlier two conferences were held in 1978 and 1983 and primarily focused on apartheid in South Africa. The forthcoming conference is going to be different. The member states of the UN will focus on the causes and consequences of various manifestation of racism. The objective is to work at strengthening existing human rights mechanisms and develop practical action-oriented measures and strategies to combat contemporary forms of racism and intolerance. At the end of the conference, the member-states will adopt a statement of principles, a programme of action and means of implementation.

Since the conference is going to discuss various manifestation of racism, Dalit groups in India have decided to present their case at the conference. Already several Dalit groups have come together to present a united stand against discrimination before the international community and the UN. They have planned common strategy, join lobbying and advocacy and have received support from concerned individuals and groups from both within and outside the country.

The Indian government has not been at ease with the move. It has declared that it would defeat any move to internationalise the issue of the caste system. The position of the government is that caste is purely an internal matter of the country and the international community should have no business to be involved in it. The UN should not interfere in the internal affairs of the country. The government has also asserted that it has been sensitive to the needs of SCs/STs and has legislated several provisions for the emancipation of SCs/STs (Dalits) in the country through abolition of untouchability, affirmative action and a large number of the economic schemes. Besides, the position of the government is that caste is not race and hence the issue is not relevant at the conference. The Dalit position has been just the opposite of the government. They just claim that the Hindutva chauvinists do not want any discussion on the caste issue because they want to continue to exult in and glorify Hindu religion, a religion based on caste. If caste discrimination gets highlighted in the international media, the 'Hindutvawadis' would not be able to pontificate and preach about the virtues of Hinduism and their heritage. At stake is the position of the ruling upper castes and classes who have thrived in the name of god and religion by oppressing the SCs/STs for centuries.

The more radical and progressive Dalit groups have attacked the present fundamentalist and fascist Hindu government that is bent upon perpetuating the caste system in the name of Hindu revivalism. A statement from one of those groups reads: "We need to let the world know how desperately and relentlessly the current Indian government is trying to prevent light being shed upon caste and the religion that is founded upon caste for continuing the hegemony of the upper caste". Dalit activists have offered six reasons why the issue must be discussed by the world conference.

One of the core themes, which will be addressed at the conference, is the issue of descent-and-occupation-based discrimination. Caste discrimination is a part of the discrimination based on descent and occupation. The position of GONGO's (a term that is used for Government of India's bureaucrats and officials) that caste is social and race is biological has had no acceptance among Dalits and their supporters. Caste is by descent and its is the children of SCs/STs and other marginalised communities that are compelled to do all kinds of menial jobs like scavenging, sweeping, bonded labour etc.

Dalit groups have refused to accept that caste is restricted only to India. Caste is prevalent all over south Asia especially in India, Nepal and Bangladesh. The Burakumin in Japan and Korea, Osu of Nigeria and similar 'untouchable' communities in other west African nations have also been experiencing discrimination. The UN therefore should discuss the issue.

The non-governmental organisation committee as well as the Asia-Pacific regional NGO coordination committee of the world conference have already officially endorsed the view that the issue of caste discrimination against Dalits is a gross human rights violation and one that need to be addressed in the WCAR.

As a member-state of the UN, India has signed and ratified a number of key international human rights agreements including the convention on the Elimination of All Forms of Racial Discrimination (CERD). Along with 162 nations, Indian government remains committed as a result of signing these agreements and convention to eradicate racial discrimination, including descent-and-occupation-based discrimination. The Dalits therefore argue that the performance of the government has to be monitored through recourse to the world organisation.

In spite of 54 years of independence caste discrimination continues in spite of laws against it. The successive governments have not been able to address the issue and have shown a lack of political will to implement the laws. Dalit activists see the world conference as an opportunity to impress upon the wider international community in the presence of their government that Dalits in south Asia still face gross discrimination and practice of untouchability which cannot be ignored by the international community.

Besides the UN is a world government. Human lives are no properties of any government. No government is permitted to violate rights of citizens. When a state fails to protect life the only alternative Dalit groups have is to bring the issue to the international community to bring pressure on the state.

UN and Caste Discrimination

In the past the UN's own committees have stated that caste fits into the conference though the world caste has not been used. They have instructed the Indian state to take steps to prevent acts of discrimination on SCs/STs. Below are a few examples:

Special measures be taken by authorities to prevent acts of discrimination towards SCs/STs and in case where such acts have been committed, to conduct through investigations, to punish those responsible and provide just and adequate reparation to the victims... A continuing campaign be under taken to educate the Indian population on human rights, in line with India's Constitution and with universal human rights instruments including CERD and aimed at eliminating the institutionalised thinking of the high caste and the low caste mentality (UN Committee on the Elimination of All Forms of Racial Discrimination, CERD/C/304/Add 13, September 17, 1996).

> Despite measures taken by the government, members of the SCs/STs as well as the so-called backward classes and ethnic and national minorities continue to endure sever social discrimination and to suffer disproportionately from many violations of their rights under the covenant, inter alia, inter-caste violence, bonded labour and discrimination of all kinds. It regrets that the de facto perpetuation of the caste system entrenches social differences and contributes to these violations. The committee also recommends that further measures be adopted, including education programmes at national- and state-levels to combat all forms of discrimination against these vulnerable groups in accordance with Article 2, paragraph 1 and 26 of the Covenant (UN Committee on Civil and Political Rights, Consideration of the Government of India Report to the Human Right Committee – CCPR/C/79/Add 81, August 4, 1997).

> The committee is concerned with the continuing discrimination, including violence suffered by women of the dalit community, despite the passage of the Scheduled Castes and Scheduled Tribes (Prevention of Atrocities) Act of 1989... The committee considers that widespread poverty, such social practices as the caste system and

> son preference, as reflected in a high incidence of violence against women, significant gender disparities and an adverse sex ratio, present major obstacles to the implementation of the convention (UN Committee on the Elimination of Discrimination Against Women – CEDAW/C/2000/1/CRP 3/ADD Dt. 31.04.2000).

> Aware that discrimination based on occupation and descent has historically been a feature of societies in different regions of the world and has affected a significant proportion overall of the world's population, acknowledging the Constitutional, legislative and administrative measure taken by relevant governments to abolish practices of discrimination based on occupation and descent in such societies, declares that the discrimination based on occupation and descent is a form of discrimination prohibited by international human rights law ... (Resolution of the Commission on Human Rights, sub-commission on the Promotion and Protection of Human Rights, 52nd Session, August 9, 2000 – E/CN4/Sub2/2000/L14).

The question therefore, is not whether caste is race or race is caste. The central issue is whether caste is a form of discrimination. The UN accepts the discriminative part of caste and places it as being similar to race though not as exactly as race. In fact, in its concluding observations on the Government of India's 1996 State Report, the CERD states that though caste may not be equivalent to race, caste-based discrimination nevertheless falls within the purview of the Article 1 of the Convention, which includes discrimination based on descent.

Dalit in India, the Ambedkarites and the progressive academic have never equated race with caste. The author writing in *The Hindu* on March 27, 2001 terms caste as variety of race and concludes Dalit oppression as worse than racial discrimination:

> Whether it is caste or race, the status is entirely ascribed, the status one obtains at birth. Segregation exists in all the three system. Shudras still remain outcastes. Even in the midst of the recent worst human tragedy that hit the country in the form of an earthquake in Gujarat, the whole institutional mechanism of the state did not

move into the dalit areas and belts while the benefits of relief went into the upper castes as fast as possible. This is no concoction. Papers have reported it. Parliament has discussed it. The Congress Party has highlighted it and NGOs have testified for it. In both caste and race those in the lowest rung are not only discriminated, but also cursed to do menial jobs. Endogamy is another feature of both. Marriages are rare and few both among different racial/caste groups. Both are stratifications, a hierarchical ordering of social categories supported by social institutions. Inequality is inter-generationally transmitted in caste and race. Prejudice and discrimination are both a part of race and caste. And what is worse is that such prejudice and discrimination are not merely personal, but institutional, a part of the structure and processes of the whole society. Basically, a system of institutionalised behaviour, norms, sanctions and vested interests are constituted in both. In both caste and race theories, there is an attitude of the so called higher or superior groups that their culture is superior to all other cultures and all the other groups should be judged according to their culture. What is the difference in the claims made by the white race in Europe and the upper caste in India? In any racial or caste society the access to the society's resources including power are proportionately larger to the pure in comparison to the impure or polluted. Take the example of the dalits in India. The Constitution has made caste illegal and abolished it in 1950. Affirmative action programme was introduced to bring the unequal to the level of equality. Regardless of official policy, the system still permeates Indian life and culture. "When we are working, they ask us not to come near them. At canteens, we have separate tea tumblers and they make us clean them ourselves and make us put the dishes away. We cannot enter temples. We cannot use upper caste water taps. Our children in schools are not treated as children of the others, we live in colonies of our own" – is a testimony of a scavenger in Ahmedabad. Caste still has limited social advancement, job and marriage choices. In spite of 50 years of independence can one still believe that the SC/ST representation in teaching jobs at the level of higher education is a mere 2% at the all India level, when the affirmative action has provided them with 22%. How do those who oppose the linkage of caste with race

> explain this? Though skin colour or physical differences may not all the time play a significant part in distinguishing caste as in race, social descent and occupation does. Apartheid exists in both. On several counts dalit oppression is worse than racial discrimination. Over 240 million people of this country have been shunned as outcastes.

The positions of Kancha Ilaiah and Gail Omvedt have been similar. A group of 40 academicians, jurists and representatives of civil society organisations mostly from Dalit communities, who met for a day's conference on May 7, 2001 in the Indian Social Institute, New Delhi, had denounced the Indian subcontinent's caste system as worse than racism and demanded an international scrutiny and debate on the plight of the victims of the pernicious caste system.

The participants in the Delhi meeting were clear that 'caste is race plus'. Inflicted by birth, sanctified by religion, glorified by tradition, caste has had brutal repercussions for a fifth of India's population through the generations. Social scientists (T.K. Oommen et al) have highlighted the Aryan conspiracy in India to subjugate the Dalit bahujans by attempting to construct the Indian nation on the basis of purity of blood, language and culture. With Hindu revivalism, a fascist culture centred on the purity of the Aryan race, superiority of Sanskrit over other languages and bramanic culture are imposed on the country.

Caste and Race in the Indian Constitution

The statement goes a step forward and even observes that the Indian Constitution recognises caste in terms of race:

> The Indian legal system has consistently recognized and acknowledged the existence in Indian society of discrimination based on caste as a form of racial discrimination. In other words, the existence of discrimination on the basis of descent and occupation has been the subject matter of a number of legislative measures including Constitutional provisions and judicial decisions of the supreme court of India and the high courts of different states. The discrimination based on caste is at least equated with, or dealt at par with discrimination based on race.

The Constitutional provisions not only juxtapose caste with race and sex as prohibited grounds of discrimination, but also equate caste discrimination with racial discrimination. Article 15 of he Constitution of India, which outlaws discrimination on grounds of religion, race, caste, sex or place of birth, treats caste at par with race as a prohibited ground of discrimination. Similarly, Article 16 while declaring equality of opportunity in matters of public employment as a fundamental right not only specifies caste a prohibited ground of discrimination at par with race, but also protects and declares the provision of reservation in educational institutions, job opportunities and legislatures (a form of affirmative action). Article 17 while declaring the abolition of untouchability has in effect accepted the existence of caste-based discrimination and its effect of untouchability as racial discrimination. Article 23 prohibits forced labour as a form of discrimination. Similarly in Article 29 while declaring the fundamental rights of protection of the interest of minority rights, caste discrimination in admission into educational institutions is prohibited at par with racial discrimination. The provisions relating to reservation of seats for SCs/STs (castes and tribes listed in the schedule appended to the Constitution of India) in the Lok Sabha and in the legislative assemblies Article 331 and 332 do recognise the mischief of caste discrimination and attempt to remedy the same, which is a clear proof of the Constitution of India acknowledging caste discrimination as a form of racial discrimination. Article 335, mandating that the claims of SCs/STs to services and posts in connection with the affairs of the union of India and the states, also reflects the acknowledgement of existence of caste discrimination as a form of racial discrimination. Article 338, which provides for a National Commission for SCs/STs, also reflects the said Constitutional acknowledgement. The provisions of Article 341 providing for the specification of SCs for the purpose of the Constitution clearly show that the castes are not only equated with races, but the Scheduled Castes include race. It is clear therefore, that according to the Indian Constitution the concept of SCs is inclusive of the concept of race. Thus caste-based discrimination is not only a form of racial discrimination, but is more than racial discrimination. Article 341 is extracted here below:

> 341. Scheduled Castes: (1) The president may with respect to any state or union territory, and where it is a state after consultation with the governor thereof, by public notification, specify the castes, races or tribes or parts of or groups within castes, races or tribes which shall for the purposes of this Constitution be deemed to be Scheduled Castes in relation to that state or union territory, as the case may be. (2) Parliament may by law include in or exclude from the list of Scheduled Castes specified in a notification issued under clause(1) any caste, race or tribe or part of said notification issued under the said clause shall be varied by any subsequent notification.

Several legislative measures relating to SCs/STs clearly prove the existence of caste discrimination even more violent and more dangerous than racial discrimination in Indian society, but also shows the ineffectiveness of the governmental measures already taken. The two particular legislations worth pointing out are (a) The Untouchability (Offence) Act, 1955 which was improved and renamed subsequently as Protection of Civil Rights Act 1976 prescribing more stringent measures, and (b) the SCs/STs (Prevention of Atrocities) Act, 1989.

The catena of judgments relating to the caste-based discrimination against SCs and the remedies against the same shows that caste is recognised and acknowledged by the judicial decisions as a prohibited ground of discrimination not only at par with race, but also as a form of racial discrimination. The different definitions of caste adopted by the several decisions of the Supreme Court of India show that for the purposes to treating caste as a prohibited ground of discrimination, caste is race in the Indian context (K.C. Vasant Kumar vs. State of Karnataka, 1985(Supp) 1 SCR 352). In the said decision caste is even identified as a race or unit of race, as per the definition of caste accepted by Justice Venkataramaiah in the said case. The nine judge Constitution bench in the case of Indira Sawhney vs Union of India (1992(Supp) 3 SCC 217 at 714) defines caste in the following terms: "a caste is nothing but a social class – a socially homogeneous class. It is also an occupational grouping, with this difference that is membership is hereditary. One is born into it. Its membership is involuntary. Even if one ceases to follow that occupation, still he remains and continues a member of that group". Thus it is evident form the Constitutional, legislative and judicial history of India that caste discrimination needs to be identified and treated as a form of racial discrimination, in fact a more virulent form of racial discrimination than the ones found in other countries

The Position of UN

The UN bodies such as International Convention on Civil and Political Rights (ICCPR), International Convention on Social, Economic and Cultural Rights (ICESCR), CERD, CEDAW and International Labour Organization (ILO) had ignored the existence of caste-based discrimination in India due to lack of awareness of the issue. This omission had negative repercussions on the lives of the Dalits in India. Since the international community was unaware of their plight, the caste forces in nexus with thee Indian state were totally insensitive to their cause. UN human rights bodies have in recent years acknowledged and addressed the existence, prevalence and persistence of caste-based discrimination in India and the rest of South Asia. This has helped the Dalit cause. The first explicit reference to caste discrimination in the CEFRD report was in 1996.The position of the Indian government was on expected lines that caste discrimination did not fall under the purview of CERD because the term descent is exclusively referred to descent based on race. However, the CERD had made it clear that the term descent mentioned in article 1 does not refer to race alone.

One of the major obstacles for gaining international recognition to the Dalit cause is the language of the UN. Being dominated by the west, the language, concepts and terms of the UN bodies have been Europe-centric. The need is not only to bring the caste issue into the UN, but to put pressure on the UN to change its language so that UN becomes representative of all countries and people. The civil society groups and NGOs active among the Dalit bahujans well understand why India has been resolutely opposing the inclusion of caste question, which is primary source of human rights violation of Dalits and the basis of economic deprivation and social degradation. The objective is to perpetuate the existing social order that has benefited the upper caste. The system has developed large social and economic interests. On apartheid in South Africa the Government of India occupied the high moral ground and was in the forefront of the campaign of sanctions and boycotts. Several civil society groups and NGOs want the global community to acknowledge and condemn the caste-based discrimination as a distinct form of racism against the position of the Indian government. UN bodies will be failing in their duty to the people of the world if they do not take this matter at the Durban conference and devise drastic steps to eradicate the caste based discrimination. The failure to include caste will, no doubt, erode the credibility of the UN and compromise its historical role.

Conclusion

There are reasons to believe that the Indian government may scuttle the attempts of the NGOs and others to highlight the issue in the UN conference. While articulating its position on the issue of inclusion of caste in the agenda in the United Nations world conference, the government has deliberately ignored Parliament and the democratic processes. It is likely to follow the same procedure in the UN. Instead of evolving a consensus on the issue through dialogue with civil society groups, it is learnt that the Indian government is working with other governments to block the discussion on caste. Apparently, the African states have decided to raise the question of colonialism and demand compensation for the sins against slavery and loot while the Palestinians backed by the Arab countries want to raise the question of racialism of Israel towards the Palestinians and some other Arab countries. The western countries are quite determined to block discussion on these issues and get India on their side and in return provide support to the Indian government to block any discussion on the caste issue. The country will be represented by a big contingent of government representatives. To present their side of the story there will be NGOs and others. Will they be able to succeed? It is quite important for the third world non government representatives to present a united front against the Indian and western states by backing the demands of the Africans, Palestinians and the Dalits in India. While Africans and Palestinians may demand compensation form colonisers what the Dalits in India need to assert is compensation from their caste masters who have oppressed them for centuries and continue to do so in the name of god and religion.

Caste, Race and Discrimination

Chapter 13

Hidden Apartheid

TEESTA SETALVAD

From August 31 - September 4, when the World Conference Against Racism, Racial Discrimination, Xenophobia and Related Intolerances (WCAR) meets in Durban, the first time since the discriminatory and centuries old regime of apartheid was overturned through much sacrifice and struggle in that country, another group of subordinated peoples, discriminated by descent and occupation, forcibly segregated by tradition and religion from access to common resources, will make their voice heard before the international community.

They will demand that caste-based discrimination, which amounts to descent and occupation based oppression, segregation and exclusion be recognised as a distinct form of racism. A distinct form of racism because it amounts to the denial of basic human rights based on prejudice, discrimination, antagonism and is justified by well-entrenched beliefs about high-low, superior and inferior.

A wide network of Dalit groups from within and outside India will voice this demand on behalf of 160 million Indians. They will make their case through public testimonies of victims and documents drawn up by the National Campaign on Dalit Human Rights (NCDHR).

Predictably, there have been strong attempts by the Indian government to resist the bid to raise the issue of caste discrimination in an international forum. At the preparatory meeting for the WCAR, on February 19 in Teheran, the government made it's stand clear – introducing caste into the ambit of the WCAR at Durban would amount to diluting the concept of racism. The government delegation was represented among others, by the Attorney General, Soli Sorabjee. More significantly perhaps, government spokesmen stress that the problem of caste was an 'internal' one and therefore out of the purview of the UN.

Using his weekly column in *The Times of India*, (March 4, 2001) to emphasise the government's position, Sorabjee endorsed the overall rational behind the theme of the forthcoming conference an acknowledgement that "no country is immune from the virus of racism whose roots lie in the hearts and the minds of the people". He mentioned the Elimination of All Forms of Racial Discrimination (ECERD) convention but commented on the "misconceived attempts by some NGO's to equate racism with caste-based discrimination which is based on birth and occupation and has nothing to do with the race of a person". Our Constitution, he said, recognises the distinction between race and caste, which are separately mentioned as prohibited grounds of discrimination.

In stark contrast to the Indian government position was the Nepal government's candor on the same issue, confronted as it is with recent assertions of Nepali Dalits who accounts for not less than 15% of the total population. The government of the only Hindu kingdom in the world openly admitted that caste is the source of acute discrimination and segregation within Nepal. This it held was serious issue that falls under the theme of the forthcoming conference and should, therefore, form part of the official deliberations at the WCAR at Durban.

Apart from the Indian government, several academics, individuals and groups have also voiced serious concern over what, in their perception, is a Dalit move to link caste to race. This, according to them, is a dangerous move that would lead to a revival of the theory of race that resulted in "Hitler's disastrous racial policies" and that was discounted decades ago (Anthropologist André Béteille in *The Hindu,* March 12).

According to Béteille, "interested parties within and outside the UN would like to bring caste discrimination in general and the practice of untouchability in particular within the purview of racial discrimination... the practice of untouchability is indeed reprehensible and must be condemned by one and all; but that does not mean that we must begin to regard it as a form of racial discrimination. The Scheduled Castes of India taken together are no more a race than are the Brahmins taken together. Every social group cannot be regarded as a race simply because we want to protect it against prejudice and discrimination.... We cannot throw out the concept of race by the front door when it is misused for asserting social superiority and bring it again through the back door to misuse it in the cause of the oppressed. The metaphor of race is a dangerous weapon whether it is used for asserting white supremacy or making demand on the basis of disadvantaged groups" (Emphasis added).

There are two substantive issues involved here. One is the theoretical rejection and support for Dalit demands by not just academics but other groups and individuals, movements and formations on the lines that Béteille argues. The other is the resistance to any attempt to take the issue of caste-based discrimination to a global forum; to solicit international condemnation of caste-based discriminatory practices and support for the struggle against it.

Put together, both amount to attempts to distort and thereby contain efforts by the Dalit movement to seek international focus and attention on caste-based discrimination, legitimised for centuries through scripture and followed in practice by notions of high and low, superior and inferior, pure and impure. Even half a century after independence, the problem continues. The Dalit condition, which was the result of such a pernicious theory, is the result of a pernicious understanding of race by perpetrators of this condition and not the other way around. It is not the metaphor of race that is being invoked but the metaphor of racism, which was the outcome of the misplaced metaphor of race.

The re-emergence of a vibrant and vocal Dalit movement (after the Dalit Panther movement of the seventies) in the mid-eighties and early nineties has formed the backbone of the national campaign whose demands are now being heard. The systematic campaigns, documentation and theorisation that have emerged reflect the painful reality of 160 million Indians (not counting Dalits of other religious denominations) even 54 years after political independence and democracy.

Even the dictionary meaning of the word racism, (Shorter Oxford: racism is the belief in or adherence to, by the perpetrator not the victims – advocacy of the theory that all members of each race possess characteristics, abilities, qualities etc. specific to their race distinguishing as inferior or superior to another race or races: prejudice, discrimination or antagonism based on this), need to hark to the theory of race to describe its consequence – the condition of racism described as antagonistic or prejudicial or discriminatory. Moreover, within political science and sociology circles, racism has come to typify and describe systems of inequality and discrimination. The condition of 160 million Dalits more than fulfils the description of the conditions used to describe racism. The terms is now being invoked to show how the same kind of dehumanising prerequisites (in terms of definition) that are used to describe, understand and protest against racism are more than fulfilled (thousand times over) when we speak of untouchability and caste-based discrimination.

Is it not time that we fill and feed such terminology with our own histories and thereby deepen their meanings?

To argue that caste-based discrimination – through exclusion, dehumanisation, segregation, violent atrocities and practices – is a distinct form of racism is surely not out of a desire to dangerously reintroduce, as Béteille seems to argue, the theory of race. Rather, the intention is to emphasise that despite the ostensible world wide rejection of the theory of race, even today, a fifth of the population in South Asia has to endure bitter prejudice, segregations, exclusion and discrimination legitimised by a tradition of superior and inferior, pure and impure. (in any case, the supposed rejection of the theory of race is obviously restricted to limited circles, as even today neo-Nazi squads in the West are a grim pointer to the awesome gap between theory and lived experience).

The very theory of the Atishudra – that even now, in the twenty-first century excludes an entire segment of men, women and children out of the Hindu caste fold, but controls this section through an elaborate system of exploitation – economic, social and political – is a theory of superior and the Mleccha, the pure and the impure. The millions so exploited are used for backbreaking manual and menial tasks. Worst of all, they are even excluded from discourse, from the minds eye.

To state that caste, descent and occupation-based discrimination is a distinct from of racism is to evocatively highlight the depth the details of the sub-human conditions that a fifth of the population of India is forced to endure – through segregation, exclusion and discrimination, hierarchy and domination.

It is racism, and not the theory of race, that the Dalit movement as a whole seeks to link it's condition and demand world understanding, international condemnation and, yes, support. There may be individual voices within the movement who hark back to the issue of Dalits being a race but for the moment, at least, the overwhelming Dalit position goes beyond it. (Incidentally, theorists associated with the movement intimately, especially Thorat of the JNU, are emphatic in pointing to Dr. B.R. Ambedkar's own rebuttal of the Brahmanical theory of race that justifies the exclusion and brutalisation of the Atishudra).

The Dalit campaign urges all people, political parties, civil liberties groups, human rights organisations, to address not the whys of caste but address it's present day existence, manifestation and reality. What continues to motivate us as people and a civilization to segregate so brutally 20% of our people and prevents us from lending support to their struggle?

Elected representatives across party formulations – RPI, Congress (I), CPI and the CPI (M) – have allied with the ongoing struggle for international condemnation of continued caste- based discrimination and exclusion. At the preparatory conference in New Delhi between March 1-4, former Prime Minister, Inder Kumar Gujral, former chairperson the National Commission for Women, Mohini Giri, CPI (M) MP, Arindam Sen, all declared allegiance to the move for international solidarity.

Yet, in the wider section of the political class, the intelligentsia, academia, progressive groups and organisations, there has been a distinct tendency to stay aloof from the issue at hand. The general fragmentation of social movements could be one of the reasons for the exclusion of the Dalit issue and it specific demands from other struggles and also the misunderstanding of the thrust and focus of the Dalit campaign. But the distance and divide is also reminiscent of what happened 50-70 years ago, when the voices of Ambedkar and Periyar were drowned in the lead-up to the national struggle against colonialism, for freedom against foreign yoke.

Then as now, Ambedkar's stance was deliberately misconstrued and ignored by the dominant discourse. Ambedkar had to bear the burden of being labelled a traitor simply because of his plea that the rights of Dalits, the 'untouchables', should be made a pre-condition for independence from the British. His own-lived experience, of having to endure the humiliation of being treated as 'impure' even after his education at Columbia University, pushed him towards the demand for separate electorates. Today, an honest look at not just the plight of Dalit but also the exclusion of the Dalit issue from other struggles is a stinging reminder of the possible validity of Ambedkar's position.

The questions raised by Ambedkar decades ago are relevant even now. They are questions about prejudicial and discriminatory methods of production and social relations, methods and relations based on principles of exclusion, denial and humiliation that have existed within the Indian sub-continent for 3,000 years before the British arrived. These centuries' old practices continue to result not only in the creation of wealth and security for half of the population at the cost of the rest, but also in the distinct dehumanisation of a fifth. This state of affairs, sanctified by religious scriptures and practice in the name of caste, is not very different even today.

Why did the national movement not lend support to Dalit concerns? Was it an internal discomfort, a discomfort in dealing with and facing the reality and shame of caste, that reduced us to denigrate and label Ambedkar then and what impels us to resist the demands and support the Dalit movement now?

In the face of growing articulations from the Dalit movement and demands put before the forthcoming WCAR, serious introspection is required over our resistance to the Dalit move to list the shame of caste, in facts and figures and to seek international solidarity and support. Our response is especially strange considering that in non-governmental circles especially, international solidarity on issues of social concern for example, the iniquitous new economic regime under GATT, displaced persons by big dams, discriminatory labour laws, gender issues, peace and de-nuclearisation is accepted practice. Why then is there such resistance to the idea of caste indignities being highlighted internationally?

The significance of the forthcoming conference should not be underrated. The abolition of apartheid in 1991 did not, of course, immediately result in the transformation of South Africa into an egalitarian society with an equitable distribution of resources. But the discrediting and abolition of such a discriminatory system within South Africa was largely due to international pressure and support.

The world has seen, before and since, a variety of exclusions, xenophobia's and intolerances that have resulted in the genocide of different sections of the peoples. The plight of Bosnian people in the very heart of Europe is an example. It will be interesting to see where and how that issue gets representation, if at all. The orchestrated genocide of the Iraqi and Afghani people suffering exclusion, death and poverty as a result of the unjust UN imposed sanctions ought to find some space in the deliberations if at all the WCAR is intended as an event meant to convey a serious commitment to the issues under deliberation. Caste-based discrimination goes back thousands of years and it is time it receives world condemnation.

And what of the other sharp and very real intolerances that have emerged in south Asia and even southeast Asia? Can we honestly look at south Asia in the context of the theme of the global conference and not reflect on or highlight the intolerances that have so sharply surfaced in the name of religion?

The crude destruction of the Bamiyan Buddha's recently cloaks what the terror of the Taliban means to it's own people especially women. In India we have been witness to the insidious movement of the Hindu rightwing, which in the name of Hindutva is manipulating the individual faith of millions to legitimise a religion-based nationalism and destroy democracy. Strife and sectarian violence within Pakistan are testimony to the failure of religion based nationalism.

Bangladesh that fought a secular liberation struggle for independence from Pakistani Punjabi domination is today grappling with it's own demons in the grab of Islamic fanatics. Farther east, for the past three years Indonesia has been torn apart as ethno religious strife (between Muslims and Christians) poses a serious threat to the polity.

Can we from South Asia really speak at the World Conference Against Racism, Racial Discrimination, Xenophobia and Related Intolerances without any mention of the intolerances and xenophobia being created in our part of the world in the name of faith?

Caste in the United Nations

The United Nations' Declaration of Human Rights, 1948 referred to race, colour gender and religion but not caste as a basis or source of discrimination.

For many years, UN bodies and international covenants, conventions such as ICCPR, ICESR, ECERD and CEDAW and ILO omitted any reference to caste. As a result, Dalits could only make little use of the space offered by human rights bodies to raise the issue of caste-based discrimination.

It was the ECERD committee in 1996 (whose convention has been ratified by India in 1969) that for the first time made explicit reference to caste discrimination, untouchability and the Scheduled Castes.

On September 17, 1996, the concluding observation of the United Nations Committee on the Elimination of All Forms of Racial Discrimination (ECERD) was "that the situation of Scheduled Castes and Scheduled Tribes falls within the scope of the convention on the elimination of all forms of racial discrimination," and that the term "descent" contained in article 1 of the convention does not refer solely to race, and encompasses the situation of Scheduled Castes and Scheduled Tribes (Document ECERD/C/304/Add.13). The present demand emanating form the Dalit movement for human right that is being strongly resisted by Indian government is an echo of the progress already made within international covenants and the law.

In 1996 and '97, the UN special Rapporteur on racism and racial discrimination had requested a visit to India to "evaluate the situation (of untouchables) in co-operation with the government and the community concerned." The Indian government has, to date, refused the request for a visit.

The CEDAW committee, in its final report 2000 had mentioned, "The committee considers (that) such social practices as the caste system present major obstacles to the implementation of the convention."

The 52nd UN Sub Commission in Geneva in August 2000 unanimously passed a resolution commissioning expert member Rajendere K. Goonasekere to prepare a working paper on 'discrimination based on descent'. The objectives of the report were to (a) identify communities who continue to experience discrimination based on occupation and descent; (b) examine existing constitutional, legislative and administrative measures for the abolition of such discrimination; (c) make any further concrete recommendations and proposals for the elimination of such discrimination. The Indian government has opposed all these resolutions.

Chapter 14

Discrimination that Must be Cast Away

SWAMI AGNIVESH AND VALSON THAMPU

The proposed "World Conference Against Racism, Racial Discrimination, Xenophoia and Related Intolerance", (Durban, South Africa, August 31 to September 7, 2001), has provoked a long-overdue debate on caste. Caste today enjoys unprecedented political leverage in this country. The political establishment argues, nonetheless, that since constitutional provisions for dealing with caste-based discrimination and disabilities are in place, caste is no longer a problem waiting to be addressed. At the same time, the protagonists of Dalit identity have had considerable success, especially in recent years, in globalising their grievances. The United Nations, in the meanwhile, has become bolder in rejecting the erstwhile dogma that the "internal affairs" of nations should not be interfered with. Those who remain stuck with the mind set of nation states, though, will take a while longer to get used to this changing reality.

Given the track record of tenacious resistance to social reform, it becomes regrettably necessary to expose the pathology of caste practices to global scrutiny. Sticking plaster over festering wounds is not known to help in healing them. They are healed best in exposure. The more we deny dignity and development to our Dalit brothers and sisters and try to keep this scandal under wraps, the surer we are to invite scrutiny and embarrassment in a globalising world.

However, the Government, stage-managed by the caste lobby, is keen to forestall the proposed debate. The strategy of obstruction in this instance is two-fold. The official objection articulated by Soli Sorabjee, Attorney General, is that caste being an issue internal to this country, the UN should refrain from meddling with it. He argues, further, that bringing caste into the ambit of this conference will dilute the focus on race. The latter in particular is a curious argument. The UN conference is not envisaged to be an academic exercise on race, but an initiative to address the evils of "intolerance and discrimination" in which ever form they exist. Else, the words "Xenophobia and Related Intolerance" would not have found a place in the ambit of the conference. The basic question is not if caste is generically identical or related to race. It is if caste perpetuates intolerance and discrimination as race does. The mandate of the world body is not to shoot down race or caste, it is to rid the world of intolerance and discrimination in its myriad forms. In the meanwhile, a segment of the intelligentsia has launched itself into endorsing the establishment's stand. André Béteille has protested vehemently against equating caste with race. "Treating caste as in form of race, "he write "is politically mischievous; what is worse, it is scientifically nonsensical". Even though he concedes that "the practice of untouchability is reprehensible and must be condemned", he feels obliged, nonetheless, to insist that caste is not "a form of racial discrimination". It is not André's case that the caste system is free from "discrimination". Like Vivekananda and Gandhiji, he finds "untouchability" repuganant. Condemn it by all means, but let not caste be polluted by having it discussed alongside race. Due to his image as an ideologue of liberal individualism, André grants that casteism deserves to be condemned. But that does not prevent him from objecting to the way the UN proposes to deal with the issue of caste. The underlying logic amounts to this "Caste is obnoxious. It must go. But the UN should leave it alone". That is clever, for if the UN does not question caste, assuredly no one else who matters would.

The Gujarat earthquake is recent illustration of the discrimination native to the casteist mindset. Kuldeep Nayyar, one of our most respected journalists, has this to say on the discrimination that vitiated relief operations in the quake affected areas. "The criteria for distribution of relief," he wrote, "are said to have been caste, creed and religion. High caste Patels did not allow relief vehicles to reach many places because the population living there belongs to lower castes, which the Patels describe as 'the disease-ridden people". This is distressingly similar to the situation in Gujarat that Ambedkar describes in his book, Annihilation of Caste. "In November 1935, some untouchable women of well-to-do families started fetching water in metal pots. The Hindus looked upon the use of metal pots by untouchables as an affront to their dignity and assaulted the untouchable women for their impudence".

India was at the forefront of globalising the opposition to Apartheid. We were among the earliest to honour Nelson Mandela for undoing this discriminatory system. Even so we are averse to debating caste objectively. In contrast, when the protagonists of the caste system began targeting a minority community in certain parts of the country, the Prime Minister found it appropriate to have a "national debate" on conversion. Given the prolonged history of caste atrocities, shouldn't there have been a series of national debates on caste, so that the Dalits too could have told their part of the story? As long as we are shying away from this long-overdue exercise, how can we convincingly argue against a global debate on caste? Swami Dayanand, founder of the Arya Samaj, blasted the citadels of orthodoxy and proved beyond doubt that the correct interpretation of the Purush Sukta of the Rig Veda not only repudiated the birth-based caste system but also supported the Varna system based on one's Guna, Karma and Swabhava, i.e., Talent, Action and Aptitude. Dayanand advocated inter-caste marriages and uplifted Dalits to the status of Aryas. He also denounced the very concept of race by insisting that all of humanity is one race and any discrimination on the basis of colour or form was an abomination. The Indian establishment should proudly appropriate the great legacy of Swami Dayanand and his Vedic insights.

As a tribute to the legacy of another of India's greatest sons. Dr. B.R. Ambedkar, India should proclaim from Durban that both race and caste are inhuman institutions and they deserve to be cast out, lock, stock and barrel.

Race and caste leave indelible marks on their victims, physically and psychologically. Various attempts have been made by their apologists to invent scriptural sanctions for them. The Dutch Reformed Church in South Africa, for instance, deceived itself into believing that Apartheid was compatible with the biblical world view. The Church of England, for long, dragged its feet in condemning this obnoxious system, largely because of the mammoth investments the Church had in South Africa. The prolonged silence of the Church universal in the face of such a scandalous treatment of human beings is at once inexplicable and inexcusable. How on earth could the Dutch Reformed Church preach that all people are created in the Image of God and also justify racism is a riddle that is hard to unravel?

Apparently, caste too claims its sanction from scripture: allegations acceptable only to those who do not either know or respect the Vedas. Ironically, the very fact that scriptural legitimacy had to be invented for caste proves that it could not have been justified or legitimised in any other way. It is not rarely that scripture is used and abused to defend the indefensible. In point of fact, caste is a post-vedic invention meant to perpetuate the religious, social and economic domination of a few over the rest. Despite the battle cry issued by social and religious reformers like Buddha, Nanak, Kabir, Dayanand, Narayana Guru, Jyotiba Phule and Ambedkar, caste discrimination continues to afflict millions in this country.

Caste, like race is exploitative, discriminatory and anti-developmental. Its virulence can be gauged from the fact that though originally a creation of the medieval Brahmanical priest-craft, the abominable caste system has spread its tentacles into those religions that admitted converts from Hinduism, such as Islam, Christianity and Buddhism. It has not spared even a great social reform movement like the Khalsa Panth, launched 300 years ago, by the warrior-saint Guru Gobind Singh. The invidious character of the caste system has even divided the Dalits into disunited fragments, disabling them from breaking out of this social prison. Decades after B.R. Ambedkar issued the clarion call for its annihilation, caste continues to dominate the social, cultural, religious and political horizon of India. The sun has set over the great British Empire; but not over the caste empire.

Hence the eagerness of our government to forestall the proposed UN Debate. It is common knowledge that the sole agenda of the Sangh Parivar is to perpetuate the iniquitous caste system under the pretext of Hindu resurgence. It is a measure of the prevalent spiritual illiteracy that this gross misrepresentation has managed to sway many in this country. In the words of Swami Vivekananda, "in religion there is no caste. A man from the highest caste and a man from the lowest may become a monk in India and the two castes become equal. The caste system is opposed to the religion of Vedanta".

In the euphoria that accompanied the birth of the republic, it was widely believed that the curses of casteism and communalism would wither away with the rise of secularism and scientific temper. Precisely the opposite has happened. An intolerant and casteist perversion of Hinduism is asserting itself politically. The major institutions of our society and culture are being ideologically colonised. Policies and priorities are being tilted in favour of the upper castes and to the disadvantage of the Dalits and minorities. The rights and guarantees enshrined in the Constitution are being eroded. A palpable allergy to dissent is becoming the order of the day. Shadows of despair are lengthening over "the India of our dreams".

In the emerging, carefully choreographed media debate on caste, it is doubtful if the voice of the victims of caste oppression will be heard at all. Even if it is, it will be formatted strictly within the academic and conceptual parameters set for this debate by the protagonists of the caste order. This is only to be expected, as they are in a position to fix the terminological and ideological framework for this debate. It is naïve in the extreme to expect that there can be a fair debate as long as one of the parties enjoys the exclusive right to fix the rules. Hence the rationale for a global debate that could ensure level playing field for both sides. The invidious trick that the social, cultural and political elite have played all through history is to invent the scruples that shape human perceptions and options from within. Once these are internalised, the advocacies of the elite seem logically inevitable. Today irrational scruples are being worked up against linking race with caste, even though discrimination and endemic injustice vitiate both. These arbitrary scruples are a far cry from the plight of the caste victims. Sadly, they do not have the polemical weapons to counter this rhetorical offensive.

The time has come to call the bluff on the immorality of the scruples of the establishment. The reeking injustice of perpetuating caste oppression and the irreligion of justifying this aberration in the name of religion must all be seen for what it is. A world free from the scandals of destitution and discrimination, a society where all are free to fulfill their potential, where none is Arya or "pariah" for being in the right or wrong wombs, is the minimum goal towards which we need to move together as a nation. If the forthcoming UN conference urges us to take a step in this direction, we should avail ourselves of that chance rather than relapse into defensive disarray.

The discriminatory nature of caste as well as race is duly recognised by the Constitution. Article 15 (which outlaws discrimination on grounds of religion, race, caste, sex or place of birth) and Article 17 (which in effect accepts the existence of caste-based discrimination and its effect of untouchability as racial discrimination) are instances in point. Likewise, Article 29 offers protection against caste-based discrimination in admission to educational institutions. The recognition of the Scheduled Castes and Scheduled Tribes as victims of caste discrimination over the centuries underlies the need to provide for reservation in the Lok Sabha and the Legislative Assemblies of the states (Articles 331 and 332). Statutory provisions for reversing the ill effects of discrimination do not make sense unless caste-based discrimination are both prevalent and rampant.

The stark reality of discrimination that plagues a fifth of India's population continues to stare us in the face. This can no longer be hidden nor justified. Our stature and future as a nation depend on the willingness to acknowledge mistakes and the readiness to correct them, rather than on the stubbornness is denying their prevalence or the droitness in defending them. At any rate, the question of masking the true nature of the caste system does not even arise. For it is not confined to Indian Territory. From here, it has spread to our neighbouring countries and, in that sense, caste-based discrimination is not, strictly speaking, an "internal affair" of our country. The fact that this sub-human pseudo-religious mechanism has survived for so long and that it continues to be ascendant does not prove that it cannot be eradicated. It is unlikely that the caste system, despite its rare genius for survival, continues to remain immune to the challenge of the global order, with the vulnerability of nation-states implied in it, and the inevitable subaltern ferment in the wake of an unprecedented celebration of human awareness.

This is not a time for academic hair-splitting. It is a time for bold and forward-looking initiatives. The hangers-on of the old order will have to realise sooner or later that their customary framework of discourse has already given way to a global frame of reference. This is bound to rob their rhetoric of the semblance of plausibility it enjoyed till the rise of the global order. Caste is a blatant anachronism in a globalising world. The sooner this is realised, the better it is for the country as a whole. The attainment of an egalitarian society free from the stains of casteism, communalism and corruption, rather than erecting some temples here and there, should be our authentic "national aspiration".

Chapter 15

We, the Other People

K.G. KANNABIRAN

The saga of "the other person has not ended. It has shifted to the international arena. They do not appear to be part of "we the people". Serious efforts to bring these "the other people", who are rotting as non-persons in a caste-ridden society, to the status of persons were on for some time prior to independence. The people emerged from subjects to citizens after August 15, 1947. After the coming into force of the Constitution all of us attained a political status with well-defined rights. The most articulate representative of the other people wrote into the Constitution human values and gave it a human face. There was recognition in the Constitution that for the other people to truly become "we the people" specific safeguards and positive measures were necessary. Caste was not abolished by the Constitution. Provisions were made to treat all castes on a par with each other. But the other people even after 50 years have remained "the other people".

Constitutions and gods have always been good. The problem has always been with the interpreters, lay and judicial. The Constitution makes untouchability an offence. And it persists. Bonded labour and child labour come from the ranks of the Dalits. Both the practices have been made penal and abolished by the Constitution and yet they persist. The entire administrative, judicial and political systems are still exercised by the "upper" castes despite large-scale movements against these hegemonic practices. A few are allowed to climb the social order as political leaders or as judges in the subordinate judiciary or as high court judges. In education and government employment, the Constitution has introduced reservation as a principle of ensuring equality for the Dalits. The present ruling party at the centre attacked reservation as the prime cause for diminishing merit and efficiency in administration, and by stoking the anti reservation stir brought down the government headed by V.P. Singh, which stood for reservation and secularism. Thus the bogie of reservation blown out of all proportion with the reality at the ground level has created a feeling of hatred for the Dalits among the middle class intelligentsia. The rights the Dalits secured after prolonged litigation appear to offer them a quasi freedom and a teasing illusion that they are reaching the stage of genuine acceptability into the social order as equal members. It is more difficult to fight this teasing illusion than to fight downright subjugation and the status as non-person.

In the rural areas, violence against the Scheduled Castes continues unabated. Recognising this, Parliament enacted the Scheduled Castes and Scheduled Tribes (Prevention of Atrocities) Act, 1989, a law creating special offences which were made triable by special court. Look at the practices which parliament has identified as offences under the act. Very few of us would have gone through the definition of "atrocity" in the Act; nor would many of us have heard about or witnessed the indignities to which Scheduled Castes and Scheduled Tribes are subjected continuously. Where social reformers have failed a Constitution may not succeed unless the words in the Constitution are transformed into deeds. Section 3 enumerates 22 categories of atrocities, which are made punishable. Unless we read the enumeration of the atrocities set out, we may not be in a position to understand why Ambedkar wanted to get out of the Hindu system, why the Scheduled Castes want the conduct of upper castes to be made an international issue.

The law was intended to afford speedy justice; the component of speed was to act as a deterrent. The lebensraum provided by the law to evade, defeated the law without any necessity for open defiance. The assault on Dalits is legitimised by the acquittal of assailants in courts. The offences under the act were made triable by a special court whose presiding officer shall be a session judge. This is entrusted to the special court for purposes of speedy trial, an aspect of Article 21 of the Constitution. This was interpreted by the apex court to mean that like all other criminal offences it should pass through the committal proceedings before a magistrate. This enactment now remains only in the statute book and will slowly fall into desuetude. All this is achieved without the hope of a loaded jury system as in the U.S. Thus we have laws, Constitutional provision showcased to tell international bodies through the obliging Attorney-Generals that the caste of the Dalits cannot be equated with race.

James Baldwin, the African-American writer, in one of his essays "letter to my nephew on the one hundredth anniversary of the emancipation", sets down the condition of the blacks which is no different form the untouchables in India. He points out to his nephew, "you were born where you were born and faced a future that you faced because you were black and for no other reason. The limits of your ambition were, thus, expected to be set forever. You were born into a society, which spelt out with brutal clarity, in as many ways as possible, that you were a worthless human being. You were not expected to aspire to excellence; you were expected to make peace with mediocrity." This is what the caste system tells the untouchable. The slaves were not transplanted in the United States to give them democracy. The promise of democracy was not made to them. In India, despite the grandiloquent declarations in the Constitution, birth and descent is the criteria. The identification of this targeted collective of 160 millions is not difficult; nor is it the issue. Racial discrimination targets the blacks for trying to rise above the subservient status allotted to them. They and the Dalits are needed for the performance of hard labour in the fields and for performing menial chores. They should be, to better function in their allotted status, quarantined and rendered invisible. Every society has such discrimination and violence and the perpetuation of such a collective can only be by descent. The principle of power is at issue and not some sociological definition or description of caste, which does not tally with the meaning of race.

The 160 million Dalits are demanding that untouchability and other forms of discrimination based on descent practiced in India be equated with or included in racial discrimination and other related intolerances. Arguments based on sovereignty to bar scrutiny of obnoxious and obscurantist practices violating human rights and dignity are irrational. Identification have never been an obstacle to employing discriminatory practices and violence against Dalits.

The caste system in India and the hereditary untouchability and the irrational and violent conduct these practices engender are crimes against humanity under the international criminal code.

Chapter 16

Annihilating Caste

MARI MARCEL THEKAEKARA

"Why do we need to take caste to the UN? Don't you know they are just waiting to humiliate India? Cut us down to size? Fumes the Indian Government. It makes sense. On an extended stay in Washington DC, 10 years ago, I scanned the *Washington Post* and *The Times* for a scrap of Indian news. Once a week or so, a little item appeared, usually on dowry deaths, Hindu-Muslim tension and Sati. I was furious at the appalling coverage.

Ten years down the line, as I listen to Dalit activists explaining why they have taken "caste" to the UN World Conference Against Racism (WCAR), I get a whole new perspective. I listen to reports from Rajasthan, Uttar Pradesh and Bihar. They are sickening. The Ranbir Sena guns down an entire Dalit village. A Dalit woman is raped in Rajasthan O.K. the cow belt is uncivilised. But then a Dalit woman sexually assaulted and tortured in normally sane Maharashtra? And finally I'm horrified to find Dalits burnt to death in Chintamani on the way to my children's school, near Bangalore.

If dear reader, you and I were a part of such a landscape, where your children, family, close friends and relatives were always in danger of being "put in their place" merely because they aspired to a normal decent life, would you not do some thing to end the torture, the precarious existence, walking on eggshells so as not to upset your "betters"?

What Dalits want to mobilise world opinion on is not for temple entry, or the roti-beti syndrome of eating together and intercaste marriage. That is something, which will take a few more generations probable. They are talking here of everyday things, like walking through the main street of the village with slippers on. Of a Dalit bridegroom in Rajasthan needing a few hundred-armed policemen to allow him to ride on horseback to his marriage. This happened for the first time because Chief Minister Ashok Gehlot ordered it on the pain of punishment to the collector and the superintendent of police. I once interviewed a Dalit collector, because he dared to study and aspire to a college degree, the elders in his village in Andhra Pradesh slapped him and attempted to cut off his right hand the hand that dared to write, instead of working in their fields. The point is all these things happen even now, in this day and age.

After 54 years of independence and in spite of a Constitution meant to safeguard the rights of our people, our poor, our Dalits, our adivasis and our women, there is no political will to stop the killing, burning, raping. Every time carnage occurs, there is a hue and cry. Politicians rush to the place to make the correct, placatory noises and get a few free photo opportunities. Then it all dies down. No one is ever punished. The culprits get off scot-free. So everyone knows you can kill Dalits and get away with it. That's what they want to change.

The government has taken the position that race is not caste.

The National Campaign on Dalit Human Rights points out that the WCAR is about discrimination in all forms. Race in terms of black versus white is an essentially euro-centric definition. The conference against racism is about discrimination and the whole world will be there working to end global discrimination of all kinds. They point out angrily that the academic debate begun by André Béteille is a futile exercise in semantics. The Dalit fight is about real issues, not a college duel to score debating points. The Dalit woman who has seen her family burnt to death in Chintamani or Bihar cares not about your academic anthropological quibbling, they remind you angrily. The killing, raping, burning, torturing of Dalit people is discrimination because of origin and descent. It is designed to maintain status quo, to keep Dalits at the bottom of the heap, as has been the case for millennia now.

The government's position that the Dalit issue should not be made international, is not consistent with our position on other international issues or on India's status as a human rights defender, the campaign points out since independence, India has always championed the cause of the oppressed, starting with African nations struggling for freedom from colonial oppression to the US Civil rights movement and hailing Martin Luther king as a hero, in recent times, we were the first to align ourselves with South Africa in the struggle against apartheid. As I write this, we have appealed to the world to help Hindus in Afghanistan fight Taliban oppression and Prime Minister Vajpayee has pledged support to the Romas at the WCAR. How then can we hypocritically try to keep caste under wraps?

As an Indian writer, it touches a raw nerve. I have thought about it long and hard. It is one thing to write about caste for my own people, in our news papers and magazines, in my own country because I want to participate in creating a better world for our children and the generations to come going international makes me a bit queasy: can we go on pretending the problem is not there?

As a nation we are champions at hypocrisy. A doctor friend once described an incident, which made her sick. She was examining a 13-year-old girl who was pregnant. She had been raped by her uncle. "Always, it's a cousin, brother-in-law, mamma. And it is hushed up to preserve the family izzat. The girl is treated as though it is her fault, though she's the victim. As a people we are sickening," she concluded.

The question here is can we go on preserving our non-existent honour when Dalits continue to be killed and tortured even as we boast of our nuclear status and IT achievements? The Dalit plea is: "in the last century we got rid of slavery and apartheid. Let this century be the one to annihilate casteism."

It is ironic that they are taking it to Durban where Gandhiji began his discovery of freedom. It is a question only you and I can answer. You and I and our country.

Chapter 17

Durban, Caste and Indian Democracy

KANCHA ILAIAH

To ascertain public opinion on the question of inclusion of caste on the agenda of the United Nations World Conference Against Racism being held in Durban, South Africa a national committee was constituted by the Prime Minister headed by Ranganath Mishra, former Chief Justice of India. The chairmen of the Scheduled Castes and Scheduled Tribes Commission and the Minorities Commission are its members. The national committee held its hearing in Hyderabad on June 4. Unfortunately, it was held in camera and initially it planned to hear only the version of carefully chosen organisations but several (about 30) SC, ST, OBC and women's organisations of Andhra Pradesh sensed this move and forced the committee to hear all opinions, which it did subsequently.

All organisations, except the few chosen ones, told the committee that caste must be allowed to go on the UN agenda. Unfortunately, the officially chosen and invited organisations had no idea about the Durban conference and what it would be all about. Only the organisations that went on their own made informed and forceful presentations. Several mass organisations gave concrete reasons why caste should be included in the Durban conference. Let me sum up some of the arguments.

The conference at Durban is against race, racial discrimination, xenophobia and related intolerance. The question is whether caste fits into this definition and India should allow caste to be debated at the UN Conference. The argument of the union government is that the UN should not interfere in our internal affairs. That India has evolved enough tools to handle the caste question. That the attention of the UN Conference should not be diverted form the question of race, about which India is deeply concerned. All these arguments sound hypocritical.

When the issue of race was put on the UN human rights agenda, Britain and America, where racial discrimination was being practiced, were permanent members of the UN and had strongly rooted Constitutional democracy in their nations. The public opinion within those nations was forcing them to enact laws that could establish mechanisms for handling racism, xenophobia and other forms of intolerance. India at that time argued that racism was too major an issue to be left to the respective countries to evolve tools to handle. Nehruvian intellectuals, who argued for pushing racism on to the UN agenda, based it on their own experience of xenophobic/intolerant treatment by whites of all coloured people, including Indians, in the west. This colonial experience of the Indian Brahminic elite itself was one of the grounds for asking for abolition of unequal race relations, the Indian upper caste elite suffered such xenophobic intolerance for about 200 years and at that time the distance between the white rulers and the lower castes was too far and was mediated by many caste in between.

Gandhi's experience in South Africa and the argument that Gandhi built against racism were India's strongest points. It is also true that Nehru and a host of other Indian leaders who studied in England carried their memories of racist treatment in their everyday life as students in the west. Nehru and other Indian leaders were strong votaries of the proposition that race must be included on the UN human rights agenda. But except Ambedkar, who had the double experience of caste xenophobic intolerance at home and racial intolerance abroad, all other Indian leaders, who experienced racial discrimination and were angry with it were upper caste men and women.

They never realised that similar, in fact more horrendous, intolerance was practiced in India because of caste. They never thought that the pain they suffered was much less than the pain the Indian lower castes suffered. The caste oppression continued for thousands of years. The Indian upper caste elite who suffered racism abroad had a liberative channel from that treatment when they came back home, but for the lower castes there was no such liberation at all. It was/is a long drawn out suffering without much hope.

Even now the union government wants an undiluted debate on racism because many NRIs are suffering racism in many Euro-American countries. All NRIs have painful stories to narrate to their parents back home; many of them are either politicians or bureaucrats even in the present ruling dispensation. Is it not true that the vast majority of NRIs are form the upper castes? Do they have the patience to listen to the Dalit narratives of pain back home? What is wrong if such Dalit narratives of suffering are talked about in all forums, national and international? When the upper castes feel relived of some pain by merely talking about it, should they not concede that much to the Dalits also in all forums?

Is it not ironical that the experience of sufferings of the Indian upper castes abroad is taken as sociologically real and the sustained suffering of the indigenous people, like that of the Blacks in the form of caste, does not become a sociological reality. Even if such a thing is acknowledged they do not want it exposed. When victims of racism want to draw international attention and seek aid and help why can the voiceless not seek such an attention, aid and help of the world community. Talking the caste issue to the UN forums is not only for the sake of debate. It would draw the attention of the world community so that more aid might flow in for taking up educational and empowerment programmes. Such programmes will go a long way in our development. Instead of taking a loan even for causes such as primary education for millions of lower caste children why not ask for charity for primary education by telling about the historical magnitude of the caste problem?

What will happen to the prestige of our democracy among the comity of nations if we talk about caste, is another question that all our ultra-nationalist theoreticians ask. By allowing the race question to be raised did the prestige of Britain and America suffer in any way? While being permanent members of the UN, by allowing racism to be debated and measures worked out their democratic credentials have been strengthened. It helped the white communities examine their own self in the context of the international critique. It gave confidence to the Blacks. They began to respect their democracy more.

The Third World countries that asked for a debate on race only shared the moral agony of the Blacks. Whereas in the case of caste and the kind of atrocities, ignorance and poverty the lower castes suffer, the capitalist West owes a moral responsibility to uplift them as much as the upper castes of India do. The colonial world benefited from the cheap labour of the adivasis, Dalits and OBCs. If the Union Government does not even concede the existence of caste how can these communities, in the context of globalisation, raise globally relevant questions of compensation? The white rulers of Britain and America could have easily vetoed any proposal on race. But that would have resulted in their democratic credentials becoming suspect in the comity of nations. More importantly, the victims of racism would have lost confidence in their own governments. But by conceding the truth of racism they gained on all fronts. Their democracies are surviving without facing any major threat.

If the Government of India conducts public hearings such as the one held in Hyderabad and uses them as an eyewash, the international community will laugh at our hypocrisy. The masses that are victims of the caste system will lose confidence in Indian democracy. It is known that at all levels of government the upper castes are holding the positions of decision making. The representatives of the victim communities, who get an opportunity to sit in such committees, may be made to endorse the decisions. How does that convince the educated among the victims? Particularly, when this Government is backed by organisations such as the VHP and the RSS, which keep arguing that abolition of caste is detrimental to the Indian tradition of Varna Dharma? The day the Dalits lose faith in it because that they cannot speak out their agony, Indian democracy will begin to crack.

Chapter 18

Caste, the Academy and Dalit Women

KALPANA KANNABIRAN

The ongoing debate on caste and race is taking place in the context of a larger advocacy on discrimination and Dalit human rights and has centred on the articulation of caste as discrimination, and the various forms of that discrimination – exclusion, untouchability, denial of Constitutional rights and guarantees, violent subjugation and histories of slavery – as resonant of internationally recognised forms of racism. This article will focus on two aspects of the issue: questions for the sociology of caste and the articulation of caste as race by Dalit women.

Caste has formed the centerpiece of sociology for close to a century now. While the practice of caste has been opposed and consistently resisted by movements in the country, caste as a knowledge system in sociology has tended to follow the well-worn paths of a depoliticised social anthropology, creating sharp disjuncture between social practice and knowledge systems within the academy. Further, the disaggregation of social practice in the curriculum of sociology, into various "topics" and "papers", by situating caste for instance in Indian society or in social institutions, and the politics of caste within social movements, erases the potential for a radical pedagogy, and renders invisible the radical politics of anti-caste movements within the academy even while "teaching" them. While this has undoubtedly begun to change, with sociologists such as Sharmila Rege raising these issues within the university system, the power of traditional authorities on caste is difficult to dismantle. We also know from our experience over the last half century at least that sociologists have periodically been called into the service of the state, particularly to supply "knowledge of society" that could then inform policy. And this knowledge must, by definition lend itself to disaggregation and be apolitical, in short, the knowledge that the sociologists generate is expected to keep the status quo.

In reiterating its stand that caste and race are not only dissimilar, but also practices that cannot be compared, let alone brought within the purview of the same international instruments, the Indian Government is relying on this knowledge that has been produced by the discipline of sociology. Several pieces that have appeared in the print media have made an often-dismissive reference to "sociological categories" but with lived experience. This feeds directly into a "Separate Spheres" argument and allows sociology to continue with its project of producing knowledge in the service of power, legitimising the exercise in the process. It is time now to call the academy into question, and to engage with systems and processes that produce knowledge, by providing alternative paradigms of knowledge, theory and understanding and asserting their legitimacy within the academy.

It is time to remind ourselves that the theorising of caste has its intellectual history, not in the "scientific" work of anthropologists of European origin and their "native" heirs, but in the political work of Indian ideologues who were committed to the establishment of an egalitarian social order, and who in that endeavour saw caste as the single most powerful obstacle to the realisation of that commitment – Jotiba Phule, Savitribai Phule, Pandita Ramabai, Periyar, and Ambedkar, to name the most influential ones. Phule's accounts of caste in the 19th century are grim. Ambedkar's concerns in the 20th century centred on finding ways in which Independence could bring freedom to the oppressed, affirmative action and positive discrimination being a first step.

At the time that Phule, Ambedkar and Periyar were articulating an understanding of caste in terms of lived experience and political reality, Risley and Guha were attempting in their own ways, a "scientific" racial classification of caste, from their respective locations within colonial administration, a fact that must enter the account. André Béteille's assertion of the conclusiveness of Boas findings on the clear separability of race as biology from social grouping is questionable, and far from settled. Guillaumin gives us a radically divergent and more plausible view, one that is strengthened and validated by the recent findings of the Human Genome Project that variations in genome sequences between ethnic (racial) groups is negligible. The physical differences between races can perhaps be accounted for by reference to environment and habitat, not biology. To restate the case, race is a social not a biological construct.

Arguments on homogeneity, the measures of likeness and commonalities and the parameters of comparison are settled within the academy, hence interventions must engage with these arguments, if for no other reason than to have a long term impact on the content of education. One of the arguments (naturally from scholars of caste) put forth against the move to bring caste within the purview of the Racism convention has been that the Scheduled Castes are not a homogenous category. Outside the realm of this scholarship, but within the realm of reality, no social group is completely homogenous across region and time. The Scheduled Castes are no exception. Yet, it is perfectly legitimate to assert the commonality of experience across cultural, linguistic, regional national and ethnic diversity. Ambedkar's coining of the word Dalit was part of this exercise in unifying the oppressed and forging a common cause. The current move to bring caste within the ambit of the Convention on the Elimination of Racial Discrimination is not a move by the United Nations alone. It is far more importantly an assertion by Dalit groups across the country, part of an effort to realise the visions of anti – caste movements.

The second concern of this article is to underscore the efforts of the National Federation of Dalit Women(henceforth NFDW) in bringing this issue into focus. In the draft Declaration on Gender and Racism drafted in February, the Federation resolved to fight the specific oppression of women from marginalised groups, whose situation as Dalit/indigenous/minority is only compounded by their being women. A part from the fact of social exclusion at various levels, the NFDW asserted that "Descent based discrimination based on caste results in the violent appropriation of and sexual control over Dalit women by men of the dominant castes evident in the systematic rape of Dalit women and the perpetuation of forced prostitution in the name of religion through the devadasi system".

In a context of increasing religious nationalism, fundamentalism and dominant caste chauvinism, globalisation and its disastrous consequences for the poor (almost exclusively Dalits), of an abdication of democratic governance by the state, the declaration asserts that the situation of Dalit Women is particularly troubling. The draft Declaration calls upon governments to review and reform national laws related to violence against women, to gather statistical information on the status of Dalit women, to offer them protection, to redistribute land to women of marginalised groups, and to work alongside the international community on issues of discrimination. An extremely significant point in the declaration and one that ties in with first part of this article, is the concern of the NFDW over the engineering of partisan hegemonic representations of history in textbooks and curricula at all levels.

The effort of the Federation to forge a broad-based common platform with other groups that suffer systematic exclusion in an increasingly virulent right wing environment is both courageous and radical, while at the same time engaging with and calling into question the disaggregation of knowledge within the academy. The campaign for the inclusion of caste within the definition of racism is, in fact, a rewriting of caste as a knowledge system that derives directly from lived experience and the politics of that experience.

Chapter 19

India's Apartheid

RAJEEV DHAVAN

It is no disservice to the heroic struggle in South Africa against apartheid to compare it with the struggle of Dalits and tribals to fight the cumulative injustice of centuries. In doing so we salute the struggles of all peoples to fight racist and related ideologies, which imprison and brutalise their lives.

It is unfortunate that we have to remind ourselves about India's apartheid through the aegis of the United Nation (UN) Conference against Racism, Racial Discrimination, Xenophobia and Related Intolerance due to be held in Durban from August 31 to September 7, 2001. It is doubly unfortunate that a cruel and ungainly controversy exists in India over whether casteism which plagues the everyday lives of Dalits, tribals and others is the same as or akin to racism? And, if misfortune can be compounded three times over, the Indian Government has obdurately taken the stance that the fight against the casteism has no place in the UN's agenda to combat racism and related phenomenon.

It was at Durban over a century ago that Mahatma Gandhi began his struggle against racism and related intolerance. It is at Durban, too, that India refuses to follow his example to confront the biggest curse that plagues around 300 million, if not more people in India with one of the most vicious ideologies and permanent social diseases the world has ever known: casteism. It was early this month that a couple from different castes were hung whilst an entire village watched the spectacle. This is not an uncommon event. Nor is the permanent isolation of Dalits who are brutalised everyday through beatings, rapes, ostracism, land grabbing, deprivation and endemic disadvantage. Casteism is not a social preference, but an ideology that affects inter-generational injustice to condemn certain castes and communities into subordination and a cycle of deprivation for decades to come.

Why is Durban important? The 20th century was remarkably creative and destructive. It enabled political but not social democracy. It moved from the bicycle to cyber space, without bypassing nuclear destruction. It created a manufacturing bonanza but perilously threatened the environment. It transmitted good and evil on an enormous scale into our time. We carry into the 21st century four critical agendas: (i) the quest for an equitable global economy, amidst the exploitative regime of the WTO; (ii) the Rio and Kyoto agendas to protect bio-diversity and all living creatures; (iii) the fight against poverty and socio-economic inequality; and (iv) the struggle against racist related and similar ideologies which victimise whole peoples on the basis of their colour, race, ethnicity or descent.

Durban is concerned with the fourth agenda to confront the ideological social enslavement of entire peoples through ideologies that viciously discriminate against them under conditions of hate and endemic social disadvantage. This is an continuing evil. Indians should know better; look at the plight of Indians abroad. In 1968, Indians were thrown out of Kenya. In 1971, Idi Amin unleashed a reign of terror against Uganda's Asians. In 2000, in Fiji, a Prime Minister of Indian origin was dethroned whilst his community lived in terror. In 1968, in England, Enoch Powell, provoked and predicted that 'rivers of blood' would flow. They did. In 2001, riots took place in the north of England. John Rex's research shows how housing patterns of immigrants perpetrate permanent disadvantages. In America, 'dot-busters' attack Indian women who wear bindis on their forehead or Indian clothes. Of all peoples, we cannot afford to ignore racism-related phenomena being the pointed target of the global agenda.

Why do we resist the inclusion of casteism in this global agenda? For this we have to understand the global agenda; and, indeed, India's own. We are concerned here not with race but racism. Not caste but casteism. Racism is not just a socio-biological phenomenon but a colonial legacy. Like casteism, it is a social construct. It exists amongst and within White communities. Spielberg's *Schindler's List* reminds us of the struggle of the Jews in our time. The English outcasted Anglo and other mixes. The Dutch did not. The Durban Conference is directed against entrenched racism and related practices which contain the following characteristics: (i) a socially constructed ideology; (ii) founded on notions of superiority (or, inversely, inferiority); (iii) directed against entire peoples; (iv) on the basis of descent, ethnicity, colour, or physical characteristics; (v) manifesting violent expressions of hostility, including vicious and violent attacks, hate and bias; (vi) to perpetrate endemic social disadvantage; and (vii) effect inter-generational injustice.

Sociologists may quibble – as, indeed, André Béteille and others have – over academic dissimilarities between 'race' and 'caste' as heuristic 'ideal types' to thrown the baby out with the bath water. But apply the seven tests which, perforce, underscore the global agenda. Caste is based on descent and birth. This is recognised as part of India's human rights constitutional dispensation in its equality provisions (Articles 15 and 16), the abolition of untouchability (Article 17), the temple entry provision (Article 25), special provisions for an SC and ST Commission (Articles 330-342 and 46), and in the scheme of Indian federalism (Articles 164 (1), 371 A-G, V and VI Schedules). Thus, the Indian Constitution has a priority constitutional commitment to fight a descent and birth based struggle against casteism and tribalism.

Our Constitution recognises that 'casteism' is a centuries-old vicious ideology founded on hate, violence and exclusion from equality, opportunity, empowerment and resources. The Protection of Civil Rights Act 1955-1976 and the SC and ST (Atrocities) Act 1989 underlie this commitment. Yet, after 50 years, despite affirmative action and other agendas, casteism continues. Rapes, beatings and deprivations reflected in government reports are the tip of the social inferno. Temple entry is accompanied by purification ceremonies before and after entry. Humiliation accompanies violence. By inclusion in the global agenda, the fight against casteism will be enhanced.

It was at India's insistence that 'descent' was included in the Convention against Racial Discrimination (CERD) in 1969. By 1996, India argued that 'casteism' was not part of CERD, but was, in effect, overruled by the UN's Human Rights Committee. Today, India flounders. It does not want to admit that 'casteism' is India's apartheid which will continue in its most vicious and persistent forms for decades to come. Even if India's stance is linked to its quest for a seat in the Security Council of the UN, this cannot mortgage human rights priorities for Dalits and tribals.

If 'casteism' is not the same as 'racism', it must be deemed to be similar. Article 25 of India's Constitution uses such a deeming provision for temple entry for Dalits by including Buddhists, Sikhs and Jains as Hindus. 'Casteism' is not a social preference, but India's apartheid. We stand on the brink of history; and, we quibble over words on whether to include 'casteism' as a related phenomenon similar to 'racism'. Durban is not just about what is to be included in the UN's remit on racism and related phenomenon. It is about how to fight these social diseases. India should concentrate on these prescriptive programmatic dimensions. Fundamental issues remain. These include fighting hate propaganda while mindful of free speech. India's programmes have concentrated on self-betterment avenues for education and jobs as part of affirmative action, and some element of administrative and political empowerment through reservation. But it has failed to distribute economic resources including land and capital which are critical for inter-generational justice. The fight over tribal lands, the Samta judgment and Balco are examples of this – as, indeed, the resourceless denotified tribals. Anti-atrocity legislation lies relatively unenforced. The police do not investigate. Courts do not convict violators. We have progressed on paper but not in fact. We should recognise and stop the horror of India's apartheid, not brush it under the carpet.

Chapter 20

Debate on Discrimination

Casteism is Racism of Another Sort

ARJUN SENGUPTA

Raising the issues of caste at the Durban conference on racial discrimination and related intolerance is perfectly consistent with the intent of that conference. Which is about human rights and their violation. It is not just for condemning racism, narrowly defined, but for fighting against all discriminatory practices that racism implies. They are, as the UN resolution, has clarified, "based on race, colour, descent or national or ethnic origin".

Casteism is one of those kinds of discrimination – even if its source is social and not biological. An individual is born to a caste, just as he is to a race, and that makes him subject to discrimination and violation of the fundamental principle of human rights, which proclaims that all men are equal, not necessarily in income, wealth or capabilities, but in dignity. To say that caste cannot be discussed in a conference on racism because caste is different from race, is not just sophistry, but misses the whole point of a human rights conference.

Such conference are meant for first, recognising certain rights or entitlement to non-discriminatory treatment as human rights. Which are universal standards of civilised behaviour of all states towards an individual. Then they try to define the obligations of the state of which the individual is a citizen and of the international community consisting of all other states and civil societies to deliver the rights by removing those discriminations. The right of all individuals to be treated as equal is universal, but the obligation of delivering that right is contextual depending upon the context in which that right is violated by specific discriminatory practices.

If casteism is accepted as a subject of the conference, it will be necessary to discuss the specific forms of discrimination that casteism implies, so that the obligations of the state parties and all other individuals can be defined, the culpability can be identified and the violators can be indicted. It is at this point that the difference between racism and casteism becomes relevant, because different discriminatory practices would call for different redressal mechanism.

Even racist practices have wide differences. What needs to be done to fight racism in America would be quite different from that in Europe or for that matter in Asia or Africa. Our scholars of caste practices should be able to design solutions fixing the responsibility of the different parties involved in the problems, and they will be quite different from the measures to solve racism problems. Caste practices may be quite different from racial practices. But the subjects of those practices are all subjects of gross violation of human rights, and every state must accept the responsibility to redress that violation.

It is no one's claim that such a conference would solve all the problems of discriminatory practices. It will take a long time to change the legal, social and economic practices and conventions. But they will not change without determined action by all concerned, and, most importantly, by the states by enacting laws and enforcing them and by positive and promotional measures to create favourable conditions.

Recognising casteism as a violation of human rights not only enhances the awareness of the problem but also raises the task of prevention of such violation to the top priority of state action. Human rights must get precedence over all other concerns of the state. The American Declaration of Independence, which was the first to proclaim human rights states that "We hold these truths to be self – evident, that all men are created equal, that they are endowed by their Creator with certain inalienable Rights, that among these are Life, Liberty and the pursuit of Happiness. That whenever any form of

Government becomes destructive of these ends, it's the Right of the People to alter or to abolish it..."

Nobody questioned if these truths were self-evident or if those rights were really inalienable. They were proclaimed as such, and that recognised the legitimacy of over-throwing a state, which fails to deliver inalienable human rights.

The inability to stop the violation of human rights through caste discrimination would also be a legitimate basis for public action to change the government. It would at least call for a concerted action by the government and all other organs of the state, and start that process by expanding awareness and public discussions of the problems and their solutions.

Since human rights belongs to individuals by virtue of their being human, irrespective of nationality, religion or geographic location they are universal and their fulfillment becomes the obligation of all states. Raising the issues of caste discrimination at a UN inter-governmental conference is motivated by getting universal recognition of the fact that freedom from the discrimination is a human right. That would place an obligation on all governments and the international community to help eradicate caste discrimination by helping the state authorities to adopt appropriate promotional measures and by punitive actions against their violation.

To suggest that raising the issues at an international forums is anti-national and is calling for international assistance when the solution lies entirely in national action, betrays a mindset of xenophobia and also a lack of understanding of the human rights movement. That mindset is even more dangerous when it affects our intellectuals. Human rights conventions always give national actions the primary responsibility for fulfilling the rights, and the international community and everybody else living in a civilised society the responsibility to help that process.

Indeed, international programmes, on their own can seldom be effective without any national programme of action. Of course, if the state authorities fail in their job, the international community must exert pressure, through public opinion, awareness and resistance and, if necessary, by concerted action, as is done against any crime against humanity. Our intellectual all supported the arrest in England of the former Chilean President Augusto Pinochet for violating human rights in Chile during his years of dictatorship in that country. I wonder how they would react if some of our political leaders are picked up by Interpol in London or Amsterdam for violating the rights of the Dalits in Bihar or for causing the death of innocent Muslims in Mumbai.

Chapter 21

Facing Up to the Facts

KULDIP NAYAR

The National Human Rights Commission (NHRC) has come out boldly on the side of the weak and the oppressed many a time. This was the purpose of its Constitution. But the NHRC has been so beholden to the government that it has often become part of the establishment.

Lately, it has been asserting itself but not to the extent human rights activists and the victims want. One expected it to be more articulate and more critical of the government, particularly in regard to the security forces. It is still a body in the making, often giving the impression that it does not want to join issue with the government. But the institution still evokes hope among those who find themselves helpless. The NHRC may only be a tiny light but even its little flicker gives some confidence.

Its diffidence has been disappointing. It was never so disappointing as now when it had to adopt, as an observer, a principled stand at the UN conference against racism in Durban. The Commission held two seminars, one in Bangalore and the other in New Delhi. Going by the pronouncements at the seminars, the NHRC should have come down heavily on the Government of India and sided with the demand for an open discussion on the caste system. Instead, it has tried to hedge the issue.

The NHRC admits that discrimination based on "race, caste and descent constitute an unacceptable assault on the dignity and worth of the human person and an egregious violation of human rights". But it pins its hopes on the "instruments of governance" which have done little in the last four years. By not taking New Delhi to task for its hidebound attitude, the NHRC has allowed the government to get away with its biased view on caste and has let down the Indian NGOs in Durban.

In fact, New Delhi's diplomatic efforts have borne fruit. New Delhi argues that caste is an internal matter and should be discussed within India, not outside. How did New Delhi arrive at such a decision without knowing public opinion, without consulting Parliament? This is where the NHRC's lead was required to chide the government. The body is either too timid or too divided. Either way it is harming its status and stature. At times, it appears to be riding two horses at the same time. It has been saved from the embarrassment of weighing caste and race at the scales.

True, caste is not race but the fallout from caste is more discriminating and devastating. Why run away from the fact of caste which has been there for more than 2000 years and which prevails in the same ugly shape as it was a longtime ago? If bias against women can be discussed at international conventions, why not caste? Do the Dalits not go through the same humiliation, the same harassment and the same horrors of living as women in many parts of the world? Borrowing words from Shakespeare, they can: if you prick us, do we not bleed? If you tickle us, do we not laugh? If you poison us, do we not die? And if you wrong us, shall we not revenge?

The fate of the Dalits has not changed at all. The NHRC should have stood by them. No doubt on the basis of 20-odd Articles in the Constitution, India can get full marks. But all that is on paper. Dalits, the lowest rung of the caste system, face discrimination every minute and at every step of their life. The government has done little to fight the caste system. Untouchability has been banned but not the caste system whose product untouchability is. All the pronouncements of equality or social justice in the preamble of the Constitution make no sense when the Dalits are no better economically after 54 years of Independence and no higher socially, the result of 2000 years of discrimination. Colour bar, however reprehensible, is better than the caste system. A black can marry a white. After two or three generations, their descendants can pass off as whites. But a Dalit cannot escape the caste system. His disability is in birth itself. Dalits remain Dalit.

Even if they marry outside their caste, which is very rare, they remain Dalit. Caste is the millstone that they have worn around their neck generation after generation. Manu divided the Hindu society into four castes. The structure has not changed – even after so many centuries. Reservation, an affirmative action of sorts, has had no effect on the attitude of the upper castes, they accept the Dalits in high positions like a tax, trying to avoid it as far as possible. That is the reason why there are so few Dalits in high positions. At present, there are no Secretary or Additional Secretary level officers from the Dalits at the Centre. In the private sector, even the fig-leaf cover of reservation is not there. Dalits are only peons or clerks. A study is long overdue to assess the plight of Dalits with regard to livelihood, equality, education, employment, security, etc. if every State in India had brought out every year a white paper on the progress of the Dalits, it might have shamed the upper Castes and goaded them to action.

The Constitution has provided for a Commissioner for Scheduled Castes and Scheduled Tribes. He produces an annual report, which is placed before the two Houses of Parliament. The perfunctory attitude towards the entire exercise shows that neither the government, nor the MP's are serious about this report. It accumulates dust on the shelves of the Home Ministry for years and then comes to Parliament for discussion. The discussion in Parliament is perfunctory. The Commissioner points out the same lapses year after year. But nothing happens, and his complaint, like that of his predecessors, is that even a Deputy Secretary in the Government of India does not gives him an appointment, let alone the Minister in charge.

True, the NHRC has its plate full. It cannot take upon itself the burden of the SC and ST Commission. But the Durban Conference is one place where it can wash away the stigma of being equivocal on the matter of caste. New Delhi is determined to sweep everything under the carpet and keep it there. Will the NHRC have the courage to retrieve it and place in the open the scourge of the caste system which has reduced the Dalits to a status less than human beings. No democratic system should be ashamed of discussing at any forum its practices which disable its own people. A free society owes its existence to the tenets of freedom. The Dalits have never had a breath of freedom in the suffocating Hindu society.

The Dalits are a wounded people, battered and broken. India is strong enough democratically to admit that it has failed somewhere, despite all the guarantees in the Constitution, to provide the same glow of freedom which the upper castes enjoy. Someone should have taken New Delhi to task for not implementing the anti-discrimination laws in letter and spirit. New Delhi would have served the country's cause better by allowing at Durban an open discussion on the caste system which continues to be a social stigma. A discussion at Durban does not mean any international interference. If the government takes what the WTO does in the spirit of improvement of economy, why is it afraid of the Durban conference? New Delhi does not accept all that comes from the WTO. Similarly, it does not have to implement the recommendations of the Durban conference if they are against the national interest.

Chapter 22

Caste, Race and Human Rights

M.N. PANINI

In a strictly formal sense, caste is not race. Race refers to physical and biological characteristics of people and the different castes in India do not form separate genotypes. Anthropological evidence reveals considerables racial inter mixture in India. Even school textbooks on Indian history support this. Over the last two millennia, the Indian subcontinent has witnessed the confluence of numerous streams of immigrants from various parts of the world bringing with them diverse racial traits and characteristics. Sociologists point out that although in theory the caste system formed a rigid hierarchy that imposed, for example, severe punishments on inter caste marriages; in practice the system was considerably fluid. It allowed upward mobility for castes lower down the hierarchy; they could emulate the lifestyles and customs of the upper castes and even lay claim to superior caste status. If such caste could back their claims would gain social acceptance. Such instances of upward mobility could have stretched and modified the rules of caste endogamy, especially for the upwardly mobile castes.

Evidence of inter mixture contrasts with the principles of caste division as enunciated in the *Dharmashastra*, the Hindu law book. The 'Purushasukta' myth expounding the four-fold varna scheme is also a colour scheme. The Brahmin occupying the highest status is associated with the colour white representing the 'satva' guna. As one goes down the hierarchy, one descends to the darkness implied in the 'tamas' guna of impurity, inactivity and ignorance and represented in the colour black of the shudra Varna.

The colour consciousness expressed thus by the theory of varna may account for the premium attached to fair skinned brides that is revealed by even a cursory scanning of matrimonial advertisements in national newspapers. Consmetic manufacturers derive huge profits by advertising and selling fairness enhancing facial creams. Indians prefer to interact with white foreigners rather than with the blacks. Many black African university and college students studying in India have bitterly complained about the harrowing treatment meted out to them by lay public. It is however, unfair to suggest that this colour prejudice is confined just to the upper caste Hindus. It has seeped into the psyche of Muslims, Christians and Jews in India; even the castes ranked at bottom of the caste hierarchy share such prejudices.

Deep colour prejudices harboured in society do not coincide with caste hierarchy. There are dark skinned Brahmins as well as fair skinned members of the shudra castes. Hence, racial considerations do not become the principal source of institutionalised oppression in the Indian context. To the sources of social oppression in India it is necessary to focus on the dynamics of inter caste relationships.

Many eminent sociologists as well as social thinkers have commented upon the oppressive features of caste hierarchy. They have pointed out that the caste order represented a system of cumulative in equalities that denied some basic human rights especially to members of castes placed at the bottom of the caste hierarchy. The ritually impure 'untouchable' castes were denied access to wells used by the upper castes. They were prohibited from entering upper caste temples and from participating as equals in village festivals. Their settlements were segregated from the main village and were usually located in low-lying areas on the outskirts of the village. There were strict sartorial prohibitions that prevented them from wearing sandals or clothes. They could not even twirl their moustaches up in the style of the upper caste kshtriyas. Their women were not allowed to wear garments to cover their upper bodies, let alone wear jewellery like women of the upper castes. If upper caste men took a fancy to any of the women of these castes and made advances, they had no power to resist. They were invariably landless and had to eke out their living as bonded labourers to the upper caste masters or perform menial services like scavenging maintaining cremation grounds and burial sites, or disposing off carcasses of the dead. They were condemned to eat carrion, left over food and leavings from plates of members of upper castes. They could not participate as equals in proceedings of village assemblies or in collective decision-making in the village social life. The untouchables were prohibited from learning the Vedas and were denied access to educational facilities.

Feminists have pointed out that as women symbolise the status and prestige of the castes in which they are born, the caste system was particularly oppressive on them. It is well known that while 'anuloma' marriages between upper caste men and lower caste women were allowed in some instances, 'pratiloma' marriages involving upper caste women and lower caste men invited harsh sanctions on the offending women. The birth of a female child is still regarded as a curse. Demographers have been worried about the sex ratio skewed in favour of men in India. Even today, in some parts of Rajasthan and Tamil Nadu, the practice of female infanticide is widespread. Women were confined mainly to household tasks and to childbearing and child raring roles. The institutions of early marriage, prohibition on widow remarriage and of sati observed among the upper caste in several regions of north India, effectively subjugated women to a life of dependence and servitude.

The arguments sketched above would inevitably lead us to the conclusion that even if in theory caste cannot be equated with racism, in practice it has all the pernicious features of racism. Racism propagates the superiority of one 'race' over the others and promotes the idea of the purity of the superior race. The traditional caste system also incorporated the ideology of hierarchy based on the ritual notion of purity. As the caste system is sanctified by scriptural injunctions it is difficult to eradicate it. Several bhakti movements that sprouted in different parts of the country preaching anti caste ideology acquired the characteristics of discrete castes over time. This line of thinking seems to have influenced the 'caste is race plus' argument put forward by some dalit intellectuals and their sympathisers in their efforts to have caste included in the agenda of forthcoming United Nation sponsored World Conference Against Racism to be held at Durban.

Policies to Eliminate Discrimination

The line of reasoning delineated above also influenced Indian political leaders at the time of independence. Hence, they set out to cleanse society of the evil of caste by adopting a Constitution that sought to incorporate progressive egalitarian ideals by including special provisions for the protection of the former untouchable castes and tribes. A schedule of castes suffering the social disability of untouchability was prepared and incorporated in the Constitution along with another schedule for the marginalised tribes. The Constitution provided these castes and tribes who came to be known as Scheduled Castes and Scheduled Tribes, with special privileges to help them overcome their social disabilities. A certain proportion of seats in the parliament and in the state legislatures was reserved for Scheduled Castes and Scheduled Tribes separately as were jobs in the government and seats in educational institutions. The Constitution abolished untouchability; the Untouchability (Offence) Act of 1955 made the practice of untouchability a punishable offence. The Act was later improved as Protection of Civil Rights Act of 1976. In 1989, to prevent atrocities from being committed on the former untouchables, the Scheduled Castes and Scheduled Tribes (Prevention of Atrocities) Act was passed, which placed the onus of proof on those charged guilty of committing atrocities on the Scheduled Castes and Scheduled Tribes. This was done to ensure that the perpetrators of atrocities could not escape punishment just because the victims were unable to produce evidence sustainable in courts of law. These were doubtless radical measures, in some ways the most radical measures to eliminate caste like discrimination anywhere in the world.

The legal provisions and measures sketched above along with the adoption of parliamentary democracy based on adult franchise and the policy of planned development have considerably changed the ideological basis of caste society. Secular trends unleashed by the policies to promote equality and developments have eroded the ritual basis of caste. Ritual considerations now no longer dominate the social life of the urbanised upper castes. Rules of endogamy are being modified. Arranged marriages now cut across the boundaries of sub castes that seemed inviolable only a generation ago. Young men and women in urban areas are increasingly choosing their own life partners and such 'love marriages' cut across 'pollution' lines and religious boundaries. At the same time, media reports have also been highlighting instances of inter caste marriages in rural areas and the exemplary punishments meted out to such couples for bringing their respective families and castes to disrepute. In some cases, such couples have even been put to death. The severity of reaction to such instances also point to the anxiety that the emerging secular trends have generated in rural society. In a way, it is an admission of the inability of the upper castes to maintain their 'purity'; in a rapidly changing world, the notion of superiority of one caste over another seems to have lost its credibility.

Rapid secularisation of caste is noticed in the shrinking role and influence of the upper castes in public affairs. The Brahmins are now no longer playing a dominant role in religious affairs. Their place has been usurped by dynamic gurus and spiritual leaders who often hail from the lower castes. The latter have become the new interpreters of Hindu values and beliefs and have been mobilising masses to promote assertive, militant and uncompromising versions of Hinduism. They have also been in the forefront of the Ram Janmabhoomi movement that led in 1992, to the destruction of the Babri Masjid that was supposedly erected on the spot where the Hindu god Rama was born.

This decline of the influence of Brahmins in religious affairs has been accompanied by a shift in the power balance in rural areas. In many parts of the country, the power and influence the upper castes enjoyed has shifted to their former tenants who became landowners, thanks to the extensive land reforms undertaken by independent India. The new dominant castes are often drawn from the 'other backward castes' a legal phrase used to refer to castes located just above the pollution line. The new dominant castes have been forthright, assertive and aggressive in exercising their power. With an intense desire to translate those who they perceive as challenging their position. Naturally, they get involved in violent clashes with members of Scheduled Castes who are beginning to assert their rights to equality. This is one reason for the rising number of 'atrocities' against the Scheduled Castes.

The rising trend of 'atrocities' in a sense is a sign of the empowerment of the Scheduled Castes. Periodic elections and parliamentary democracy have taught the Scheduled Castes and Scheduled Tribes the arithmetic of caste. They have realised that by pooling their caste votes and casting them in favour of one or the other electoral candidate, they can make a significant difference to the election outcome. Hence they now assert their rights and even openly challenge the hegemony of the upper castes. Recently in Andhra Pradesh the Dalits (or oppressed – the term members of Scheduled Castes prefer to describe themselves) in some villages challenged the upper castes to prevent them from drawing water from the wells located in upper caste settlements. Such acts often lead to violent backlashes from the upper castes. In some regions of Bihar; the landowning dominant castes have even organised private armies to put down the Dalits with force. The Dalits in Bihar have also organised themselves under the aegis of political organisations that preach armed insurgency and revolution to resist the oppression of dominant castes. In the face of the growing self-awareness of Dalits the dominant castes are on the retreat as they find themselves fighting a losing battle. The success of certain Dalit organisations in persuading to include caste in its agenda despite the resistance of the Government of India is also indicative of the reach that Dalit ideology has acquired in the recent years.

Politics of Caste

The politics of caste-based reservations gained an added edge with the decision of the union government in 1989 to implement the recommendations of the Mandal Commission Report extending the reservation of government jobs for the 'other backward classes'. The reservation of jobs and seats in educational institutions has now become a politically sensitive issue. No political party can afford to oppose reservations as it may lose its popular base by doing so. To gain popular support, political parties now compete with each other to extend reservations to castes hitherto excluded from the list of Scheduled Castes or backward classes. Just as pressure to accommodate more and more castes in the reserved categories grows, resentment has been building among castes that have not been able to take advantages of the reservation policy. Leaders of these castes complain that the more educated and socially advantaged castes in the reserved categories have monopolised the privileges of reservation. Hence, there is now a trend to demand separate quotas for each of the castes within the reserved categories. This trend is sharpening the identity of castes and of even sub-castes within castes. In Tamil Nadu, widespread caste riots of early 1990s demonstrated the emotional appeal that these identities have acquired as well as the inability of the state apparatus to put them down. Another recent trend in Tamil Nadu politics is the emergence of political parties formed specifically to cater to the interests of particular castes or sub-castes among the backward classes and the Scheduled Castes. Thus, the policies aimed at eradicating caste seem to have succeeded in reinventing a state sponsored caste system that is elaborating itself along caste and even sub-caste lines. The difference that this new officially recognised version of caste system has vis-à-vis the traditional caste system is that it is organised around modern, egalitarian politics.

Another dimension of the politics of reservations has been the demand for extension of reservation to members of backward castes and of former untouchable castes among the Muslims and Christians. This demand also reflects the reality that conversion does not wipe out caste discrimination. Not so long ago, Church leaders as well as Muslim clergy were unwilling to admit that widespread caste discrimination prevailed in their respective religions. Unfortunately, this demand does not find favour with the castes that are already enjoying the privileged. If the forthcoming Durban conference accepts the view that caste discrimination is a form of racial discrimination, the demand of Christian Dalits for inclusion in the Scheduled Castes category will gain strength.

Overriding some of the fissiparous tendencies within castes as noted above, the politics of reservation has acquired a new integrative momentum, especially after the implementation of Mandal Commission recommendations in 1989. Some political leaders and intellectuals have been busy crafting a new Dalit-bahujan ideology that seeks to overturn the monopoly of power and privilege hitherto enjoyed by the upper castes who only formed a minority of the population. The ideology calls for the unity of Dalits or the oppressed castes, backward castes and religious minorities to form a formidable political force that can wipe out the remnants of upper caste Hindu hegemony. The ideology elaborates the concept of social justice to build a secular egalitarian society that upholds human dignity by destroying the foundations of caste-based hierarchy. It espouses 'Dalitisation' or the social process that upholds the communitarian, egalitarian and work-oriented values of the Dalits.

The Dalit-bahujan ideology has also produced contradictory social trends. As mentioned earlier, the recent success of some Christian and Dalit organisations on the inclusion of caste in the agenda of the forthcoming Durban conference reflects the power of this ideology. While discussion of caste as a form of racial discrimination will give worldwide publicity to the Dalit-bahujan cause, the manner in which the argument is presented may produce contrary results. The proponents of the Dalit view that 'caste is race plus' tend to overlook secularisation processes that have indeed freed Dalits from the ritualistic grip of caste hierarchy. The argument suspecting a conspiracy of the upper castes in implementing progressive government policies does not take account of the structural changes that have subverted the position of the upper castes. It also overlooks the fact that the rhetoric of caste has become more strident by adopting an approach that recognised certain castes for special treatment. There is the distinct danger that by insisting that the principle of caste remains the basis of social discrimination and oppression, secular factors that perpetuate the wretchedness of the deprived castes will be ignored. A caste-based approach to the elimination of caste discrimination will only succeed in perpetuating caste discrimination.

Conclusion

The idea that 'caste is race plus' may prove effective in drawing the world attention to bear on the practice of caste. The practice of caste cannot, however, be easily eradicated by strategies that merely legitimise caste and caste-based politics. Further, the strategy may also divert attention from secular deprivations that lock deprived castes in casteism and caste politics. Indian electoral politics has developed a vested interest in the perpetuation of caste identities because it glosses over the failure of political parties and the state in addressing the basic issue of development. As one prominent political leader said sometime ago, 'development does not bring in votes but caste does'.

Hence, if we are intent on gaining more than mere political mileage from the proceedings of the Durban conference, it is time to recognise that non-caste secular strategies need to translate political empowerment of the Dalits into social empowerment. Special efforts need to be made not just by the government but also by non-government organisations to educate and train Dalits and other poor and vulnerable sections of society. The need is to ensure that a new generation of Dalits rises provide role models for not just the members of their own castes but for the whole society.

Caste, Race and Internationalisation

Chapter 23

The UN, Racism and Caste

GAIL OMVEDT

The World Conference Against Racism, Racial Discrimination, Xenophobia and Related Intolerance will be held in South Africa from August 31 to September 7, marking the culmination of the International Year of the Elimination of Racial Discrimination. The conference itself is a testimony to an ongoing fight for social justice, to battles won as well as battles remaining. The very fact that it is being held in south Africa is a tribute to Nelson Mandela and a symbol of the victory won when the apartheid regime, representing one of the most extreme examples of racism, yielded to world wide democratic movements. The decision to hold such a conference marks the determination no to be content with a few significant steps forward, but to move ahead and annihilate all the vestiges and forms of the brutal discrimination that for so long has tyrannised over the majority of the peoples of the world.

The South Africa conference also marks a big step ahead for the global Dalits movement. After over two and a half decades of organising, caste is being recognised as a form of racist related discrimination and will be discussed in United Nations forums. Two and half decades of obstructionism by the Indian government and the Indian elite is being overcome.

The beginnings of this world level Dalit organising can be traced to the period of the emergency, when in August 1975 Dalits in the US under the leadership of Laxmi Berwa organised a demonstration against the visit of Indira Gandhi. Dr. Berwa, a physician practicing in Washington D.C. has mobilised under the banner of VISION. "Volunteers in service to India, suppressed and neglected." Berwa's organising had also illustrated one of the first examples of unity between Dalits and Black Americans (African-Americans),for he was offered the chance to present his case on radio stations controlled by African Americans in Washington. For perhaps the first time, in the very backyard of the Indian embassy, stories of atrocities on Dalits and the continuing burden of Casteism cold be heard by Americans, whose image of India had been only that of the "land of Gandhi." About the same time, a small businessman in Toronto, Yogesh Warhade, founded the Ambedkar Mission and began efforts to take the cause of Dalits to the forums of the United Nations. In England, Hirekar began to work along similar lines and Buddhist groups began to organise. Gradually, a worldwide Dalit movement began to take shape.

It has not been easy. Since Dalits are among the poorest sections of India, migration has been a rare option for them; even among migrants to the Gulf, Dalits from Kerala have been very under-represented compared to the general population. In the US, the situation is even more severe. Historically speaking, there were never large sections of working class Indians who migrated to the US, unlike Chinese and Japanese populations; those who did (Sikhs to California) were forbidden to bring their wives. For this reason, the NRI community in the US today is one of the most affluent among minorities, and it is even more upper caste dominated than India as a whole. Perhaps this explains why, when NRIs in the New York area raised money to finance a chair of South Asian studies at the University of Columbia, they refused suggestions to let it be named after Columbia university's most famous Indian graduate, Dr. Ambedkar. The Vishwa Hindu Parishad and similar organisations have found fertile field among Indian in the US, and sites relating to India on the internet are clearly Hindutva dominated. Those Dalits going abroad have rarely been in the universities, more often working outside as engineers, doctors, or occasional small businessmen.

However, long years of organising work by groups such as Vision and the Ambedkar Mission have paid off, and the growing human rights movement has begun to hear the slogan, "Dalit rights are human rights." Not only have Dalit-oriented NGOs sprung up to take the issue to the new World Conference Against Racism, but a group of enterprising activists has begun Dalit and bahujan e-mail forums and an excellent website, www.ambedkar.org. Similarly, efforts to build connections between African Americans and Dalits have gone on. One of the first attempts was a conference in 1986, also organised at Columbia University, dealing with Untouchability and Racism, drawing together black scholars and Indian Dalit scholars as well as non Dalit scholars dealing with issue of caste. In more recent years, journals such as Dalit Voice have organised tours of India by representatives of African-American groups. The Conference Against Racism is one example of such linkages being recognised.

Unfortunately, the union government has from the beginning offered adamant resistance to taking up the issue of caste at the UN just as it has resisted the efforts of adivasis to be included among "indigenous peoples." Scholarly study of caste issues has been discouraged (students proposing to do their Ph.D. work on this issue tend to get their visa applications refused) and, following the Columbia conference not only did the government refuse to let a follow up conference be held in India, but American organisers of the Columbia conference were denied research visas.

This unwillingness to recognise that caste is a persisting problem of Indian society, with global implications, has continued during recent years, and government spokesmen have opposed having it taken up at the South Africa conference, arguing that this would only lead to "diluting" the efforts to eliminate racism. This official position has most recently been put by the Attorney-General, Soli Sorabjee, who argues in addition that the issue of caste is an "internal" matter. It is sad that the country which has not hesitated to condemn racism and apartheid elsewhere should be so sensitive on the issue of caste that it should oppose this form of "globalisation" and try to retreat behind a saffron curtain on the issue of human rights within the country. As Smita Nirula, a well-known activists on the issue of Dalit rights, has argued, India is a signatory to many UN rights documents condemning discrimination on the basis of "descent"; yet in this case it has made every effort to block the issue and has never been ready to have it discussed in Parliament. "While countries may ignore the pronouncements of UN treaty bodies, they cannot ignore their own Constitutions or the voices of their citizens. The spirit of this conference and own Constitutional commitment to freedom of expression, equality, and the abolishment of untouchability demands no less.' Indians may find it demeaning to be condemned for forms of racism, but what is truly demeaning is the effort to block discussion, the refusal to have social transparency before the world.

Unfortunately, leading intellectuals too have supported the government position. A major example was an article in *The Hindu* on March 10, 2001 by André Béteille. Béteille, however, indulges in some rhetorical overkill; for he not only denies that caste has anything to do with racism, but even appears to be against the effort by the UN to deal with racism. "What is neither understandable nor excusable," he writes, "is the attempt by the United Nations to revive and expand the idea of race, ostensibly to combat the many forms of social and political discrimination prevalent in the world," Béteille has taken an extreme position, but it would still be useful to deal with the question raised by his arguments: what is racism, what is race, and what is the relation between race and caste, or racism and casteism?

André Béteille has argued two major points in his article, "race and caste"(*The Hindu*, March 10). One is that racism was based on false science; there are no genetically and biologically different races among human beings. The other is that caste has nothing to do with race, and therefore to include caste in a discussion of racism is erroneous, however politically useful it may seem to some people. In fact his two points contradict one another. Neither caste as a social system nor "racism" are based on actual biological differences among human beings. Both, though, are systems of discrimination that attribute "natural" or essential qualities to people born in specific social groups. In other words, while caste has nothing to do with "race", the justifications of caste discrimination have a lot to do with the social phenomenon of "racism".

As Béteille has argued, "race" in terms of naturally different species does not exist among human beings. The science of genetics is now strikingly clear on this – there are no significant genetic differences among socially identifiable groups of people; the genetic variation among individuals is by far greater than any among any society group. But, this is only to say that "racism" as a social phenomenon is based on a lie; it does not provide us an analysis of why the lie has come to exist.

Racism, which is the attribution of "natural" characteristics to groups of human beings, came into full scale existence in the last few centuries, largely in connection with imperialism. In order to justify the brutalities of conquest and subjugation, the non-white peoples conquered by the colonial powers had to be viewed, and were viewed, as less than human. The new biological sciences and even genetics came in handy for this purpose. Suddenly skin colour and the shape of heads could be taken as representing some inherent biological and genetic features which had larger implications. Dominance was asserted to be the result of the "natural" (biological, genetic) superiority of white European peoples, who had the god given charge of caring for the "lesser" peoples of the world.

This connection of racism with recent European based imperialism is not to say that cultures of non white peoples, whether Chinese or Japanese or the Africans themselves, have lacked systems of discrimination similar to "racism". It is simply that the European form has been dominant in the world over most of the last centuries, and has been linked with the strongest forms of oppression.

Racism, or ideas of innate, biological superiority and inferiority is, as Béteille himself has noted, a very "plastic" concept. All kinds of "races" have been postulated; class differences themselves were even interpreted at times in terms of race. It was quite natural, then, that when the British conquered India at the time of the full-fledged flourishing of racist concepts, when they were puzzled by the phenomenon of caste, that they should interpret it in terms of race. Thus, linguistic similarities among many of the languages of India and European languages were linked to groups such as the Aryans, identified as racial types, and using the notion of an "Aryan conquest," the argument was made that the upper three varnas were descendent from the Indo-European "Aryans", and the shudras, adivasis and Dalits from non-Aryan indigenous ethnic groups. In fact, racism in India has been as much a lie as elsewhere; the millennia of mixing of linguistic-ethnic groups, Aryan, Dravidian, Sino Tibetan, Austro Asiatic, had resulted in little clear distinction between caste categories. Ambedkar himself was categoric in rejecting the "Aryan theory" or the racial theory of caste. Caste was not a racial division of races but a division of races, he said (still using the category); Punjabi Brahmans and Punjabi Untouchables were ethnically the same, the Tamil Brahmans and Tamil untouchables were not racially different.

However, what has to be answered is why this "Aryan theory" proved so attractive to Indians themselves, why interpreting caste in terms of race has been so pervasive. The reason is precisely because of its resonance with indigenous themes of caste. For caste, like race, is based on the notion that socially defined groups of people have inherent, natural qualities or "essences" that assign them to social positions, make them fit for specific duties and occupations; it is their swadharma to carry out these duties. The word jati has been applied to species of plants and animals; and quite naturally many Indians thought of human castes as similar to such species. Thus, when the Buddha sought to refute the notion of birth determined caste, two and a half millennia ago, he referred to the basic physical similarity of all human beings.

According to the Sutta Nipata, when asked by Vasettha, a Brahman, to settle a debate between him and a friend about whether it is "birth" or "life" that makes a Brahman, the Buddha replies that whereas grass and trees, insects, snakes, fish and birds have diverse species, he uses the term jati among humans this is not so. "Men alone show not that nature stamps them as different Jatis. They differ not in hair, head, ears or eyes, in mouth or nostrils, not in eyebrows, lips, throat, shoulders, belly, buttocks, back or chest." He then goes on to say that one who lives by keeping cows is a farmer or Kassako: on who lives by handicrafts is a tradesman or Sippiko; one who lives by selling merchandise is a Vanijjo; one who lives by services done for hire is a Pessiko or wage-worker; one who lives by taking things not his is a robber; one who live by warfare is a Yodhajivao or solider; one who lives by sacrificial rites is a Yajako or priest; one who rules is a monarch or raja. This denial of innate, inborn differences between Jatis contrasted with arguments in the *Manusmriti* that for example, Shudras were by essence, by nature, designed to serve, that they were created as servants. Thus, because such notions of "natural" differences lay behind justification of the varnas, it is perhaps not so surprising that when the British put forward their racial theory of caste, it was accepted by so many Indians also. The original theological justification – varnas created out of the original Purusha could be replaced by a pseudo-scientific justification. Thus, caste is not based on race; but the theories justifying caste, or caste as an ideological construct, were similar enough to racism to allow a racial interpretation of caste (It has to be added also that many of the Indian elite, including Gandhi, used sociologically themes of a harmoniously functioning society to justify an idealised Varna system).

The fact that the United Nations is holding a conference against racism is not a matter of perpetuating notions of "race". Indeed, significant progress in most countries has been made over the last decade in fighting existing forms of racism, caste discrimination and similar social forms. This is true also in India. Yet it would be foolhardy to say that racism or caste discrimination do not exist, whether we are talking about the United States, South Africa itself, Japan where an indigenous groups similar to Untouchables, the Burakumin, have been organising, or India. Racism and casteism cannot be annihilated by ignoring their existence. Policies to eradicate these social evils require full consciousness of their extent, knowledge of their various expressions and will to take public action. In a global age, fighting racism, caste discrimination and similar phenomenon means global alliances and international as well as national policies. There is no reason for a government representing the Indian people to fight this; if the government does so, that means it is representing very different interests.

Chapter 24

Caste and the World Conference Against Racism

DAVID HASLAM

The first major World Conference Against Racism (WCAR) is to be held in Durban, South Africa, at the beginning of September. It is being organised under the auspices of the United Nations Human Rights Commission, based in Geneva. It is being held in South Africa partly to celebrate the ending of the apartheid, and to look forward to a world where racial discrimination is eliminated.

The conference is to be held between August 31 and September 7, 2001. It will be preceded by a Non-Governmental Organization's (NGO) Forum, from August 28-31. This event will be held in a sports stadium in Durban, and an exhibition of campaigns against racially-based discrimination from around the world will be held.

Some have questioned whether the issue of "caste" should be associated with that of "race". There are, however, many similarities between the two, and it has been interesting to note that the South African organisers are particularly interested in including caste as an issue at the WCAR. It could be argued that both "race" and "caste" are social constructs. They are created by forces in society who seek to divide the powerful from the powerless. In fact, biologically there are no such thing as separate races and the same could be said of castes. These systems are a biological invention.

It is true to say that racial discrimination, and the ideology of racism, are based more on colour and so-called facial features than is caste, although there is a colour element in caste and "Varna" – one of the words used to describe caste in India – means "colour".

However despite that modest difference, both the systems of racial and caste discrimination use the same mechanisms of oppression. These include economic oppression over jobs, land ownership and access to capital, and social oppression such as access to education, health, decent housing and all the other expected equalities of treatment in life. The one additional factor used in caste discrimination is the concept of "purity/pollution", in which one group is said to be pure and other groups regarded as polluted. This creates the kind of psychological oppression to which Dalits so strongly object.

National Campaign on Dalit Human Rights (NCDHR)

Over the last two years, the NCDHR has emerged to try to coordinate activity of Dalits against caste discrimination, and more recently to organise preparation for the WCAR. The Dalit communities who have organised as the NCDHR have begun to attend international UN meetings, in company with supportive national and international NGOs. Representations have been made to the UN Committee to Eliminate Racial Discrimination (CERD), and to the UN Human Rights Commission, in particular. A short presentation was made by the author of this article to the UNHRC in Geneva in March 2000, with the support of NCDHR and other agencies such as Anti Slavery International.

The NCDHR has been working hard within India to draw attention to the issue of caste in the context of the WCAR. A major conference was held in Tamil Nadu in November 2000, which drew scores of participants. Then at the beginning of March 2001, a "Global Conference Against Racism" was held in New Delhi in order to prepare for the WCAR. Over 200 participants attended, including senior figures from Indian life and a UN Human Rights Commissioner from South Africa. Representatives of international NGOs were also present. The conference made a strong statement about the necessity of including caste discrimination in the agenda and program of action of the WCAR.

International Dalit Solidarity Network (IDSN)

The development of the NCDHR within India has been parallelled by the growth of an international network of NGO's representing a wide range of countries. The International Dalit Solidarity Network (IDSN) began its life at a meeting in London in March 2000. Since then it defined it's purpose as, among other things, to "raise consciousness" about Dalit people nationally and internationally, and to "advocate, separately and together, Dalit human rights in international forums." The IDSN has continued to lobby UN organisations, particularly CERD and UNHRC in Geneva. Representatives of sympathetic NGO's such as Human Rights Watch, International Movement Against All Forms of Discrimination and Racism (IMADR) and the Lutheran World Federation have been active particularly around the Preparatory Committees of the WCAR. Over the same period they have been developing contacts with Western European and US governments, both to try and inform on the issue of caste and also to get support for inclusion of caste at the WCAR. In May 2000 a small delegation from four European countries and India visited politicians and officials in Strasbourg and Brussels to encourage the European Union to press harder on the caste issue at the WCAR.

Reaction from India

This pressure has not gone unnoticed in India. In early February the Indian Foreign Minister Jaswant Singh, called together a 15-member committee to seek to block the introduction of caste into the WCAR. Jaswant Singh said some in India were trying to broaden the scope of the WCAR by bringing racial connotations to caste. This defensive reaction caused international interest to rise and on February 14th *The London Times* ran an article which drew attention to India's defensive reaction, and went on the describe the caste system in some detail. The story was picked up by a number of Indian newspapers.

Indian academics and intellectuals responded to this by organising a conference in April in New Delhi which again discussed the issue. They subsequently put out a statement indicating that there were parallels between caste and race, and stating that the Indian government was trying to cover up international discussion on caste discrimination. They strongly urged that caste be included on the WCAR agenda.

Discussion on the issue has been sharpened by widespread reports of discrimination in the distribution of relief resources after the Gujarat earthquake. A major article appeared in the UK Guardian. The article drew attention to refusal by the higher caste Patel community to move into emergency tended camps with Dalits. In other places Dalits claimed that although the higher caste people obtained relief within a couple of days in the aftermath of the earthquake, it took much longer for assistance to reach them. Aid agencies also drew attention to the presence of the RSS (National Volunteer Force), which is avowedly Hindu-supporting in the relief operation. There were reports of non-Hindus being required to make pro-Hindu statements before receiving help.

Back to Geneva

In the meantime, the UN Human Rights Commission Intercessional Meeting was taking place in Geneva. This was again lobbied by NCDHR and IDSN representatives. As a result the smaller countries of Barbados and Switzerland were persuaded to put forward an amendment on caste into the WCAR program of action. However, within 24 hours heavy pressure, apparently by the Indian government on Barbados, had caused the proposal to be withdrawn.

This clash laid the foundation for the final Preparatory Committee for the WCAR to meet in mid-May. Strenuous efforts were being made by the campaigners to reinsert the wording on caste into the draft Program of Action. The way such things work means that, unless such phrasing is at least included in draft documents, it is very unlikely to emerge as part of the conference outcome. Campaigners were hoping that, as a result of what happened to Barbados, European Union governments might be more willing to take a principled stand on caste.

This, however, was proving difficult, as the main thrust of the conference from the countries of the South appears to be to put the countries of Europe and North America in the dock over slavery and colonialism and their results, and to seek reparation for all the peoples of past centuries. The European Union governments are therefore on the defensive, and do not want to antagonise India which is the Chair of the Asia Group. If they do, India may more actively support the demands of African, Latin American and other Asia countries for reparations.

Conclusion

Whether or not cast appears in the final statements of the Durban WCAR, it will undoubtedly have been pushed up the international agenda by the lobbying and campaigning between 2000/2001. After Durban, the NCDHR and IDSN will need to review progress so far, and to work out the next steps for the international campaign. Positive signs are that, as well as CERD and UNHRC taking up caste, the Committee on the Elimination of Discrimination Against Women (CEDAW) and the Committee on the Rights, of the Child (overseeing the Convention of the Rights of Children), and the International Labor Organization (ILO) are all taking an increasing interest in the caste issue. There is no doubt that concern will continue to rise, and that caste discrimination is rapidly becoming an international human rights issue.

Chapter 25

Racial Discrimination as a Grave Violation of Human Rights

P.N. BHAGWATI

I am deeply grateful to the UN Information Centre for inviting me to speak at this meeting, which has been organised in the context of the World Conference against Racism, Racial Discrimination, Xenophobia and Related Intolerance. It is a Conference in which I am deeply interested. Both in my capacity as Regional Advisor for the Asia-Pacific region of the High Commissioner for Human Rights and also as a human rights activist which has contributed in some measure to the development of human rights jurisprudence in India and who is engaged in the promotion and protection of human rights throughout the world.

The Third World Conference is going to be held in Durban, South Africa from 31st August to 7th September of this year. The convening of the world Conference has been preceded by 50 years of activity by the United Nations in its efforts to eradicate all forms of racism and racial discrimination. It would be worthwhile to refer briefly to the efforts made by the United Nations in this connection during the last 50 years.

When the international community adopted the United Nations Charter in 1945, it accepted the obligation to pursue the realisation of human rights and fundamental freedoms for all, without distinction as to race, sex, language, or religion. In December 1948 the United Nations General Assembly adopted the Universal Declaration of Human Rights, which declares in Article 1 that "all human beings are born free and equal in dignity and rights".

On 20 November 1963, the General Assembly adopted the UN Declaration on the Elimination of All Forms of Racial Discrimination. It was that might be called a "soft" international human rights instrument. In its preamble, the declaration recognised that, in spite of progress, discrimination based on race, colour or ethnic origin continued to give cause for serious concern.

Article 1 reaffirmed the principles of the UN Charter and the Universal Declaration of Human Rights, and their fundamental importance to good international relations: "Discrimination between human beings on the ground of race, colour or ethnic origin is an offence to human dignity and shall be condemned as a denial of the principles of the Charter of the United Nations, as a violation of the human rights and fundamental freedoms proclaimed in the universal declaration of Human Rights, as an obstacle to friendly and peaceful relations among nations and as a fact capable of disturbing peace and security among nation". The Declaration, however, was not legally binding.

On 21 December 1965, the General Assembly adopted the International Convention on the Elimination of All Forms of Racial Discrimination. The Convention, which is a legally binding instrument, entered into force on 4 January 1969 and now has 155 State parties. It defies racial discrimination as any distinction, exclusion, restriction or preference based on race, colour, descent, or national or ethnic origin which has the purpose or effect of nullifying or impairing the recognition, enjoyment for exercise… of human rights and fundamental freedoms..." States parties agree to condemn racism and to undertake measures to eliminate it in all its forms. The Convention also established the Committee on the Elimination of Racial Discrimination, the first such human rights treaty monitoring body. It overseas implementation of the Convention by reviewing reports of the States parties to the Convention.

Thereafter, on 11 December 1969, The General Assembly designated 1971 as the International Year for Action to Combat Racial

Discrimination. It asked that the Year "be observed in the name of the ever-growing struggle against racial discrimination in all its forms and manifestations and in the name of the international solidarity with those struggling against racism." It appealed urgently to States to intensify their efforts to eradicate racial discrimination in all its contemporary forms, including Nazism and apartheid.

On 2 November 1972, the General Assembly designated the ten-year period beginning on 10 December 1973 as the Decade for Action to Combat Racism and Racial Discrimination. The programme decade was structured around a worldwide education campaign and measures to be taken to implement United Nations instruments promoting the elimination of racial discrimination. Its goals were to promote human rights and fundamental freedoms for all, without distinction of any kind on grounds of race, colour, descent or national or ethnic origin, by eradicating racial prejudice, racism and racial discrimination; to prevent the continuation of expansion of racist policies, to discourage the strengthening of racist regimes, to "isolate and dispel the fallacious and mythical beliefs, policies and practices that contribute to racism and racial discrimination: and to put an end to racist regimes."

The First World Conference to Combat Racism and Racial Discrimination was held in Geneva in 1978 at the midpoint of the First Decade. It adopted a declaration and a programme of Action reaffirming the inherent falsity to racism and the threat it posed to friendly relations among people. It specifically condemned apartheid, branding it as the extreme form of institutionalised racism and a crime against humanity.

This was followed by the Second World Conference to Combat Racism and Racial Discrimination held in Geneva in August 1983. It reviewed and assessed the activities undertaken during the Decade and formulated specific measures to ensure implementation of UN instruments to eliminate, racism, racial discrimination and apartheid. It took various decisions for combating racism and racial discrimination but it was found that despite the Declarations made at the first and Second World Conferences and the efforts of the International community, the principal objectives had not been attained and that millions of human beings continued to be the victims of varied forms of racism and racial discrimination. The General Assembly, therefore, proclaimed the Second Decade for Action to Combat Racism and Racial Discrimination. But, as the subsequent events showed, the efforts of the international community to eliminate racism and racial discrimination did not succeed in achieving a racism free society.

As I shall presently show, racism, racial discrimination and xenophobia and related intolerance still continue to bedevil humanity throughout the world. There is indeed no country, which is free from racism or racist tendencies. The scourge of racial discrimination is not confined or concentrated in any one part of the world but it is to be found in all parts of the world. Aided by the process of globalisation, the contemporary international system is now characterised by economic centres of power within nations, in countries around the world. These industrialised centres attract trafficking of women, cheap labour, and illegal migrants. Individuals within these groups suffer not only exploitation but also become the victims of racist and xenophobic resentment by nationals, long-term residents and those who have benefited from past privileges in the economy. These conditions exist in several parts of the world, including some of the developed countries. The office of the High Commissioner had organised a meeting of experts in Bangkok during 5 to 7 September 2000 to consider the situation with regard to the trafficking in women and children and migrant workers and the discussions by the experts showed that racism and xenophobia was rampant in regard to these victims of violations of human rights. In addition to these economic realities, complex cultural and political situation gave rise to the worst forms of racial discrimination such as the racist coup in Fiji, the Chinese occupation of Tibet, increasing violence against Jews in Russia, mass rapes of Chinese women in Indonesia during the 1998 riots, systematic and severe discrimination against the Roma in Europe and police abuses against African-American males in the US on a continuing basis. Efforts to address these and similar others should form the agenda of the Third World Conference.

This was emphasised by Mary Robinson, United Nations High Commissioner for Human Rights in the following statement made by her on 24 March 1999:

"As we see all around us, racism and racial discrimination continue unabated. Although we refer to our world as a global village, it is a world sadly lacking in the sense of closeness towards neighbour and community, which the word village implies. In each region, and within all countries, there are problems stemming from either a lack of respect for, or lack of acceptance of, the inherent dignity and equality of all human beings. Our world is witness to serious ethnic conflict; to discrimination against minorities, indigenous peoples and migrant workers; the accusation of institutionalised racism in police forces; harsh immigration and asylum policies; hate sites on the internet and youth groups promoting intolerance and xenophobia".

The Third World Conference is intended to awaken in human kind throughout the world sensitivity against racism, racial discrimination, and xenophobia and spur humanity to action. We have for long given lectures, speeches, and sermons condemning racism and racial discrimination but precious little has been done despite all our protestations. Today, we find still continuing discrimination and exploitation of large numbers of people throughout North America, South America, Western Europe arising from the perception entertained by the countries of Western Europe that they are being invaded by hoards of immigrants from Asia and non-Christian countries in Eastern Europe and the Middle East. There is also resurgence of anti-Semitism in some parts of Western Europe. "In the majority of European countries" according to a UN Report, "racist or xenophobic sentiments are shared by an increasingly large percentage of the population". The mass media also sometimes adopts a racist approach in the guise of protecting national identity by describing immigrants as criminals or destabilising influences. The immigrants are often described by the media as perpetrators of violence, although in fact they are most often its victims and they are banded as incapable of adapting to traditional national values. Even more chilling are the racist video games, which are being distributed in Austria, Germany and Sweden. These games, inter-alia, portray Turks as dangerous non-Aryans who destroy society. The Internet also plays a highly dangerous role in promoting racism and racial prejudices.

We find that racism: racial discrimination and xenophobia are widely prevalent in Latin America where total discrimination against the indigenous groups and total exploitation of the indigenous communities. The human rights committee had occasion to observe, while considering the report of Brazil, that the Committee was concerned over the existence of racial and other discrimination against black and indigenous persons. The same situation prevails in other countries of Latin America. While considering the report of Chile, the human rights committee had occasion to point out that the Committee was concerned by hydro-electric and other development projects that might affect the way of life and the rights of persons belonging to the Mapuche and other indigenous communities.

The publication of the Asia Pacific Human Rights Network sets the situation prevailing in several countries of Asia and Africa where the societies are afflicted by racism, race prejudices, and xenophobia. I will refer only to a few of them for lack of time. About 3 million Burakus who are considered outcastes by ethnic Japanese because of their traditional professions like butchering, continue to face similar societal discrimination. There are a large number of Koreans in Japan who have no right to hold public positions whether it be a job in the government service or an elected post in a local municipality, solely because of their Korean ethnic origin. Until 1993, approximately 7,00,000 Koreans who were born, brought up and educated in Japan were required to give finger prints like criminals to the Japanese law enforcing authorities until this was abolished as a result of the criticism made by the Human Rights Committee. Similarly, the Chinese in Indonesia face discrimination in public life. There still continue curbs on the teaching of Chinese in schools or its usage in the Public domain.

The situation of indigenous people across Asia is also alarming. The hill tribes of Thailand such as Akahs, Lahus, Lisus and Karens are barred from participation in the political process although their ancestors have been residing in the territory of Thailand for more than 200 years. Only half of the estimated 5,00,000 to 6,00,000 members of the hill tribes in Northern Thailand possess official documentation that enlists them as citizens and gives them other basic rights. They cannot even own land and they are not entitled to the benefit of labour laws and consequently, they are vulnerable to exploitation.

So also in India, despite affirmative action provided in the Constitution and taken by the government, there remains a yawning gap between rhetoric and reality. The Dalits still continue to face discrimination and prejudice including ill treatment, neglect, and exploitation particularly in the rural areas. The enactment of the 1989 Scheduled Castes and Scheduled Tribes Atrocities (Prevention) Act does not appear to have made the anticipated impact on the situation of the Dalits. The Adivasis or indigenous communities in India are still in the eastern sector subjected to the harsh provisions of the Criminal Tribes Act and though the National Human Rights Commission recommended its abolition, no action seems to have been taken so far by the government. Indigenous peoples in Indonesia and Bangladesh such as Chakmas have also been the victims of government sponsored trans-migrants policies and serious human right abuses.

I have given only a few instances where racism, racial prejudices, and xenophobia still prevail in their most devastating forms in all parts of the world. The Third World Conference is intended to be action oriented and positive measures have to be adopted by all states, law enforcement agencies, NGOs, Civil Society organisations, and other associations in order to eradicate racism, racial prejudice and xenophobia from the minds of the people. What is necessary is to change in the attitudes of men and women. They must be made to realise that we are all part of one common humanity, whatever be the race to which we belong, whatever be the colour of the our skin and whatever be the religion we practice. A new culture what I call the humanist culture, must be cultivated, and instilled in the minds of our youth. This can be done only through education, not only education in the schools and colleges but also education at home. Our school and college curricula must be oriented against racism, xenophobia, and five human values, which are essential humanity and the imperative necessity of one world community. The Great Master whom I follow has always said that there are five human values which are essential if humanity is to live in peace and harmony, free from all negative tendencies on race, colour, descent or national or ethnic origin and they are truth, righteousness, love, peace and non violence.

Let us hope that the Third World Conference will be able to inspire and motivate human beings around the world to practise these five virtues and bring about a new world order.

The Third World Conference must lay down firm and strong foundation for respect for equality and human dignity in the society.

The Third World Conference has the potential to be among the most significant gatherings at the start of this century, as it can shape and embody the spirit of a new century based on the shared conviction of the human race. It is bound to be landmark in the new century, as it will provide an ideal opportunity to craft a new vision for the fight against the racism for the future generations. It must focus action oriented and practical steps to eradicate racism, including measures of prevention; education and protection and the provision for effective remedies.

The evil of racism is a shame on humanity. Mere mechanisms of control and regulation cannot eliminate a complex phenomenon. It just cannot be wished away. It demands evolving a culture, which is responsive, sensitive, and reflective of human dignity and human justice. In other words, it must be a culture, which demands elimination of all kinds of exploitation not only by the state but also by members of civil society. The members of civil society should use their social status to eradicate practices, which are derogatory to human dignity. The goal of evolving human rights culture aimed at waging of war against racism has to be fought at many levels. Education is the most powerful means of influencing and bringing attitudinal change in people. Being a tool to spread awareness, information and knowledge amongst its recipients, education can play a crucial role in making us shed some of our prejudices and reform some of our attitudes and thereby eradicate the scourge of racism.

Chapter 26

Caste at Durban

Why and How

A.S. NARANG

Recently there has started a debate about the inclusion or otherwise of the issue of caste/Dalits in the forthcoming World Conference against Racism, Racial Discrimination, Xenophobia and Related Intolerance (WCAR) at Durban. The debate has unfortunately got limited to whether caste falls within or outside the definition and purview of racial discrimination. Within that race is being defined in a very limited way. The background of the Conference, the issues being raised, the processes being followed clearly suggest that the purpose and agenda of the Conference is quite comprehensive and the meaning assigned to race for this is quite wide. In the words of Mary Robinson, the United Nations High Commissioner for Human Rights and Secretary-General of the World Conference, the title of the Conference extends its scope to the many forms of racism and bigotry in our modern world, to xenophobia in all its manifestations, to anti-Semitism: Negrophobia, discrimination against indigenous peoples, migrants, refugees, displaced persons and the minority communities.

Definition of Racial Discrimination

For the purpose of WCAR and in general at present racial discrimination is defined in accordance with Article 1(i) of the

International Convention on the Elimination of Racial Discrimination. It says:

> Any distinction, exclusion, restriction or preference based on race, colour, descent, or national or ethnic origin which has the purpose or effect of nullifying or impairing the recognition, enjoyment or exercise, on an equal footing, of human rights and fundamental freedoms in the political, economic, social cultural or any other field of public life.

This definition of social discrimination, Ion Diaconu, a member of the UN Committee on the Elimination of Racial Discrimination, points out, is based on objective elements: it involves any distinction, exclusion, restriction or preference; that means, one has to identify an appropriate comparator; as they are based on race, colour, descent, or national or ethnic origin. By this enumeration the definition is suitable to protect all persons, as well as racial or ethnic groups.

Interestingly, the term "descent", which is not found in any other international document, was suggested by India during the elaboration of the Convention. Of course, it dose not indicate in what way it is different from "national" or "ethnic" origin. Some scholars, however, commented that it would include the notion of caste. The UN Committee on the Elimination of Racial Discrimination in its forty-ninth session in 1996 observed that the term 'descent' mentioned in Article 1 of the Convention does not solely refer to race. The Committee affirmed that the situation of the Scheduled Caste and Scheduled Tribes falls within the scope of the Convention.

It is thus clear that the definition of racial discrimination is broad and comprehensive and by its reference to race, colour, descent, national or ethnic origin covers persons belonging to various social groups including based on descent. It presents racial discrimination as a human conduct – by public authorities and institutions, by organisations and persons – which has to be eliminated.

Objectives of the Conference

The main objective of the WCAR is to review the progress made in the fight against racism, racial discrimination, xenophobia and related intolerance, particularly since the adoption of the Universal Declaration of Human Rights, and to reappraise the obstacles to future progress in the field and ways to overcome them. The approach here is not of conflict but for redressal and reconciliation. Calls for redress and reconciliation emerge out of historical resistance and struggle against repression and the processes for reconciliation take a variety of shapes and forms as they are fitted to different political situations. The most important component of a process of reconciliation is an accurate, public and official documentation of past human rights abuses. Collective remembering of the past, Rosemary Nagy of University of Toronto suggests, accomplishes a number of things. First, it gives victims a chance to tell their stories. Psychological healing is enabled "through providing the space for survivors of violence to feel heard and for every detail of the event to be re-experienced in a safe environment". Secondly, remembering and renouncing the past sets the foundations for a democratic culture and respect for rights that will deter future abuses. Thirdly, victims are given the opportunity to confront the official rhetoric, which proclaimed them guilty of terrible crimes and justified what was done to them. Finally, remembering the past is crucial because it is impossible to expect 'reconciliation' if part of the population refuses to accept that anything was ever wrong, and that other part has never received any acknowledgment of the suffering it has undergone or of the ultimate responsibility for that suffering". A shared memory is the starting point of reconciliation, the assumption of responsibility, contrition, forgiveness, healing and national unity.

Caste Discrimination

In the backdrop of the state of facts of being economically dependent and exploited, victims of many kinds of discrimination and ritually polluted in a permanent way, the feeling of alienation among the Dalits are deeper and intense. Although Constitutional provisions and legal texts exist to abolish untouchability and to protect the members of the Scheduled Castes and Tribes, and although social and educational policies have been adopted to improve the situation of members of the Scheduled Castes and Tribes and to protect them from abuses, widespread discrimination against them and the relative impunity of those who abuse them point of the limited effect of these measures.

Also it is important to look at both de jure and de facto segregation. In that sense whereas de jure discrimination against lower castes has disappeared, de facto segregation remain particularly at the social level not only in rural areas but also in cities; and they are treated even today in many parts of India as untouchables. As we are aware, many theories have been woven around the origin of this in human practice, but the effort to change it has not yet been successful.

In this situation putting up the issue of caste on the WCAR agenda apart from giving an opportunity to the Dalits to highlight their oppression in the international forum, will bring out with precision and insistence that the rights of persons belonging to lower castes, like such others elsewhere in the world, are human rights. This in turn will help the Government of India in its efforts to address social behaviour, attitudes, cultural stereotypes and interpersonal discrimination. When the issues are debated at international fora governments get, if they are serious, additional source to educate and reform societies. We all know that issues like environment, gender, child labour, poverty, etc. became important social issues at the national level in many countries after having been raised and discussed at international fora. Let us not shy away from the reality that caste is an intolerance and that it is a social evil which results in discrimination and needs extra efforts for eradication. Paulo Sergio Pinheirio, a member of the Sub-Commission on Promotion and Protection of Human Rights, in a working paper prepared for the Preparatory Committee of the WCAR, points out that when we consider the diverse forms of racism, its victims and manifestations – and discrimination on the basis of colour, ethnic origin and caste, discrimination against indigenous peoples, ethnic groups, the Roma, xenophobia and religious intolerance – we may conclude that in every society there is present a 'vicious circle' where such factors as race, poverty and lack of education interact for the oppression of many groups of people. But we must not overlook that many elements of a 'virtuous circle' by which transformation can occur, also exist. The WCAR can help the virtuous circle to prevail. By allowing caste to be discussed at the Conference we will only get help to locate such a virtuous circle as additional inputs in our efforts for effective elimination of such discrimination.

Chapter 27

UN's Record on Caste Rights

SIRAJ M. SAIT

Introduction

The 2001 WCAR must set the international agenda for addressing caste discrimination. Caste distinctions, fixed indelibly at birth, lead to widespread and serious forms of discrimination for generations, caste-based discrimination has persisted due to under-reporting, resistance from 'individuals who benefited from the caste system[1] and the acute disempowerment, silencing and social exclusion of those born with historically discredited identities. Caste was sidelined at the UN world conferences against racism in 1978 and 1983, at the 1993 Vienna Conference on Human Rights, as well as at the 2000 Millennium Summit. By integrating the caste dimension into programmes addressing racial discrimination and human rights initiatives, the WCAR would give effect to the principles of equal rights and freedoms, and the inherent dignity of every human being.

The prevalence of caste hierarchies is not confined to the well-documented case of Dalits (so-called 'untouchables')[2] in India, or the Buraku people in Japan[3], for as the UN working paper notes, 'discrimination based on work and descent (which manifests itself most notably in caste- or tribe-based distinctions) is a long-standing practice in many societies throughout the world and affects a large proportion of the world's population.[4] Caste or caste-like systems operate in, for example, Bangladesh, Burkina Faso, Burundi, Cameroon, Guinea, India, Japan, Madagascar, Mali, Mauritania, Micronesia, Nepal, Nigeria, Pakistan, Senegal and Sri Lanka. This Briefing evaluates the consideration of caste issues by relevant UN treaty monitoring bodies with respect to some of these states, with reference to State Reports, which have been reviewed.

This briefing also deals with the UN Charter based bodies examining thematic issues related to caste. Caste considerations impact on personal relations, access to public places, land and water, the provision of public services, health and educational facilities, the judicial system and employment practices. Caste distinctions result in extreme cultural, economic, religion mechanisms under the UN Charter based bodies are not designed or specifically mandated to examine caste, many violations linked to membership in low castes fall within their mandates. The extent to which these mechanisms acknowledge and address the impact of caste distinction is discussed below.

The UN Human Rights System

That discrimination so gross as caste has survived to this day is not only an indictment against the countries where the practice exists but [also] against the international community itself (Asian Legal Resource Centre).[5]

Since its first session in 1974, the UN Commission on Human Rights (Commission) has focused on both standard setting and monitoring human rights situations through its special procedures. Thought the Commission has focused on a wide range of human rights violations and has expressed concern about the incessant growth of racism 'adopting new forms including tendencies to establish policies based on racial, religious, ethnic, cultural and national superiority or exclusivity[6], caste discrimination rarely receives a mention. None of the special procedures established by the Commission has specifically or substantially addressed caste or similar forms of human rights violations. However, the recent work through its Sub-Commission has provided a breakthrough.

After years of failing to refer to caste discrimination, the Sub-Commission in August 2000, issued a significant resolution declaring discrimination based on work and descent as prohibited by international human rights law, and called on governments to take measures to eliminate this type of discrimination.[7] Though the resolution did not specific caste, it unmistakably made reference to some of the basic characteristics of the caste system. Moreover, in his recent working paper, the expert member appointed by the Sub-commission, does make a link to caste. He refers to the 'most widespread discrimination on the basis of work and descent [which] occurs in societies in which at least a portion of the population is influenced by the tradition of caste, including the Asian countries of Bangladesh, India, Nepal, Pakistan and Sri Lanka'.[8]

The working paper also discusses the discrimination against the Buraku people in Japan; the expert member notes that the paper 'which is introductory in nature' has not been able to deal with similar practices in other parts of the world, including Africa and perhaps South America'.[9] The Sub-Commission has only just begun the process of studying the global dimension and implications of caste and similar practices, and hopefully will undertake further studies to analyses the extent of this complex problem. Other mechanisms of the Sub-Commission have alluded to the practice during their work. The Working Group on Contemporary Forms of Slavery notes that those in bondage 'very often belong to minority groups exposed to discrimination such as indigenous populations and persons from lower castes'.[10] The Working Group on Minorities also engaged with caste issues while discussing the situation in India, but has not dealt with the thematic and global dimensions of the practice.[11]

The Office of the UN High Commissioner for Human Rights (OHCHR), which coordinates the UN Human Rights Agenda has, with respect to India, raised the question of 'social inequalities relating to the caste system'[12] and generally acknowledges that 'victims of slavery and slavery-like practices frequently belong to minority groups, particularly racial group... including people of "low" caste status.[13] However, despite NGO interventions, the elimination of caste discrimination does not feature in any substantial manner in the OHCHR's human rights reports, the Programme of Action for the

Third Decade to Combat Racism and Racial Discrimination, or, to date, in the draft WCAR official documents.

Caste Discrimination as Racial Discrimination

It was discovered in 1998 that private detective agencies in Osaka, Japan [with over 1,400 private companies as client] had conducted investigations into the [complete background] of job applicants to find out they were from Buraku area (Buraku Liberation League).[14]

ICERD provides five grounds for direct or indirect 'racial discrimination': 'any distinction, exclusion, restriction or preference based on race, colour, descent, or national or ethnic origin'[15] CERD has interpreted 'descent' under Article 1 of ICERD as also covering caste situations.[16] It has focused on caste discrimination and other descent-related discrimination with respect to India, Japan and Nepal, noting the limited effect of legal and/or constitutional measures to prevent such discrimination or deal with its perpetrators.[17] In its 1993 General Recommendation XIV on the interpretation of Article 1, CERD noted that States have the responsibility to address systemic discrimination and structural impediments to substantive equality, and to refrain from any action having disparate impact on the group (s) concerned.[18]

However, in reviewing other countries including Bangladesh, Burkina Faso, Burundi, Cameroon, guinea, Madagascar, Mali, Mauritania, Mauritius, Nigeria, Pakistan and Sri Lanka, CERD either does not proactively examine caste-like practices, or merely notes existing legislation and declares that caste is covered by the convention. Despite the Committee's pioneering role, in clarifying caste and similar forms of discrimination as violating the Convention, the caste system must be discussed more fully by CERD.

The Commission's Special Rapporteur on Racism, Racial Discrimination, Xenophobia and Related Intolerance has recently included the caste issue within his broad mandate. However, his engagement with caste-based discrimination has been country-specific and limited, rather than a worldwide initiative. The Rapporteur has sought to study the Dalit situation in India through a country visit[19] and has called for their integration into society and action against 'violence perpetrated against them in several parts of the country'.[20] He has also asked that 'special attention be given to the situation of the untouchables in India'.[21] India has not responded positively to the Special Rapporteur's request to visit.

Civil and Political Rights

[A government report] describe a number of social manifestations of caste-based discrimination in the 1990's: restrictions in marriage traditions; restrictions on] drawing water from common wells and hand-pumps; and... the use of] separate crockery and cutlery... for serving the flow] Castes (Human Rights Watch).[22]

The 1966 International Covenant on Civil and Political Rights (ICCPR) is wider in its anti-discrimination provisions that ICERD. The Human Rights Committee (HRC) monitoring the ICCPR has highlighted how 'the de facto perpetuation of the caste system entrenches social differences in India, which contribute to 'inter alia inter-caste violence, bonded labour and discrimination of all kinds'.[23] On Nepal, it observes that 'the principle of non-discrimination and equality of rights suffers serious violations in practice' through 'inadequacies in the implementation of the prohibition of the system of castes'.[24]

With Japan, the HRC, while acknowledging 'the acceptance by the State Party [Japan] of the discrimination that persists vis-à-vis members of the Buraku minority with regard to education, income, and the system of effective remedies', recommends that the government 'takes measures to put an end to such discrimination'.[25] The HRC does not frame questions on caste or related practices while engaging with Burundi, Cameroon, Guinea, Mauritius, Nigeria, Senegal or Sri Lanka. Moreover, none of the HRC's General Comments have touched on caste.

The Commission's Special Rapporteur on Extra-Judicial, Summary or Arbitrary Executions notes that 'social stratification in Burundi is based primarily upon class or caste differentiation rather than rigid ethnic differentiation'.[26] In a recent report on Nepal, the Rapporteur stated that 'social and economic inequalities between sexes, classes and regions are different [and, though the caste system has been abolished by law], these serious human rights problems still persist and continue to dominate social, economic and political life, particularly in the rural areas'.[27] On the other hand, the Commission's Working Groups on Arbitrary Detention,[28] and on Enforced or Involuntary Disappearances,[29] do not give attention to the caste factors underlying violations. Neither does the Special Rapporteur on the question of religious intolerance fully deal with the implications of caste discrimination.[30]

Torture and Inhuman Treatment

Dalit [so-called 'untouchables'] are particularly vulnerable to torture and ill-treatment and there is much evidence of blatant anti-Dalit discrimination within the police system. Physical land verbal abuse and intimidation on the basis of caste is common (Amnesty International).[31]

Members of low castes face a compounded risk of violations of physical integrity, inhuman treatment such as derogatory references, abusive language and, in some cases, public stripping, and further victimisation within the criminal justice system. The 1984 Convention Against Torture and Other Cruel, Inhuman, Degrading Treatment or Punishment contemplates that torture could be carried out 'for any reason based on discrimination of any kind'. Yet, the Committee against Torture (CAT) does not seem to have been interested in the caste factor. Its Concluding Observations on Bangladesh, Burundi, Cameroon, Mauritius, Nepal, Senegal and Sri Lanka do not explore caste or similar forms of discrimination as creating a greater propensity towards torture.

The Commission's Special Rapporteur on Torture and Other Cruel, Inhuman or Degrading Treatment or Punishment investigates, highlights complaints, profiles methods, perpetrators and victims, and details conditions conducive to torture and factors affecting the ability of torture victims to obtain redress. Despite his pioneering work, caste-specific and caste-motivated offences are absent in the conceptual study of the link between poverty and torture[32] and 'low' castes do not figure in a list of over three dozen categories of victims identified.

Economic, Social and Cultural Rights

Several aspects of exclusion cannot be characterised as [the result of] simply being poor or unemployed caste, fixed at birth, is one category that sociologists typically study, and economists tend to ignore, but its importance [in excluding people from development] can hardly be overemphasised (ILO Consultancy Paper).[33]

Discrimination grounds listed in the 1966 International Covenant on Economic, Social and Cultural Rights are identical to those in the ICCPR. However, the Committee on Economic, Social and Cultural Rights (CESCR), in its Concluding Observations on Cameroon, guinea, Mali, Mauritius, Nigeria, Senegal and Sri Lanka, Has yet to recognise caste discrimination as a relevant factor. In its list of questions for forthcoming dialogues, CESCR does express concern over the caste system in Nepal, but while referring to the situation regarding the Buraku people of Japan, makes no links to caste like discrimination.[34] It queries Cameroon on caste but has no comment on the issue in its Concluding Observations.[35] Its General Comments – on issues ranging from education to health – also do not deal with caste as a factor in the denial of socio-economic rights to those of 'low' caste.

The Sub-Commission's Working Group on Contemporary Forms of Slavery (as mentioned above), finds that those in debt bondage are very often from minorities, including people from lower castes. Such persons are also subjected to caste-based restrictions on work, and are employed in menial work such as manual scavenging.

However, the relevant International Labour Organization (ILO) conventions and programmes,[36] and UN development initiatives, understate caste vulnerability. Clearly, those at the low end of the caste hierarchy have significantly lower levels of education, health and enjoyment of other basic rights. Yet caste did not figure at the World Conference on Population and Development (Cairo 1994) or the World Summit for Social Development (Copenhagen 1995), nor is it included in follow-up measures. Moreover, the Commission's Independent Expert on the Right to Development,[37] the Independent Expert on Human Rights and Extreme Poverty,[38] and the Special Rapporteurs on Adequate Housing[39] and the Right to Education,[40] have so far largely ignored the case for the development of members of those 'low' castes excluded from social and economic opportunities.

Women's Rights

Devadasi means 'female servant of God' – a label that condemns many thousands of low-caste girls [yet to attain puberty] to a life of sexual servitude and subsequently prostitution. Unable to marry, she is forced to become a prostitute for (higher) caste Hindus (National Campaign on Dalit Human Rights).[41]

The 1979 convention on the Elimination of All Forms of Discrimination Against Women targets sex-based discrimination and allows for the intersection of gender and caste discrimination in the interpretation of its provisions. On India, the Committee on the Elimination of Discrimination Against Women (CEDAW) recognises the caste system as a factor impeding implementation of the convention. It notes that 'discrimination against women who belong to particular castes, ethnic or religious groups is also manifest in extreme forms of physical and sexual violence and harassment' and urges implementation of legislation against caste-based discrimination.[42] It is also concerned at 'the existence of caste-based discrimination' in Nepal.[43] However, in its Concluding Observations on Bangladesh, Burkina Faso, Burundi, Cameroon, Japan, Madagascar, Mauritius, Nigeria and Senegal it forgoes consideration of this form of multiple discrimination. CEDAW's General Recommendations on Violence Against Women (XII, XIX) do not recognise the added vulnerability of women facing caste discrimination.

The 1995 Beijing Conference on Women and its follow-up processes do not address the problems of women made more vulnerable through caste. UN resolutions, for example, on women's equal ownership of land and equal rights to own property and to adequate housing leave out 'low-caste' women.[44] The Commission's Special Rapporteur on Violence Against Women notes that women's lives are 'mediated by class, caste, race, ethnicity, access to resources...', and that women are subject to exploitation through a 'skewed, gender, caste and class based resource distribution'.[45] But the UN Division on the Advancement of Women makes no effort to include caste-discriminated women in its several programmes on gender empowerment and participation.

Children's Rights

Owners of bonded labourers believe that low-caste children should work rather than go to school [:] 'Once they are allowed to come up to an equal level, nobody will go to the fields. We have to keep them under our thumbs.' (UNICEF Report on Child Labour).[46]

The anti-discrimination clause in the widely ratified 1989 convention on the Rights of the Child is comprehensive. The Committee on the Rights of the Child (CRC) has recognised the caste system as 'an obstacle to combat [ing] discrimination... [that] compounds inter alia poverty, illiteracy, child labour, child sexual exploitation, and children living and or working on the streets'.[47] It notes the link between caste and child prostitution and other forms of exploitation in Nepal.[48] Dialogue with Micronesia led to the notable admission by the government representative that 'the caste system [is] accepted as an integral part of social and political life' and that those in lower castes [have] fewer privileges and sometimes more obligations'.[49] On the other hand, despite the Sri Lankan State Report acknowledging that 'any generalisations can be misleading... unless they take account of socio-cultural diversity of ethnicity, religion and caste', the CRC's Concluding Observations on Sri Lanka omit any reference to caste.[50] Neither does the Committee specifically investigate caste issues or similar forms of discrimination while dealing with countries such as Bangladesh, Burkina Faso, Burundi, Guinea, Japan, Pakistan or Senegal.[51] The General Comments issued by the CRC do not adequately address the exceptional problems encountered by children born into marginalised castes.

The CRC has in the case of India expressed concern over 'striking disparities' in terms of access to education and opportunity between children belonging to different castes.[52] The Commissions s Special Rapporteur on the sale of children, child prostitution and child pornography has found that 'children of the untouchables" are most often victimised in child labour situations'[53]," while the Sub-Commission's Special Rapporteur on traditional practices affecting the health of women and the girl child refers to the debilitating role of the caste system.[54] however, despite evidence and occasional recognition, the relevant UN mechanisms have failed to address comprehensively the additional risk to children due to their birth into a 'low' caste.

Conclusions

The UN documents tell a story of selective perception, tepid reactions and token gestures. It may be that one must read 'caste' into the broad references to harmful 'traditions and customs', but it is not clear whether the UN human rights bodies do take into consideration the wider ramifications of the caste phenomenon. The caste narrative does surface in descriptions, but is rarely considered in recommendations and is disregarded where standards need to be developed. Generally, the UN acknowledges the practice in countries where it is well documented but is hardly proactive with regard to other countries where evidence of caste and caste-like discrimination has been emerging.

UN human rights bodies are often hampered by the absence of disaggregated data on caste[55] (this is not provided by the UNDP Human Development Indicators)[56] and limited reporting on caste issues. This is all the more reason why thematic mechanisms must fully explore and investigate caste issues rather than merely append references to caste almost as a footnote or after though. The WCAR, by recognising work and descent-based caste discrimination as a form of racial discrimination, and including it in it Declaration and Programme of Action, would pave the way for a much-needed, systematic analysis and monitoring of a widespread and complex manifestation of racial discrimination.

Notes

1. See Report of the UN Special Rapporteur on Contemporary form of Racism A154/347/para. 19, 8 September 1999.
2. See Human Rights Watch, *Broken People: Caste Violations Against India's 'Untouchables'*, New York, Human Rights Watch, 1999; see also Susan Bayley, *Caste, Society and Politics in India: From the Eighteenth Century to the Modern Age*, Cambridge, Cambridge University Press 1999.

3. See Buraku Liberation and Human Rights Research Institute and Buraku Liberation League, Reality of Discrimination against Buraku People in Japan and the Challenge Aiming for the Elimination of Discrimination, Osaka: BLIJ BLHRRI, 2001.
4. Working Paper on Discrimination Based on Work and Descent, op. cit.
5. Asian Legal Resource Centre, 'Caste-based Discrimination in South Asia', in Human Rights Solidarity, vol.-10, no. 8, pp. 24-6 (Asian Human Rights Commission, August 2000), vol. 10, no. 8, pp24-6.
6. E/CN.4/RES/1999/78;

   E/CN.4IRES/2000/l 4;

   E/CN.4/2000/l 5
7. E/CN.4/SUB.2/RES/2000/4.
8. E/CN.4/SUB.2/2001/l 6/para.8.
9. E/CN.4/SUB.2/200 1/1 6/para.49.
10. E/CN.4/SUB.2/2000/23, para.17. (Working Group on Contemporary Forms of Slavery).
11. E/CN.4/SUB.212000/27/para 53-4. (Working Group on Minorities).
12. A150/36 (Supp. No. 36) para.31.
13. E/CN.4/2000/l 2/para.53.
14. Buraku Liberation and Human Rights Research Institute and Buraku Liberation League, op.cit.
15. International convention on the Elimination of All Forms of Racial Discrimination, adopted 21 December 1965, 660 UNTS *195.* See Michael Banton, Combating Racial Discrimination: The UN and its Member States, London, Minority Rights Group International, 2000.
16. CERD/C/304/Add.13/paras 14, 36 (India); CERD/C/304/Add.l 14/paras 4, 7 and 8 (Japan); A/55/18, paras289-306 (Nepal). See also Masanao Murakumi, Meaning of 'Descent' in the International Convention on the elimination of All Forms of Racial Discrimination and its applicability to Caste and Buraku Discrimination, Osaka, IMADR, 2001.
17. CERD/C/304/Add. 1 3/para.23 (India). For example, despite specific legislation and a complaints system, less than 1% of the legal petitions related to atrocities against 'low' castes result in conviction in Tamil Nadu, India. See M. Siraj Salt, 'Are Civil Rights for All? In *The Hindu*, 10 November 1996.
18. HRJIGEN/lfRev.4, p. 144(E), para. 2.
19. See for ex~mp1e the position taken by former CERD member Mr. Woifrum CERD/C/SR.1 165/para. 50.

20. UNGAA/541347.
21. UN GA A/55/304/para.26: see also E/CN.4/1998/79/paras 148-9.
22. E/CN.4/1999/15/paras. 88-100.
23. See Human Rights Watch, *Broken People*, op. cit.
24. CCPRIC/79/Add.8 1/para. 15 (India)
25. CCPR/C/79/Add.42/para. 7 (Nepal)
26. CCPR/C/79/Add. 102/paras. 9,15 (Japan)
27. E/CN.4/1996/Add.1/para.13. Also see Special Rapporteur on Burundi alluding to caste, E/CN.4/1 996/1 6/para. 19.
28. E/CN.4/201/9~Add.2/para. 14 (Nepal).
29. E/CN.4/2000/4; E/CN.4/200 1/14.
30. E/CN.4/1 999/62/paras 146-54 (India).
31. E/CN.4/2000/65 (Religious Intolerance). The title of the Special Rapporteur has been changed to the Special Rapporteur on freedom of religion or belief (Commission resolution 2001/42).
32. Amnesty International, Racism and the Administration of Justice, London, July 2001, p. 84.
33. See E/CN.4/2000/9;AJ55/290.
34. Arjan de Haan and Pulin Nayak, *Social Exclusion and South Asia*, Geneva, International Institute for Labour Studies, 1995, chapter 2.
35. E/C.12/A/JAP/1/ques.7 (List of Issues, Japan); E/C.12/QINEP/1 (List of Issues, Nepal).
36. E/C.12/1/Add.40 (Cameroon) but see E/C.12/Q/CAMER/lpara.1 1 (List of Issues, Cameroon).
37. See 1998 ILO Declaration on Fundamental Rights and Principles at Work C and its Follow-up initiative, which so far has not paid due attention to caste-based discrimination.
38. UN GA *54/175* (Development).
39. E/CN.4/2000/52 (Human Rights and Extreme Poverty).
40. E/CN.4/2001/51 (Adequate Housing).
41. E/CN.4/2000/6 (Education).
42. National Campaign on Dalit Human Rights, Dalit Human Rights Violations: Atrocities against Dalits in India, Case Papers, Chennai, NCDHR, 2000, pp. 196-7.
43. A155/38/paras. 52, 68-9, 74-5 (India).
44. A/S 5/18/paras 289-3 06 (Nepal)

45. E/CN.4/RES/2000/l 3
46. E/CN.4/i 999/68/para.9; E/CN. 4/2000/68/para.57 (Violence Against Women).
47. UNICEF, *State of the World's Children*, Oxford, Oxford University Press, 1997, pp. 27-8, 31.
48. CRC/C/15/Add. 11 5/para.9 (India).
49. CRC/C/15Add.57/paras 12,23 (Nepal).
50. CRC/C/SR.440/para.82, CRC/C/SR,441/para.9 (Summary of Proceedings, Micronesia).
51. CRC/C/8/Add.13/para.38 (State Report); CRC/C/15/Add.40 (Concluding Observations, Sri Lanka)
52. RC/C/15/Add.1 15/para.56 (India)
53. E/CN.4/l994/84/para. 14.
54. E/CN.4/SUB.2/2000/17/paras 65-7.
55. See for example

    CERD/C/3 04/Add. 1 3/para.4 (India);

    CRC/C/15/Add. 1 15/para. 16 (India)
56. See UNDP, *Human Development Report 2000*, Oxford, Oxford University Press, 2000

Dalit Discourse

Chapter 28

Regaining Our Lost Faith

PRAKASH LOUIS

The attempt to include caste discrimination as one of the agenda items in the World Conference Against Racism, Racial Discrimination, Xenophobia and Related Intolerances (WCAR) has unearthed many basic issues about the polity and society the subcontinent.

The WCAR, held in Durban from 28 August to 7 September 2001, witnessed the concerted efforts of Dalit and human rights activists from India to lobby and pursue the issue of 'including' the 'exclusion of the Dalits' as one of the subject-matter of human rights violation to be discussed in the conference. They received overwhelming support not only from the NGO fraternity but from delegates representing various governments as well as national and international organisations. The official delegation handpicked by the Government of India was isolated whenever it tried to denounce and decry the efforts of activists to introduce caste discrimination as a more horrendous form of racial discrimination and hence a heinous human rights violation.

The starting point of Dalit discourse are the atrocities and brutalities that are heaped upon them in everyday existence.[1] It is this individual and collective socio-historical experience of oppression and exploitation that provides the fodder for Dalit movements as also shapes the direction of Dalit discourse. It is a given fact that the Dalit movements and discourse begin with the atrocities that they are subjected to from birth in day to day operations, and the mind-set that controls and colours their behaviour. Coupled with this is their immense and inalienable innate power and prowess which equally defines the scope and space for Dalit struggles and discourse.

There are various interpretations about the nature of the WCAR, the expediency of presenting caste discrimination for discussion at the global arena. There are some who express strong indignation for 'internationalising' an 'internal reality'. But anyone who examines the pre-Durban phase, the Durban conference and post-Durban scenario would be overwhelmed by the fact that the discourse about discrimination of Dalits has moved from the internal arena to the international forum. This is not due to what happened in Durban alone, but because of the years of struggle that the Dalits waged against every form of oppression and domination. Further, those who highlighted the caste question in Durban also raised another historico-social issue before the international community – that race is only one form of discrimination. Since race is the western form of social stratification, other horrendous forms of discrimination known as 'hidden apartheid' are excluded from the purview of global discussion.

This has gone contrary to the stand of the Indian government which continues to treat caste discrimination as an 'internal matter'.[2] The ruling class, which had till now projected itself as a crusader against apartheid, found its hypocrisy challenged from within. The Dalit and human rights activists forced the Indian ruling castes and class to 'set their own house in order'. This reduced the space for the Indian rulers to cry hoarse about apartheid out there. This is a major achievement for the Dalit and human rights activists and all those who perceive the validity and legitimacy of this struggle. Above all, it is a victory for the Dalits and downtrodden who have entered into a protracted struggle for maintaining human rights at all cost. It is here that the national and inter national solidarity to root out all forms of discriminations has come into central focus.

It is in the fitness of things to state that due to the clarity of the issue and unity of purpose the proponents of this cause managed to highlight in the international forum the historical discriminatory principles and behaviour towards Dalits. The NGO forum, which preceded the WCAR, in an unprecedented manner, took note of caste discrimination and the deprivation of Dalits. The practice of untouchability, rooted in the caste system, stigmatises 260 million Dalits in South Asia as "polluted" or "impure", thereby denying them entry into places of religious worship, participation in religious festivals, assigning them menial and degrading work including cleaning toilets, skinning and disposal of dead animals, digging graves and sweeping, and the forced prostitution of Dalit women and girls through the traditional system of temple prostitution.[3]

Along with the declaration, the NGO forum's programme of action demanded that various governments 'enact suitable legislation to recognise and eradicate discrimination based on work and descent, including caste discrimination and untouchability against Dalits, Buraku people and other affected communities in those countries where such legislation does not exist; and in countries where legislation banning such discrimination already exists, take immediate steps to create transparent and effective monitoring mechanisms including the establishment of time-bound programmes to ensure effective implementation of such legislation, even where the perpetrators are states or state agents.[4]

The programme of action identifies caste discrimination as a crime against humanity and calls for time bound action for the removal of atrocities. It demands redistribution of land, and legal provisions to protect the rights of Dalits and other discriminated communities. It advocates that sufficient financial provisions be made for the upliftment of the Dalits in a time bound manner. Alongside, the NGO forum called for international enforcements like the appointment of a special rapporteur to examine the complaints about various forms of discrimination and human rights violation. The Indian government, incidentally, has refused permission to the special rapporteur from 1996.

The National Human Rights Commission's (NHRC) uncompromising stand to include the Dalit issue on the agenda of the WCAR gave unprecedented support to the struggle. Justice K. Ramaswamy in his address stated, 'The National Human Rights Commission of India has considered it its duty to listen attentively to those, that is, the Dalits and the adivasis, in our country who have been victims of historical injustices.' The commission also proposed concrete measures for its eradication. 'The commission believes deeply in the value of engaging governments, non-governmental organisations, national institutions, and all concerned elements of civil society in the process of fighting discriminations, and urges that these processes be conducted at all levels in a spirit that is genuinely interested in the furtherance of human rights and not vitiated by self-righteousness or by political and other extraneous considerations.[5]

Significantly, this is contrary to the government's stand, which continued to consider caste discrimination as internal issue or engaged in the debate 'caste is not race'. Thus, the Indian establishment obfuscates the issue of caste discrimination. The bold stand of the NHRC was lauded by Mary Robinson, Commissioner for the United Nations Human Rights Commission. Robinson declared, 'I congratulate the principled stand taken by the NHRC which stood up to help the Dalits and extended moral support.' She also took note of the manner in which Dalit and human rights activists highlighted the plight of the Dalits and other discriminated masses. 'The NGOs have raised what they called discrimination against the Dalits in India, and the issue has been brought before the international community.[6]

The Indian government stood exposed on another ground too. Minster of State for External Affairs, Omar Abdullah, in his address to the WCAR, criticised those who spearheaded the Dalit cause. 'In the run up to the World Conference, there has been propaganda, highly exaggerated and misleading, often based on anecdotal evidence, regarding caste-based discrimination in India. We in India have faced this evil squarely.[7] Abdullah instead of being applauded for his statement was decried by many delegates.

The WCAR held in Durban has once again brought the issues and struggles of the Dalits to centre-stage. It is not that Dalit discourse is a new phenomenon. Those who raised this issue at the international forum were under no illusion that the Durban conference would put an end to all the ills of the Dalits. In fact, the Dalit discourse is as old as the caste system and caste discrimination. But it is at this global conference that caste discrimination was made visible, though the intergovernmental conference that preceded the NGO forum did not include caste as a form of discrimination that cries for global retribution.

It would be appropriate to examine some of the dominant Dalit discourses. Some economists claim that Dalits were never landholders but historically landless agricultural labourers. These social scientists assert that the Dalits who were given land under land reform measures sold the land and' squandered the money'.[8] This is because they do not have a sense of private property and saving for tomorrow as they are a happy-go-lucky people. Dalit intellectuals have attempted to explore and explode myths of this type. From the Dalit perspective, since most other avenues are closed to them, the agricultural sector provides the only economically gainful occupation. This is not in terms of adding assets, but to just ensure survival.

Land reform laws have been in force for the last 50 years. If one looks at the election manifestos of the political parties[9] and Independence Day proclamations, one is overwhelmed by the pronouncements. But the track record over 50 years reveals an abominable picture: out of 78 lakh acres that were declared surplus only 66 lakh acres, that is 83.68% of the land, was taken into possession by the government. Further, out of the 78 lakh acres of land declared surplus only 52 lakh acres, that is 65.85% was distributed. The total amount of land distributed among the Dalits was only 28 lakhs, that is 35.60%.[10] This empirical data disproves the tall claims of the ruling establishment, the dominant castes and social scientists that the Dalits.

Another area where Dalit discourse has made a contribution is by unraveling the phenomenon of litigation, the root cause for non distribution of land. Over 48% of land was not distributed because of litigation.[11] Nevertheless, the rulers have already announced the need to introduce changes in land legislation policies. The National Agricultural Policy states that 'the legislative and regulatory framework will be appropriately amended and strengthened to achieve these objectives.[12]

This anti-people and anti-Dalit policy has been criticised by Dalit intellectuals. Anand Teltumbde argues that 'the impetus to export agriculture in the reforms is bringing in corporate and contract system in agriculture. The government has already declared that the Land Ceiling Act, identified as the main obstacle in the process, would be suitably changed. Directionally, the emergent corporate farms will gobble up small holdings of the marginal to middle farmers and push them into the herd of job-seeking millions... This emergent scenario will cel1ainly aggravate the unemployment problem further rather than solving it.[13]

There are indications that untouchability did not take this tyrannical form as long as it was practiced only by the upper castes. But when the lower castes began to practice untouchability towards each other, it adopted this rigid, inhuman form.[14]

We need to investigate the social conditions and social forces that contributed to the harsh enforcement of untouchability, both among the Dalits and between the Dalits and non-Dalits. This investigation would also unravel the root cause behind polarisation among the Dalits.

Thousands of Dalits embrace Buddhism.[15] 'Defying the ban, thousands of Dalits attend a conversion rally in Delhi on 4 November.' The numbers game apart, such announcements are indicative of the social processes at work within the Dalit community. Conversion in general poses two fundamental threats to the existing religious realities. On the one hand, it demonstrates to the majority religious community that its boundaries are penetrable and vulnerable to external forces. On the other, it registers the social fact that what were earlier held as unshakable and unalterable beliefs and practices stand shattered. For Dalit intellectuals, conversion is not just moving from one religion to another, but provides a paradigm for social change.

One of the overarching strengths of the Dalit community is that Dalit women customarily enjoyed considerable freedom, both spatially and temporally. One is not arguing that Dalit women were equal to Dalit men. But as one moves down the social order, one can recognise the comparatively free existence and operation of Dalit women, for instance, in the absence of dowry exchange and the consequent dowry deaths. But as Dalits get educated, urbanised and economically mobile, they fall into the trap of non-Dalit practices. Interestingly, there are some emerging voices demanding that the dominant castes should learn from the Dalits about the principles and practices of providing freedom to their women.[16]

The Dalit discourse should seriously and comprehensively take note of the polarisation around leadership in Dalit movements. The question being raised is: Should Dalit movements be led exclusively by Dalits? Dalit intellectuals also need to examine the root cause of emergence (and extinction) of Dalit movements. The emergence of the Dalit Panthers in the early 1970s was an unprecedented assertion. This appeared to be a spark, which would set the forest aflame.

According to Anand Teltumbde, there could be varied explanations for the paradigm shift in Dalit politics marked by the Dalit Panthers. Remarkably, they spoke the language of defiance and militancy which shook the foundations of the established order in the country and demonstrated what the wrath of the wretched could be. Going by their manifesto, the Panthers radicalised the political space for the movement by imparting a proletarian radical class identity to Dalits, linking their struggles to those of oppressed people all over the globe.[17] Though a radical move, it soon died out because of a failure to provide adequate substance Dalit and human rights activists will have to address these burning issues. Their discourse needs to begin from the lives and struggles of the Dalit masses. But its legitimacy can be sustained only in the context of its contribution to the liberation and emancipation of the excluded, exploited and subjugated masses. The Dalits will have to comprehend the various methods used by the dominant castes to throttle any attempt to stage protests against the existing social order through time-tested weapons like repression, co-option and distortion

Above all, the Dalit discourse has to engage in a protracted battle for the mobilisation and organisation of Dalits and the downtrodden to strengthen the struggle for basic issues such as rights over natural resources, proper wages, social dignity and self actualisation. Thus, Dalit movements are not directed towards elimination of caste discrimination alone but work ultimately for the restructuring of the social order. In this sense, Dalit emancipator struggles are not just 'freedom from'[18] subjugation but also 'freedom to' liberation. This attempt has to be at all levels – local, regional, state, national and international. If those who raised the issue of caste discrimination at the

WCAR are satisfied that the issue has been made visible at the international level, they would be betraying the Dalit cause.

Alongside the mobilisation and organisation of Dalits, activists have to engage in forging a broader alliance with other exploited masses-tribals, women, backward castes and minorities. Any exercise outside this framework would defeat the very purpose of engaging in a struggle against forces of oppression and exploitation. There is no denying that there are some differences among these communities, but there is a common unifying factor among them: they are the exploited masses of this subcontinent

For instance, the Dalits in Jharkhand are more vulnerable than the tribals of the area. The tribals are protested by the Chotanagpur Tenancy Act and the Santhal Pargana Tenancy Act. They are also protected under the Fifth Schedule, which upholds their constitutional rights. But the Dalits in Jharkhand are not protected by any of these provisions. Similarly, the tribals in Bihar are more defenseless than the Dalits of Bihar. The Dalits can claim their legitimate rights due to the reservation policy. But the tribals, who are in a minority in five out of 34 districts of Bihar, are in no position to demand proper implementation of the reservation policy. Women from all these communities are the worst exploited segment of the population.

Moreover, it is only a broad alliance that can protect the exploited masses from the onslaught of the ruling dispensation. Since the forces of castes and upper classes are powerful and resourceful, any independent struggle would only weaken the exploited masses. The experiment in Kerala where the Dalits and fisher folk showed solidarity with the tribals and thereby achieved their objectives, demonstrates the scope for a united struggle.

The Durban conference on racial discrimination did mark a watershed, showing that despite internal differences and polarisation, a broad-based united, struggle alone can help the liberation and emancipation of the Dalits. It is crucial to note that this liberation struggle is not directed to Dalits alone but for restructuring an unequal and hierarchical social order.

'We have begun a new life
we have found our new temples
Regained our lost faith
All are equal here"

Harish Bansode, a Dalit poet[19]

Notes

1. Prakash Louis, 'Casteism is More Horrendous than Racism: Durban and Dalit Discourse.' Mimeo, Indian Social Institute, New Delhi, 2001. Also Shiv Visvanathan, Durban and Dalit Discourse', *Economic and Political Weekly*, 18 August 2001, pp. 3123-3127.
2. Shiv Visvanathan, 'The Race for Caste: Prolegomena to the Durban Conference' *Economic and Political Weekly*, 7 July 2001 pp. 2512-2516.
3. The Declaration and the Programme of Action of the WCAR NGO Forum, Durban 3 September 2001.
4. Ibid.
5. Abstract of the Statement of the National Human Rights Commission of India.
6. NHRC support for Dalits praised. *The Hindu*, 6 September 2001.
7. Statement by Omar Abdullah, Minister of State for External Affairs, India, at the WCAR, Durban, 2 Sep 01.
8. Prakash Louis, 'People's Perception of Land Reform Policies and Practices: A Comparative Study of Eastern, Western and Central Regions of Uttar Pradesh, Ministry of Rural Development, Government of India 2001.
9. Election Manifesto of Indian National Congress (I) Party, 1999, p.18.
10. B.B. Mohanty, 'Land Distribution among the Scheduled Castes and Tribes', Economic and Political Weekly, 6 October 2001, p. 3863.
11. Ibid., p.3864.
12. The National Agricultural Policy, Department of Agriculture and Cooperation, Ministry of Agriculture, Government of India, July 2000, p.13.
13. Anand Teltumbde, Impact of New Economic Reforms on Dalits in India. Paper presented at a seminar on Electoral Reforms and Dalits in India organised by the University of Oxford, November 1996.

14. Kancha Ilaiah, *God as Political Philosopher: Buddha's Challenge to Brahminism.* Samya, Calcutta, 2000, p. 32.
15. *The Hindustan Times,* 5 November 2001.
16. Manisha, 'Avarna se kuch seekhen savarna'. *Rashtriya Sahara* (Hindi), 8 December 2000.
17. Anand Teltumbde, *Ambedkar and Post-Ambedkar Dalit Movements.* Sugawa Prakashan, Pune. 1997.
18. Jan Nederveen Pieterse, *Emancipations, Modern and Post-Modern.* Sage Publications, London, 1992, p. 13.
19. Steven M. Parish, *Hierarchy and its Discontents: Culture and The Politics of Consciousness in Caste Society,* University of Pennsylvania Press. Philadelphia, 1996, p. 82.

Chapter 29

Caste and the UN Meet

KANCHA ILAIAH

Now that the World Conference on Racism is allowing caste discrimination on the agenda as "work and descent based discrimination", the semanticists must stop hair-splitting debates on caste and race and allow the UN to focus on eradicating all forms of discrimination. The National Human Rights Commission must help in strengthening the agenda and see that caste discrimination is abolished in India in spheres, social, economic and spiritual.

It is laudable that the NHRC decided to take an independent stand. Its chairman, J.S. Verma, refused to join the national committee constituted by the Prime Minister, headed by Ranganath Mishra, to assist the Government in formulating its position on the question of inclusion of caste in the agenda of the Durban conference. The NHRC can and should formulate its own position on whether caste, as an institution that constructed descent-based intolerance and xenophobic discrimination, was a problem of human rights or not. Once the NHRC formulates its position and suggests instruments to eradicate this pernicious practice, steps by the Government of India have to follow.

To ascertain informed opinion about the caste-race relationship, the NHRC conducted a national seminar on August 3 at the National

Law School, Bangalore. A public hearing on the intensity of caste discrimination was organised by it at Bangalore University. It also conducted a national seminar in New Delhi on August 11. Studies showing the historical relationship between caste and race and those holding that the caste system had no relationship with race were presented. However, it is important to look at the mindset of the Brahmanic castes in clinching this issue.

Many reform movements including that of Swamy Dayananda Saraswati used the hegemonic racist notion of Aryan (the brown race of India) to construct an upper caste nationalist ideology. The social forces that joined these organisations even in South India came from hegemonic castes. The movements that sprung up from the South owning the Dravida (black) racial identity were joined and owned by social forces from Sudra and Dalit castes. The South Indian Brahmins and Vaisyas who share dark skin with other lower castes named their organisations Arya Brahmin Samajam and Arya Vaisya Sangham. We can see a very strong racist psyche in constructing symbols of sacredness and nationalism based on colour and caste.

Take, for example, the notion of the sacredness of the cow. The cow became a sacred animal with the Brahmanic Aryanism that got constructed as hegemonic in civil society. Even now, the average Brahmanic psyche treats the cow as sacred, but not the buffalo. The cow was the prime sacrificial animal when the priests were beef-eaters; it remains a sacred animal even after the priestly class gave up beef-eating.

In both the Gandhian and the RSS mode of nationalist thought, though both of them are vastly different, the cow not only remains sacred but is constructed as a constitutional animal as well. It is a known fact that in economic terms the buffalo contributes more to the Indian milk economy than the cow. Why then does the buffalo remain a non-sacred and most invisible animal? Why did it not get constitutional protection as the cow did in the Directive Principles of State Policy? Simply because the cow belongs to the white race in the animal kingdom and the buffalo belongs to the black race. This is an Indian variety of racism. All white races constructed their colour as superior, the Indian Aryans also made the colour sacred. The colour black in general and dark people, buffaloes and other animals, irrespective of their utility or beauty were/are condemned both in social and spiritual realms.

This psyche was not only ancient and historic but is continuously operating in our day-to-day life rendering black humans and animals unworthy of occupying national and international space. The Western mode of racism did not sink into the spiritual realm. It is this Indian racist spiritual and social psyche that is at the core of the caste system. Indian civil society, the state and the institutions such as the NHRC that operate as negotiating agencies between the state and civil society must address this racist and casteist psyche.

The Indian Government took an undemocratic stand and the national committee has failed in telling the nation, even after so many days of its Hyderabad hearing, what its opinion is. The NHRC being an independent body did well as Verma himself said that it did not mortgage its mind to any preconceived notion or thought on this issue. By formulating both short term and long term policies on the question of caste, as a historical institution of oppression, it can help the nation and keep the morale of Scheduled Castes, Scheduled Tribes and Other Backward Castes up.

Human rights organisations in this country have not so far realised that civil societal oppression and systemic subjugation of SCs, STs, OBCs and women have more dangerous implications for social change and development than state oppression. With the help of UN bodies, the Government of India must evolve more instruments to tackle this historical problem.

If the NHRC takes a position on the question of caste and defines its very existence and day-to-day operation as a problem of human rights, it then becomes the bounden duty of the state to work out much stronger instruments to abolish this institution in all its forms. In fact, the NHRC should have formulated its position and educated the Government of India much before the world forums took it up.

It is an absurd argument that governments, even though elected democratically, become responsive without pressure from both national and international agencies. The oppressive institutions that came into operation through the process of civil societal structuring need the pressure of outside agencies such as the UN, because it is more difficult to address the civil societal agencies than the governmental agencies from within. The UN Human Rights charter has been worked out to serve that purpose also. It hence thought of addressing the civil societal oppressions that emanate from race, religion, language, gender and so on. Unfortunately, caste as an institution of social oppression was not included in the charter at that time.

A body like the NHRC should have realised this and recommended to the Government of India a long time back that caste discrimination has many traits of racial discrimination and, hence, must become part of the UN Human Rights charter. Then the World Conference on Racism would have automatically included caste in its agenda. In this respect, the National SC, ST Commission and the Backward Class Commission have failed in putting caste discrimination on the UN agenda. The SC, ST and OBC MPs and political leaders have not shown any maturity in understanding the role of UN bodies in resolving certain historical problems and have remained blissfully indifferent to this process. They could have easily forced the Government of India to avoid all somersaults in the meetings of the Preparatory Committees of the World Conference.

Caste will be discussed in the inter-Governmental Conference at Durban under para 109 of the agenda which reads: "to ensure all necessary constitutional, legislative and administrative measures, including appropriate form of affirmative action, are in place to prohibit and address discrimination on the basis of work and descent and such that measures are respected and implemented by all states, authorities at all levels". The government and other state bodies such as the NHRC must tell the nation that they will abide by the mandate of the UN Conference.

Chapter 30

Politics of Representation

GOPAL GURU

The UN conference on Race, Xenophobia and other Related Forms of Discrimination was recently held at Durban in South Africa. A central issue that assumed 'flaming' importance both before and during the conference was whether caste should be included in the formal agenda of the conference. The NGOs, led primarily by Dalits, tried hard to force the government to accept their demand, which the latter opposed by all the means at its disposal. While one appreciated the efforts of the Dalit camp and their friends in achieving a certain amount of visibility to the issue of caste discrimination, both at national and international level, conspicuously missing from the debate was the question: who is entitled to talk about the caste issue and represent it in Durban?

It was suggested by some that since India is a democratic state which believes in equality, I should represent the Dalits at the Durban conference. The government itself suggested that it was only Hindu Dalits who had the right to speak on behalf of the Dalits. Still others argued that all those who believed in equality could speak about the caste question at Durban. But most Dalits felt that they alone had the natural right to speak on behalf of the Dalits any where in the world. Unfortunately, this question of representation got relegated to the background; it was overshadowed by the central issue of whether caste could be included in the agenda of the conference. Since the question of representation is both complicated and of enduring importance for our understanding, it will be worth while to discuss it in some detail.

Let us begin by raising certain questions about the representation claims, particularly in the context of the Durban conference. Does a formal, if not firm, commitment to the ideal of equality establish an automatic right to talk of the issue at different forums, including Durban? Does this privileging of certain ideals as an adequate condition make the representation claim valid? Does talking of issues concerning caste and the Dalits become automatically valid just because of an ability to write in the English print media? Or is the case for speaking on Dalits and caste at Durban enhanced because one has the right body language and TV-friendly face? And finally, does one's ascribed Dalithood make the claim for representation automatically valid and authentic?

Let us begin by discussing whether commitment to equality by itself makes the representation claims acceptable. There should be little disagreement about accepting the representation claims of those who not only peach but practice equality. This accords a secular and universal status to one's representation claims. But if the commitment is only to formal equality, then the representation claims certainly become less defensible.

For example, as the experience of the last 50 years demonstrates, the Indian state by and large has shown only a formal and rhetorical commitment to equality as far as Dalit are concerned. Hence, even had it chosen to speak for the Dalits at the conference, it would have had a weak moral case to defend its assertions. On the contrary, it showed extraordinary brazenness in asserting that there was no caste discrimination, (juridically if not in practice) in India, thus sliding further down on the morality scale. Moreover, it chose to handle the issue with Machiavellian tricks thereby deploying the discursive element.

For example, it sought to push the issue of caste discrimination perpetuated by civil society of the twice born (CSTB) into the domain of patriarchal morality, arguing that since caste was a family (Hindu) matter, it would be sorted out within the family. Instead of launching a critique of CSTB, the Indian state sought to make concessions (justify?) to a society which is, in fact, responsible for committing caste atrocities against the Dalits.

The question that needs to be asked is: Why was this moral deficiency further reinforced by the use of Machiavellian tricks? There could be two possible explanations of this moral downsizing of the state. The Indian government did not want to publicly blame or shame the Hindu community whose belligerent members are primarily responsible for the perpetuation of the hydra-headed monster of caste atrocities against the Dalits. Second, it perhaps was worried about loosing some material benefits from the international agencies who may haul the Indian state over the coals for its malignant social face. If civil society in India is a part of the problem, then this resource is not available to Dalits for speaking on their behalf. How could one have expected civil society to represent the case of the Dalits at Durban, particularly when it does not have a stake in the equality question?

It is shocking to note that many of its members, particularly the upper middle class, seem unaware about the existential dimensions of caste. As a social reality, caste just does not exist for this section. Their sociological blindness is evident in their reactions to caste related issues in the print or electronic media: it sends them into cultural shock. The lower rung of this growing class, though aware, remains largely callous about the caste question, thanks to globalisation. This is partly because avenues generated by globalisation have created new aspirations of mobility among this class and diverted their attention from the search for reservations to international migration.

As for the rest of rural society in India, since caste discrimination is treated as a natural phenomena why should they bother about Durban? However, it must be admitted that there are some fragile voices from this society trying to articulate the Dalit question through the media, both print and electronic. But is this representation of caste and Dalit at Durban valid and authentic?

If we focus on the social background criterion of representation, it was difficult to come across any Dalits representing their own case in the mainstream press electronic media. It was clear from reading the press that it was the non-Dalits who spoke on the issue of caste. In fact, since the media took the initiative to approach 'experts' it is clearly not their fault either. But why did the media, by and large, contribute to the exclusion of Dalits on Durban?

In fact, it is a combination of both political economy and modernity, and to some extent the biased reading of body language, which contributed to keeping Dalits out from the media-driven debate on Durban. Appropriate accent and pronunciation, speed of speech delivery that is required for maintaining efficiency in communication – these supposedly constitute the lifeline of the electronic media. Thus, permitting a philosophical or poetic pause on TV is not economically acceptable. The media does not make any concession to such pauses, of course with certain exceptions.

It is assumed that since the Dalits do not have the three SSS – skill, sound and speed – they are misfits on TV, which privileges speed over philosophical pause, sound over sensibility and skill over serious scholarship. Second, the subordination of serious scholarship to efficiency of presentation also mitigates against a deeper understanding of the issue. Since the three S's demand certain selective rhetoric and terminology, they tend to screen out the serious and deeper content of the discourse.

If we examine the debate on whether caste should be included in Durban, it is clear that the media experts used audience friendly rhetoric and academic jargon without, however, touching the threshold of the problem. The debate no doubt achieved sophistication, but lacked depth. For example, the question of nationalism, state and civil society and caste in the context of Durban were hardly ever discussed on TV.

A key reason why Dalits were excluded from the discourse is that they lack the necessary body language and a camera-friendly face. To state it bluntly, you must have fair skin, a sharp nose and expressive eyes that are a must for any TV appearance. Dalits become the object of TV camera not so much for any intrinsic aesthetic value that they may possess, but for their idiosyncrasy or incoherent use of language, or bizarre physical movements, which only serve the purpose of presenting them as a caricature. In the final analysis, the stereotype that is constructed around the caricatured body language of the Dalits keeps them out, thus leaving an uncontested space for the darlings of TV to hegemonise the discourse.

The exclusion of the Dalits was equally marked in the print media, particularly the English press. This exclusion, whether intentional or otherwise, definitely suggests that the Dalits lack the necessary language competence, if not the content. This, however, deprived audiences of an alternative reading of the issues being discussed. The discourse on caste and Durban remained academic and had little relation to the mobilisation of Dalits who were directly making a political point to embarrass the Indian government. Thus, there was a serious mismatch between the discourse in the print media and Dalit mobilisation, without giving us an authentic sense of the people's perceptions.

Scholars wrote on the issue without bothering to take any feedback from those who are victims. Since they have language competence they have the privilege of being invited by the media, which is bothered more about form than content. These 'privileged darlings' of the press are able to write on anything and everything. Their interventions, however, raised more dust at the polemical level than elevating our understanding through the sociological expansion of the debate.

The polemic in English journalism on issues raised at Durban was only vertically sensitive; it remained sociologically blind towards the horizontal level of the vernacular public. For example this debate was confined to the English press and English electronic media. There was a total silence in the vernacular press, barring few exceptions. Was this debate, therefore, informed by the perception of the common people? The answer unfortunately, is no. Thus, the above scenario indicates the comprehensive exclusion of Dalits from the intellectual domain that was built up around the issue of Durban.

Does this exclusion, therefore, make the claim or representation, as advance by certain Dalit NGOs, automatically valid? The answer to this question cannot be given in black and white terms, because framing the question in such dichotomous ways traps us into a patronising essentialisation of Dalits. In order to overcome these dangers let us approach the issue in the following manner.

The Dalit claims for being legitimate representatives of their issues, including at Durban, can be justified on the grounds that it is they who took the initiative to bring caste into the forefront of the public domain, howsoever elitist and limited the frame work of this domain may be. Thus, at an epistemic level, privileging the Dalit voice on the Dalit question can be justified. Second, the representation of Dalits by non-Dalits becomes problematic since it accords to the claimant a kind of morally superior position without realising that it sustains itself on the basis of a permanent exclusion of Dalits from the intellectual domain. It reproduces new forms of intellectual hierarchy, thus making difficult the democratisation of intellectual representation. It marks the continuation of the alien. It is primarily in this sense that a Dalit speaking for the Dalit can be justified; it helps the historical recovery of Dalit voices.

However, such culturally specific claims of representation, though initially desirable, remain problematic for two reasons. First, they do not create a sufficient condition for a transformative Dalit politics as they tend to foreclose the possibility of Dalits acquiring the intellectual leadership to speak in the universal language of emancipation. In order to claim a moral status to their representation claim, Dalits have to acquire the moral capacity to question themselves vis-à-vis both their intellectual and political moves. In other words, they are supposed to substantiate their claim not only on the basis of external reasoning, but an internal ethic informed by public accountability, a historicisation of Dalit reality and tolerance towards internal intellectual dissent.

The Durban initiative was hegemonised more by the opinion makers among Dalits based in the metropolis rather than the people's initiative. Had they only gone to the people for political education, they would have got a response since ordinary Dalits are invariably generous in extending support to their leader on public issues, even those which may be of a scholarly nature.

The Dalits may not object to an elite representation of their general aspirations for three reasons. First, they feel empowered if someone from their community speaks or writes in a scholarly language that confronts the language of the adversary, in our case the twice born. In this regard, it is important to remember the pride with which the Dalits quote the 17 volumes that Ambedkar wrote both in English and Marathi in order to silence upper caste adversaries. Often they also feel that they are incapable of producing the more complex arguments that their community intellectuals might provide in order to answer the adversaries.

Such an approach to difficult and complicated issues, however, lacks good common sense (a la Gramsci), since the cognitive map of the people is marked more by thick emotions than reason and leads to a critical distancing of the masses from their 'smart' leaders. No wonder, the common Dalits make huge concessions to these leaders to speak on their behalf. The moral question still remains: Should Dalit leaders claim public support for their intellectual moves? Is there not a greater need to go to the people again and again, not only with promises but also problems? But, unfortunately Dalit leaders only make promises, thus making the discourse absolutely easy and free flowing.

Second, valid Dalit representation claims should be informed by a historicised projection of social reality, meaning that the claimant should not shy away from depicting the reality in its fullness without avoiding the uneasy or inconvenient dimensions of social reality. Did Dalit representatives show this moral courage of confronting their reality in its totality? For example, some of the Dalits did show sensitivity in criticising caste discrimination within the Christian and Muslim establishments. But it was dealt with only at the theoretical and academic level, that too only in the NGO sector and thereby missed out the opportunity to expand the social base of the critical understanding of the Dalits masses. The reality once again failed to travel into the public domain in its fullness.

Such a partial representation of the issue may have been necessitated for pragmatic reasons. Nevertheless it continuously worked to deny moral consistency to transformative politics. This pragmatic politics does sometimes acquire a sharp edge, as it should, against the external adversary but fails to show the same tenacious criticism against the internal one. Any claims to representation, including by Dalits, can be valid only when they have the moral capacity to confront reality, howsoever ugly it may be. They become authentic only when their claimants resolve the uneasy tension between the pragmatic and the moral component of politics.

If the representation claims are driven primarily by the force of pragmatic considerations and the sense of easy and quick political victory, then they have the tendency to render the claimant less tolerant of internal criticism. In fact, they can drive them to eliminate the internal adversaries, not so much by force of argument but by deploying extra-intellectual factors. The representation claims established through these methods necessarily become self-limiting, in as much as they keep the concerned interrogators from the non-Dalit groups out of the discourse. In a way such claims are ultimately converted into self-evident truths to be believed without question. Such claims also lack a unity of purpose in as much as they are exclusionary in character. The paradox is that such representation claims reproduce the very same processes of exclusion against which they had emerged in the first instance.

It is not the that language of moral uprightness is deployed only in order to hold onto the representation claim; the Dalits are also fond of using language which is full of rhetoric and little substance. For example, during the Durban mobilisation one came across statistics and narratives of Dalit atrocities that were being dished out by Dalit ideologues and repeated by activists from below. This, while certainly useful for mobilisation, creates an empistemic closure within those who employ such rhetoric.

Similarly, during the Ambedkar centenary year (1991), one came across a plethora of writings on Ambedkar. But most of it was marked by mere rhetoric, thus doing double disservice to the intellectual universe of the Dalits. In the first sense they focused on Ambedkar's philosophy, but without establishing its relevance in the changing times. Thus, they operated in a fixed notion of time and space. Second, they failed to provide a fresh reading of Ambedkar to those Dalits who, though small in number, sought a new interpretation of his writings. Unfortunately, such writings cannot be representative as they travel in different, and often self-serving, directions without links to the intellectual and political need of Dalits.

The spheres of representation are also spheres of intense political contestation. They are advanced sincerely and seriously contest the representative claims that are made by adversaries with the hegemonic intention of assimilation. But they are also advanced to assign exclusionary boundaries around the Dalit constituency. Ambedkar tried, both at the intellectual and political levels, to enlarge the horizons of such claims without fear and favour. This quality is absent in the current instance.

Chapter 31

The Race for Caste

Prolegomena to the Durban Conference

SHIV VISVANATHAN

One of the most gripping detective stories I have read in recent times is Friedrich Durrenmatt's *The Judge and His Hangman* [Durrenmatt 1954]. It is a classic tale of an encounter between a dedicated policeman and a criminal who is convinced he cannot be caught. So confident is the latter of his prowess that he murders a man in front of the policemen and defies him to convict him. The criminal gets away and the duel goes on. One day the policeman realises he has stomach cancer and therefore little time to pin his opponent down. Gloatingly the criminal says "you will never convict me for a crime I have committed". For once the policeman has the better lines and he replies, "I will convict you for a crime you have not". And he does. Content he orders a huge dinner when he realises justice has been done. A crime has been punished. At last. Justice is justice. It matters little whether the gangster AI Capone was caught for kidnapping, murder or income tax evasion. He was caught and it is the consequences that are important.

There is an eerie touch of Durrenmatt to the recent battles between Dalit activists and GoI relating to a definition of caste as race. Suddenly before the Durban conference Dalits, or a vocal section of them, are claiming caste should be treated like race or more succinctly 'caste is race in India'. It is dramatic manoeuvre which has caught the government flatfooted. There is an element of play in it which we can realise if we abandon our stuffy brahminism. After all conference on apartheid and racialism always gave the Government of India 'a feel good feeling.' It brought back memories of Gandhi in South Africa, of India's support for Mandela, the PLO and other independence struggles, of the Gandhian roots of Steve Biko and Martin Luther King. Freedom was part of our genealogy and we were official advocates condemning racism, colonialism, apartheid in every international conference. Suddenly our great role is being threatened and threatened from within. India is being condemned in the name of universal freedom as a violator and all along for what we glibly thought was 'an internal affair' – caste.

Suddenly Dalit activists want to see caste as a fragment of race – not conceptually, not analytically, not even empirically but legally. Dalits exclaim we know caste and race are different yet treating one like the other might make the difference. It is a breath taking move that we must understand. It needs a full hermeneutics. Lining up professors of sociology or exemplars of law won't quite do. If some sociologist says, 'that's bad sociology'. Macwan et al, aren't bothered. Their answer is, it is a bad society and your sociology does little to improve it. One needs a more playful entry into this.

We need to ask – what is the argument? What is the method and manner of the argument? And will this 'tricksters' move succeed as politics? This time it is not Louis Dumont or M.N. Srinivas we begin with. There are no reports by Mandal or Rane, no meeting of important committees but only mimeographed handouts or printouts downloaded from NGO websites. There is no university forum. This function is in fact performed by newspaper *The Hindu* (how apt) with its visiting faculty of Gopal Guru, Gail Omvedt, Swami Agnivesh and so on.

II

The background documents appear crucial in this context. The first is Advocacy Update's issue on Dalit human rights [Prakasam, Bhopatkar and Samuel 2001] and the second is Martin Macwan's piece (mimeo)

'Caste May Not be Race', a title wicked enough to turn sociology department inside out. 'Koi jawab hai?'

Advocacy Update's 15th issue demands a careful reading. It emphasises three points in its opening paragraphs. There is first a compressed history of the movements against caste. The social – reform movements, the Gandhian movements, the Marxists have all fought and failed. The importance of movements is not denied. It is supplemented with NGO as agency and interpreter.

The NGO moves all levels "grass roots, state, national and international" reflecting on the efficacy of movements and strategies. This self-reflexiveness reveals that the state is not only the agency of reform, but also a violator of Dalit dignity. So the question is how does one fight the state? Strategically the answer is two fold. Change the discourse. The domain is not one of reform but of rights. The locus is not only local or national but international. The human rights movement despite attacks on it claims to universality is international in scope and effectiveness. Therefore the Dalit movement must become an international human rights movement. The agency changes, the discourse changes, the levels alter and with it comes the possibility of a more effective politics of empowerment. Or, is this wishful thinking? Advocacy Update sees its work as a value addition to this campaign of empowerment. The tactic is simple. It is to argue "that caste and caste-based discriminations have a similar impact to that of race and racial discrimination. Therefore, caste and caste-based discrimination should come within the purview of the International Convention for Elimination of Race, Racial Discrimination, Xenophobia and Related Intolerance." (p.2). There seems to be a political shuffling of cards here. Is it the logic of analogy being pushed to the logic of identity? Is it a self-fulfilling prophecy or plain wishful thinking? Is it bad sociology and bad politics or something else? Gnana Prakasam et al, proceed with their argument by providing a historical perspective.

They argue that the history of Dalits is a geneology of pain captured in the very etymology of the word. The word Dalit was coined by Jotirao Phule. "The word 'Dalit' means broken people." (p.3) It is a Marathi word derived from Sanskrit. Its synonyms capture its poetics. 'Dal' means to break, to crack, open, split, scatter, crush, and destroy. The thesaurus is overwhelming.

The journey of the word is interesting. Originally used by Phule to describe outcastes and untouchables, it found a resonance in Ambedkar. For a while, it got restricted to the mahar community of Maharashtra. In the 1970s, the Dalit panthers used it as a generic terms for poor peasants, tribals, landless. Present in it was a sense that Dalit referred to all marginal and exploited people. The government sought its domestication by equating it to Scheduled Castes. Now as a rights' terms, 'Dalit' must begin another journey beyond India and beyond the classificatory confines of bureaucratic legalism.

In the Dalit history of pain, words are important, names are crucial and most classifications life denying. Dalit oppression was a naming exercise, Consider the roll call of names – avarnas, chandalas, achhuts, pariahs, untouchables, unapproachable, outcaste, exterior castes, ex-untouchables. It was humiliation through naming. As Prakasam et al, state "Their identity was defined by the upper castes and the Dalits internalised this identity" (p.3). Step one is clear. If the name of the game is naming and classification, Dalit tacticians can also change the rules of the game and have to.

The next few paragraphs of Advocacy Update are straight sociology out of a Pune or JNU department. As one academic primly note, it seems adequate for *Sociological Bulletin* or *EPW* but it is not quite Contributions to Indian Sociology. The ghosts of Dumont or Srinivas do not quite haunt these pages. Sanskritisation does not eke out a footnote. But the structural principles of the caste system – hierarchy, separation and interdependence are clearly recognised. Step two is a historical sociology that recognises the correlation between hereditary occupations, pollution and powerlessness.

Step three seeks a structural resonance between race and caste. The goal is not identity but affinity, a search for similarity between caste and race. Untouchability is a 'hidden apartheid' and what marks the similarity is the link between deprivation and distance, Segregation is a key characteristic of both. Fundamental to the grammar of 'distance' are the notions of pollution, dirt, 'touch'. Any form of closeness is repulsive or defiling. A defiance of segregation leads to violence. Three key terms determine segregation. First is the ritual order of pollution or dirt. The Dalits were regarded as impure and faced restrictions in marriage, dining, and in encounters in public places. Identified with dirt and impurity, they were associated with the lowest and dirtiest of occupations like tanning and scavenging. Their touch was defiling, their occupation polluting. Dalits were prohibited from public bathing places. Dirt also legitimised the sexual abuse of Dalit women. The final seal was set by violence against Dalits including atrocities, forceful eviction from land, arson and rape. The picture resonates with South Africa. However apartheid was an official state ideology, while in India the state was Constitutionally responsible for the welfare of Dalits. The ambiguity was heightened at the level of civil society where rituals of pollution were legitimised on religious or hygienic grounds.

The terms 'hidden apartheid' was basically invented to smoke out the Indian state which they felt hypocritically proclaimed itself an agent of Dalit welfare. The Dalits realised that protesting at the level of the state was futile. Not only did the state lack political will, its administrative set-up was high caste and had internalised caste value. "As a result complaints against atrocities were either not registered or if registered no action was taken" (p.7).

How does one fight such a cunning state? The politics of guilt does not work. Gandhi attempted it through the idea of Harijan. It was an attempt to locate Dalit as a Hindu problem and a Hindu responsibility. Gandhi's was a pre-emptive politics which sought to redefine strategies but worse robbed the Dalits of their prized possession, their legacy – anger. The state played at the politics of humiliation which became a politics of waiting. The strategy now was to create a politics of embarrassment to counter the politics of the state. The theatre could not be electoral politics but international forums.

To create such a politics of embarrassment, one had to master the politics of definitions and procedures. The international Esperanto of UN politics had become reduced to two terms – genocide and rights. The politics of genocide was seen as premature but the politics of rights was timely and for two reasons. The resurgence of democracy in Africa and Europe made rights as a courant as the market. Rights was the one universalism everybody from G-7 to the UN was ready to recognise. But there were three barriers to such an affinity. First was the fragmentation of the Dalit problem into gender poverty and other issues. Issues of poverty dissolved into the logic of development and the sexual violation of Dalit women became a gender problem but not a Dalit one. The parts were political but the whole was not internationalised enough to be political. Secondly, the Indian state was seen as a democratic welfare state which projected the caste issue as temporary, processual and internal. Thirdly, the world of scholarship had reduced caste to a sub continental phenomenon, to an ethics of particularism rather than universalism. How does one fight an opponent who not only defines the discourse, the rules of the game but claims to be well-wisher, patron and referee?

There were several models of sleight of hand. The Kurds had used internet to create a virtual community. The Chiappas in Mexico had mastered internet and created an international politics through websites. But politically, India preferred public forums, international meetings to websites. One needed to capture not an internet of nations but affiliate to a discursive space. Race was the most universal language of condemnation. Race moved mountains like the UN, the foundations and the corporations. If caste were defined as 'race in India', one retained local turfs but could use international forums to embarrass the official Indian image. A moralistic, moralising state could be caught flatfooted in international forums. The politics of definition became central. How does one outplay the upper caste at a textual level? There is no idiot talk about Dalit epistemology because this was time and place for legal definitions. Step four – how does one enter the politics of rights?

One begins with the obvious. "Human rights are rights possessed by all human beings merely by virtue of being human. In this sense, all Dalits are human beings, they do possess rights" (p.12). or, has the obvious eluded the Indian elite? Should we reiterate it again in Jeffersonian style we hold these truths to be self-evident. The document states, "Biologically, Dalits are human beings but socially and culturally they are lesser humans", (p.12). Therefore, Dalits, to recover the humanness, have to reinsert themselves into a human rights discourse.

Rights are universal but histories and experiences are particular. To find the right resonance Advocacy Update claims, "that the whole discourse on human rights needs to be reinvented and redefined particularly from the Dalit point of view". As an intellectual project, it has to be placed along two other projects. There is, first, the arguments publicised over the last decade which deny that human rights are universal and claim that it is antithetical to Asian values. Here the Dalit challenges this claim of the Khomeini's and lee Kwan yews to represent Asian values. There is then the effort to see caste as part of civilisation project. For the Dalits, this civilisation is an iron cage. Yet, the Dalit claim to the modernity of rights as an emancipatory project is not an uncritical one. It realise that the state's approach to rights has been atomistic or individualistic in perspective. This attitude led to redefining the 'individual rights' as 'group rights'. Advocacy Update claims that Dalit human rights are distinct because of their group character.

As concepts become clear and campaigns build up. The activists realise the greatest chance for success lies in arguing in terms of consequences. It is a pragmatic approach not an analytical or ideological one. Internationally it is race and racial discrimination that has created a banyan tree of regulations. All one has to do is a bit of conceptual and political grafting to consider caste as race under the international convention for the elimination of racism, racial discrimination, xenophobia and related intolerance. It is a request for classificatory hospitality justified by a claim to belong to the same family of suffering identified by the nature of violence, the corrosion of identity, the sexual abuse, the weight of history.

The claim to entry is at two levels. Why is caste like race? The answer is because our history says so and because we feel so. Beyond the objective history of the world of Dalits, there is a lived history of suffering which argues for a twinning, a siblingship of consequences. If caste is like race in consequences, can't caste join race in a similar track of liberation? Welcome to the UN. But narratives of feeling won't only do. Not in a world of lawyers and bureaucrats. One must seek the right term. The caste/race equation is weak till they discover the third term in the legal text - descent.

A life saving term. Descent is about blood and blood lines. It is hereditary. It is through descent that caste becomes synonymous with race. Advocacy update adds to it the folk theory of colour. Blood is present not only in the Varna theory, but in the notion of Aryan and

Dravidian races. It argues 'varna means colour' and that "the origin of the varna system seems to be based on the colour of skin. Gradually due to intermarriage and mixing of blood, this changed to breed and blood. In south India, contrary to other parts of the country, there is a strong belief that the people belong to the Dravidian race and not the Aryan race...There have been very strong political movements in the south against Aryan supremacy. In this reference, caste-based discrimination can be called racism.' (p.12)

The final argument is thus threefold. There is the lived experience of Dalits who see a racism in caste. There is the folk theory of skin and blood, which is racial in framework. There is also the politics, which feels race might be the liberatory framework for rescuing the impasse of caste as oppression.

But frames shift quickly. What is argued in terms of phenomenology of oppression is also represented as a history of tactics. But the writers are quick tc emphasise that even tactics involve a comparative sociology. Constituency politics implies a comparative politics of affinity and distance.

III

Advocacy update admits that efforts at the grass roots level were not critical enough to mobilise sufficient public opinion. But the strategy took off at the international level by "using all available spaces". The logic of numbers helped with 160 million Dalits and three million Burakumin forging conceptual and demographic solidarity eventually of 240 million Dalit Asians. Dalit NGOs have taken a south Asian phenomenon and temporarily globalised it.

There is a clear understanding that globalised politics thrived on networking and lobbying. But one must ask whether the logic NGO politics will alter the framework of politics, as UN agencies, foundations, courts start changing the discourse at the international level. The logic of NGO politics, especially as it extends to health, disasters, development also carries a touch of suspicion. Many NGO groups are seen as self serving or even narcissistic. Should one get embroiled in a confusion between Dalit politics and NGO politics which operate on different assumptions? Of course, the writers emphasise that their work is at three levels local, national and international. The hint eventually is that these advocacy efforts are global strategies, a sandwich of the local and global to pressure the national in certain directions.

The Dalit activists are clear about two issues. The emerging public discourse of castes being explained as cultural difference is not acceptable. The logic of multiculturalism merely sees them as antiseptically different 'like Maggi sauce'. The Asian Legal Resource Center argues that difference is only acceptable if it "is another name for equality". The document argues that the state has produced a hegemonising discourse, which has been dominant and oppressive. They suggest that the idea of caste as race be seen as another dissenting discourse and read and accepted as one. The document claims "the right to freedom of expression will entail the right to dissent and to produce countervailing discourses by Dalits".

While the right and the need for dissenting and countervailing discourses on caste is acceptable, the Dalit critique of the state appears naïve. It begins with a realist critique of the state as a high caste state lacking political will to tackle atrocities and yet it demands "reservations must be ensured for Dalits in all private bodies even if they do not receive a subsidy from the government". Such a demand in the period of liberalisation appears hurried. Reservation by itself appears mechanical strategy. Would not a claim for loans for a new style of entrepreneurship be more powerful? Shouldn't Dalits express their claims to private industry including MNCs through an 'international' strategy? Would a Dalit evaluation of private firms and multinationals be too elusive a lobbying tactic? As Dalit political tactics get globalised, one needs to ask how this move is to be located within a Dalit theory of globalisation?

The Dalit documents are passionate, clear-cut in analysis and intentions. How does one respond to these theories of oppression? Does one do as Durkheim (1959) did in Socialism and St Simon where he dismissed socialism as not being a science, but a cry of grief uttered by a creature in pain. Do we treat as 'voice' but refuse to recognise it as science? Do we respond professorially by claiming Dumont and Srinivas knew better? The situation is made more difficult in this day of political correctness. Would my criticism be dismissed as brahminic or seen as engaged? When André Béteille insists caste is not race, one cannot shrug it off as his credentials and intentions are impeccable.

Providentially it is at this point that Martin Macwan's 'caste may not be race' becomes important. Macwan's paper moves between system and life world, between objective statements, lists of atrocities, everyday events asking the reader to react. He is also asking what should be the Archimedean point of discursive change-Dalit suffering or the taxidermy of analytical distinctions? Macwan's paper reads like a power point presentation with quick facts about atrocities and everyday behaviours. Try it as a response test before one demands a deeper Gandhian or Levinasian response.

(1) "A high court judge in the north Indian state of UP caused his chamber to be washed with the holy water from the river Ganges to purify it, as the previous occupant happened to be a Dalit judge." Just a case of hygiene? (p.1)

(2) "When a judge of Gujarat High court wanted to know the police response, had the police been the victim, from a prosecutor fiercely defending police action of causing death of a Dalit through merciless beating, the response was, 'My lord, the law differs from person to person'." Would you promote the prosecutor? Incidentally he was (p.1).

(3) "Dalit children have to sit separately in a corner of the class, there are separate cups in the village hotels for tea for Dalits." Separate but equal? (p.2)

(4) "After the mid-day meal in some schools, while the non-Dalit children shall be playing, the Dalit children will be made to clean the utensils." A permissible case of child labour? (p.3)

(5) "There have been incidents where parents of the non-Dalit children have come to class and beaten up Dalit teachers including women teachers, because the latter have scolded children for not doing homework". Did you say Dalits as teachers, what more do you guys want? (p.3)

By moving between lived experiences and objective indices, Macwan creates a sense of how far reforms have had effect or even changed the attitudes of people. In fact, he locates the current reactions to the Dalit rewriting of caste to this same mindset. Dalit activists cite a historical precedent.

At the 1930-31 Round Table Conference in London, when "leading representatives of various communities ... met to discuss the future Constitution, Ambedkar bluntly told the conference that the depressed classes would not accept any Constitution for self rule which did not guarantee them equal citizenship and fundamental rights" [Divakar and Mathew 2001:3]. Ambedkar's stand was resented by dominant caste leaders. In fact, he was accused of dividing the independence movement and being a stooge of the British raj..." They lectured him that the situation of "untouchables was an internal matter and urge him to wait until independence was achieved"[Divakar and Mathew 2001:3]. Ambedkar's stand was resented by dominant caste leaders. In fact, he was accused of dividing then dependence movement and being a stooge of the British raj..." They lectured him that the situation of "untouchables was an internal matter and urge him to wait until independence was achieved" [Divakar and Mathew 2001:3]. The sequence is the same. It is the politics of waiting and the politics of right spaces. The argument is that caste is an internal matter and that raising the issue only creates a source of divisiveness and embarrassment. Of course, the timing was all wrong.

Dalits argue that the current objections to the welding of caste and race and the attempts to raise caste at the Durban conference on race, has a similar ring. Added to it is the politics of correctness, a sense of a good thing ruined. The bureaucrats must be seething. "Imagine just as we and our wives were looking forward to Durban...Imagine making a spectacle of caste internationally". Washing dirty linen in Durban is a messy affair.

IV

It is around Ambedkar's dramatic stance at the Round Table that Dalit activists build the legitimacy for their current politics. For instance, Paul Divakar and Ajai Mathew observe;

Ambedkar showed that boundaries for solutions to the problems of caste discrimination are not to be drawn around the village, district state or nation. What is an internal solution or an external solution should not be determined by geographic borders or national boundaries. A solution is internal when it makes use of democratic, Constitutional and legal space, bodies and mechanisms to which the state by its own volition is obligated. The United Nations World Conference Against Racism is an internal mechanism with respect to India, because India freely chose to ratify CERD in 1969, thus making it binding upon the nation. Terrorism or some other undemocratic methods are external solutions.

Therefore, to raise the problem of caste discrimination for attention and action by CERD and the WCAR is not to seek an external solution. It is rather a Constitutional, lawful and democratic means to by which Dalits and other similarly discriminated communities hope to strengthen laws which until now have failed to protect them from discrimination: Utilising international human rights mechanisms can only empower their respective governments to fulfill their own Constitutional and legislative obligations, thus strengthening the national integrity and renewing the nation in its striving to approach the ideals conceived in its Constitution" [Divakar and Mathew 2001:10]

Yet is the argument that globally simple? For instance, how would Dalits react to a backlash from their well-wishers who feel that as nationalists Dalits should have worked out a solution in India within an internal democratic framework. The question is how much dialogicity is there in these arguments even with Dalits who dissent with the current tactics. There is also the danger of the current debate acquiring a communalist or fundamentalist slant from both sides. In a political sense one has to still ask whether Durban will initiate a new cycle of reform or merely open a Pandora's box of intransigence, tokenism, fundamentalism, misunderstanding on both sides? One would be very interested to ask what is the post-Durban scenario? Is it the politics of a zero-sum game? What will be the relationship between NGO inspired activists and Dalits in the electoral domain? How does one relate to Dalits supporting the government? Are they uncle Tom or is their politics also genuine?

How does one respond to all this? Does one toe the official line and play the politics of waiting? Does one play the new-found convert and say with greater enthusiasm that all this is not about science or biology and insist it is only political. Does it mean the political is illiterate? If it is an internal matter, is the Government of India bringing it to the National Review of Constitution, producing at least a mea culpa report on bonded labour? Has a group of social scientists or technocrats gone into the issue of scavenging and what it means? Does saying it is an internal matter exhaust the politics of responsibility? Have we committed ourselves as state and civil society to respond to even one issue, such as scavenging? Can the imagination leap so we move from a reform of scavenging to a new vision of the city that incorporates Dalit imaginations?

There is also the practical question. Will the move succeed? Will there be a backlash? It is at this level that one is doubtful about success. At one level, one sees the Dalit manoeuvre as symbolic politics. Symbols are crucial in global world. The symbolic insertion of caste into race will be a victory. But of what kind?

One wants to respond at several levels. In a very instructive sense Dalit politicians have not only been our great modernists, but our first globalists. Think of Ambedkars critique of the village as a sink of regression and entrapment and contrast it to Gandhi's view of the village. Similarly Dalits were among the first to appeal to what Michael Ignatieff and Martha Nussbaum have called a civic internationalism. It is an appeal to a wider ethic of responsibility that goes beyond the state to international civil society. Such a civic internationalism might be necessary for India as a mirror and as a cultural counter to our diaspora's involvement in nostalgia or a mechanical globalism. A civic internationalism that addresses issues like scavenging and bonded labour might be different from those that the diaspora is involved in. The latter with its 'subaltern' idea of suffering may not find these interesting enough or even discursive enough to deconstruct.

Dalits were also the first to realise the link between globalisation and the politics of rights. It is true that the Dalit interventions are sometimes pragmatic but Dalits realise the power of human rights and its international appeal. They would resonate with Norberto Bobbio observations on the idea of human rights:

I do not know whether this idea is ambitious, sublime, merely consolatory, or naively hopeful, but it invites you to cancel the image of the twisted piece of wood or the mistaken animal, and no longer depicts the contradictory and ambiguous being called man solely in terms of his wretchedness, but also in terms of his potential grandeur" [Bobbio 1996:63].

Bobbio dubs human rights a great innovation. The question one must ask is the poetics of universalism powerful enough in India where caste speaks the voice of particularism? Or, do we need manifold and multiple voices which understand the particular, the universal and the plural? One believes this a great challenge to Dalit speech. How will it evade its potential univocality. There is a double responsibility. There is first their commitment to thickening the universalist argument but they must also contribute to south Asian voice and identity, to the south Asian project on alternatives. In their anger, one senses an erasure of this problem.

There is the question of scholarship. For instance, there is a serious problem of time in Macwan's paper. He cites Risley (1915) Madras Census Report (1911) the latest Dalit atrocities as if they were all simultaneous. Synchrony erases diachrony despite dates in footnotes but diachrony is crucial to understand the nature of change. In a more fundamental sense a dialogue with scholars about caste is required. If the Dalit understanding challenges the current understanding of the flexibility, mobility and political possibilities of caste, then there must be more debate and the Dalit reading located within this wider social science and civilisation reading. Dalit scholarship should not get caught in the anti-intellectualism of the Mandalist frame. It needs to be open even when it is talking of closures.

Consider a second example. Advocacy Update derives the term Dalit from a politics of pain but Gopal Guru (1998) shows that such an understanding of the politics of naming is not enough. Dalit as category had a much more variegated journey. Every act of naming had a social and political context we must understand to comprehend how the category was arrived at.

The historical journey begins with upper caste social reformers like S.M. Mate using 'asprustha' (untouched), and V.R. Shinde using 'depressed classes'. Then Gandhi introduces the term Harijan. Ambedkar uses Dalit first in his fortnightly Bahishkrut Bharat but even he did not use it often preferring different terms for different settings. It was a process of epistemic and political experimentation, an effort to combine identity and distributive politics, an attempt to blend caste, class and gender identities that Dalit as a term was eventually arrived at. It is an active construction reaching beyond the passivity of state sponsored categories and it is precisely such a political journey one misses in Advocacy Update's argument.

There is also a dramatistic quality to the Dalit movement where a symbolic landscape has been created even if the goal of Durban is not achieved. The polarity is that of Dalit and state but one believes there is a third terms in the drama – the Indian citizen as spectator. I think we need to see the Dalit manifestos not just as legal arguments, political manifestos but as a 'secular prayer'. What can be read as gestures of differentiation can be also turned into as gestures of unity if we intervene between the government and the Dalits and accept responsibility. It would be sad if we produce a politics of resentment claiming that Dalits like Muslims, etc, have got enough. The tragedy lies here in every city in India and not in playing fields of Durban. May be one has to go to Durban to reinvent a post Gandhian, post-Ambedkarite politics. If the Dalit crusade triggers this, it has done enough, for now.

References

Bobbio, Norberto (1996): *The Age of Rights*, Polity Press, Cambridge, p. 63.

Divakar, Paul and Ajai Mathew (2001): 'A Historical Overview of Achievements and Future Action Agenda', presented at Global Conference Against Racism and Caste-Based Discrimination, March 1-4, Teen Murti House, New Delhi.

Durkhiem, Emile (1959): *Socialism and St. Simon*, Routledge and Kegan Paul, London.

Durrenmatt, Friedrich (1954): *The Judge and His Hangman*, Jonathan Cape, London.

Guru, Gopal (1998): 'The Politics of Naming', *Seminar*, 47, November, pp. 14-18.

Prakasam, Gnana, Gauri Bhopatkar and John Samuel (2001): 'Campaign for Dalit Human Rights', Advocacy Update, No. 15, January-March.

Chapter 32

Durban and Dalit Discourse

SHIV VISVANATHAN

There is something antiseptic about Indian sociology. It has been marked by a search for competence, even exactitude but with achieving a deeper sense of the problematic. We write like clerks about our subjects clear about the consensus that brings us together, measuring change with little pipettes. One can read 20 years of contributions to Indian sociology and think that Mandal, Narmada, Bhopal or the turmoil in Punjab were all events that have not touched our social imagination. In fact, the only time our elite sociologists turn violent is when someone disturbs their consensus as when the Mandal report arose Rip-Van-Winkle like to challenge the amiable sociology of Dumont and Srinivas and the middle class dreams of mobility.

Today the prospect of the Durban conference on racism is threatening to do something similar by juxtaposing and even assimilating the categories of caste and race. The writings of NGO activists like Martin Macwan, Gnana Prakasam, Ambrose Pinto, Gail Omvedt have addressed to problem. Sociologists like André Béteille have replied to them. But each side treats the other as if it is correcting a bunch of poor tutorials. It is an act of distancing that condemns each to their own ghettos of illiteracy. We need a different point of entry, something that sees Dalit sociology not through the eyes of the academe but in terms of its own emic categories.

This point once arose in the aftermath of a seminar at Vidya Jyoti, Delhi. The theme was 'forgiveness and reconciliation' as ideals. The conversation began in an elliptical style with one speaker talking of his favourite handbook of metaphors, the *Mahabharata.* He talked of Draupadi and the humiliation of Draupadi. After her disrobing Draupadi chose to leave her hair open claiming that she would tie her hair only after washing it in the blood of Duryodhana. She wanted vengeance. The argument was that vengeance as a category can lead to a creative politics. Another speaker suggested that in this context one can contrast the politics of Gandhi and Ambedkar. Gandhi's politics was a politics of exorcising anger. He wanted Harijans to be part of the community and worked for methods of embracement and understanding. Ambedkar did not want to cleanse anger but stoke it like into a powerful politics. It reminded another of D.R. Nagraj's complaint that Gandhi's politics of love often denied Dalits the creativity of hate. One can add – of anger, of horror, of despair.

Of course, one can see caste as a fascinating intellectual order like Levi-Strauss or Octavia Paz did, treating as a geometry to be enjoyed. One can read it as an exotic ideology a la Louis Dumont and contrast it to the homo equalis of western individualism. One can read it like M.N. Srinivas or McKim Marriot and talk of caste interactions, Sanskritisation, pollution or be a trifle more aggressive and creative a Mandalist electoral sociology a la D.L. Sheth, where one sees caste as vertical than horizontal organisations, considering them not merely as endogamous units but as political alliances. But in none of these will one experience despair, horror, hate as original categories of a sociology. Anger is crucial for sociology of this kind. If sociology is science of empathy then such an understanding is crucial.

In Dalits and the Durban Discourse, Prakash Louis (2001) who has written sensitively on Jharkhand argues forcefully for a Dalit discourse at the Durban conference. I think the choice of terms is crucial. Durban as a city represents South Africa of apartheid: Durban also represents the Indian presence in South Africa, and Durban historically represents Gandhi's involvement in the battles against racism. Durban thus is an old theatre for recurrent battles and interpretations. Today it is a site in post-apartheid Africa where the question of caste as a 'glocal' phenomenon will be debated.

The word 'Dalit discourse' is also crucial. It is an emphasis not on voices or borrowed theory but an autonomous language to articulate a Dalit view of the world. It is not Dalit in the voice of academic sociology, or western categories but it is Dalit world in Dalit eyes. What this implies is not a borrowed sociology, or western categories but it is a Dalit world in Dalit eyes. What this implies is not standard textbook categories but the lived world of Dalit oppression and not a borrowed sociology locating itself Seymour Martin Lipset like between caste, class and race. It is a sociology which use emotions to create a cognitive world, a sociology born out of anger.

Consider the examples Prakash Louis (2001:1) describes:

A Dalit woman was stripped naked and beaten to death by two upper backward caste men in Negla village in Agra district. This woman made the mistake of crossing the path of Virendra Pal and Vijay Pal, carrying an empty pot. Six persons belonging to the Dalit community in Barabanki district, barely 22 km from Lucknow the capital of Uttar Pradesh were subjected to a brutal acid attack on the October 24, 2000. The dominant caste thakurs who are also the landed gentry of the area carried out this barbarous assault because they were infuriated by the failure to procure a tender for fishing rights in a nearby pond. The Dalits who dared to challenge the hegemony and the monopoly of the thakurs were 'taught the historical lesson'. Similarly in Hasanpur of Varanasi district, five Dalits were beaten to death by the thakurs because one of the them 'defied the dictates of the rajputs' and filed an FIR against the criminal assault of a rajput of the village. This enraged the dominant caste rajputs and they took laws into their hands against the 'erring untouchables of the village'.

For Louis, the sociology of Dalit discourse emerges out of the atrocity as an act of violence. The atrocity as an event stands between two forms of violence: the uniqueness of torture and the collective violence of genocide. If you begin with atrocity ideas of mobility, pollution, 'passing' recede to a corner. A sociology of atrocities is central to the Dalit discourse. Confronting atrocity and horror, academic sociology seems antiseptic and trite. The latter also valorises the voice of the experts over the voice of the victim leading to a reaction that combines scream and critique. Louis implies that categories like hate, oppression, despair, humiliation, horror, could rewrite Indian sociology fed on Marxists, functionalist or semiotic staples of class, order, mobility, deprivation, pollution. The question of anger and humiliation must be underlinked.

One has to understand the atrocity as a social fact. As an act of violence, an atrocity stands between torture of an individual and genocide involving the collective erasure of a people or community. The violence of an atrocity is totally out of scale triggered by some sense of threat or difference which could be an imagined slur or a simulated threat. If the scale of violence is totally disproportionate, the nature of the response is also left wanting. The state usually institutes a committee of enquiry which is belated in response offering little in terms of justice or even compensation. What marks the event is the varieties of violence including stoning, beating, arson, rape, branding and the sheer sense of horror and helplessness, a sense of violation far beyond any act of pollution. An atrocity cannot be understood in the usual opposition of academic sociology between functional and conflict theory because an atrocity needs not merely be a sociology of conflict but an understanding of evil and a phenomenology of humiliation which standard sociology has so far not captured. Finally, an atrocity as a victim's narrative often falls afoul of the expert discourse because the victim's testimony is often in discordance with the expert's assessment. Calibrating an atrocity with standard sociological tools often leads to surreal results.

It is in this context that one has to look at academic sociology squarely in the face. One of its great exemplars is undoubtedly André Béteille (2001). Béteille's approach is textbook perfect. He cites Ashley Montagu's classic textbook *Man's Most Dangerous Myths: The Fallacy of Race*. It was adequate for his college days and seems adequate for students now. And that is precisely the problem. Textbooks are cognitive regimes which often acknowledge the victor. Defeated knowledge's are erased or condemned as unscientific. What Béteille fails to project is that race itself was seen as a science. Eleven major universities in America taught race as a respectable scientific subject till the 1920s. Race has been interwoven with science over the last 50 years. It is not as Béteille claims only a 19th century affliction. Béteille ignores the history of science which show how complex the relation of science to race has been both in imperialism and Nazism and even anthropology [Chorover 1979; Wertheim 1966]. Béteille's exorcism of race might thus seem simplistic. When Béteille claims, 'treating caste as a form of race is politically mischievous; what is worse, it is scientifically nonsensical' he is indulging in naivete about the historical relation of science to race.

At another level, Béteille's conceptual wardenship of caste and race is welcome. His warning that we are opening a Pandora's box balances the Dalit objections to upper caste definitions of caste as a Procrustean bed. One wishes he had accompanied his spring cleaning with some proactive stand on caste oppression. One is tempted to compare Béteille's writing with what Helene Cixous [Seller 2001] wrote in *Manna from Mandelstams to the Mandelas.*

This book is an attempt at compassion. Only an attempt, for I am capable of going to the foot of the olive trees, but I will never manage to feel in my feet the nails Sergeant Visser drove into the feet of old Willie Smit, in spite of the supplications and tears. Only the supplications pass through my heart. I hear and do not feel, I weep and do not bleed. The next day my tears come no more. I have spent all I had... [Sellers 2001:165]

When Alfios Sibisi was tortured on March 1, 1962, in the Dundee countryside near Natal (But I shouldn't recount this here, so as not to cause too much anguish)... It is not the pain that hurt him, it is seeing wickedness face to face, and having the devil for a witness.

As for Alfios Sibisi, I know nothing of him save this name and the date of his death. Neither his age nor his face. I know the list of tortures, in order, I know the club, the nails, the ladder, the chains – I know he did not cry out. All night he wept, he was heard weeping.

And the price of the axe he did not steal was: £ 1.5s.9d. Through his nostrils, his ears, his throat, through his oesophagus, his entrails, his anus, he gave the axe back, in tears, in blood, in flesh, and in vomit. But this, no one can understand.

> Your suffering is beyond my strength. Your solitary face is beyond my gaze. And meanwhile crouched, my runny nose between my knees, rolled up under the rock of Dolor, I try to hoist up my insufficient soul toward you,

You innocent initiate of atrocious mysteries, you living inhabitant of insane hells. You meat hung alive on nights hooks [Sellers 2001:167]

But beyond the question of academic sociology there is the question of whether pride in a nation can be put to creative use. Rather than seeing this only in an Indian context, let us do a bit of comparative sociology by looking at similar attitudes in America around race. I summon as by expert one of my favourite philosophers Richard Rorty. In his *Achieving our Country*, Rorty (1997) begins by contending that "national pride is to countries what self-respect is to individuals: a necessary condition for self-improvement" [Rorty 2001:37]. Rorty then contrasts the view points of Elijah Muhammed the Black Muslim leader who wanted a separate black nation and the writer James Baldwin. Baldwin's work is a superb meditation on humiliation. In fire Next Time, Baldwin [Rorty 1997:12] says, "This is the crime of which I accuse my countrymen, and for which neither I nor time nor history will forgive them, that they have destroyed and are destroying hundreds of thousands of lives and do not know it and do not want to know it" (italics mine). Rorty remarks that this lack of forgiveness may take two forms, that of outright condemnation, disgust and a withdrawal from certain forms of politics as Elijah Muhammed and Black Panthers did or it can take the way of Baldwin. Rorty notes that "as Baldwin's narrative of self-creation unfolds, we watch him combine a continued identification with the country that brought over his ancestors in chains" [Rorty 1997:12]. Baldwin holds, "We, black and white deeply need each other here if we are really to become a nation… that is to achieve our identity, our maturity, as men and women" [Rorty 1997:12]. In one sense, Rorty gets it wrong when he claims that one is the way of the spectator and the other of the agent. Both can be ways of active engagement but with different political consequences. However, Rorty sums it up beautifully when he adds "there is no point in arguing that Elijah Muhammed made the right decision and Baldwin the wrong one, or vice versa. Neither forgave. Either can be made plausible. But there are no neutral, objective criteria which dictate one rather than the other" [Rorty 1997:13].

This point I think is important. The issue is not only of objective social science. The issue is one of creative myths and storytelling. As

Rorty says, "Stories about what a nation but rather attempts to forge a moral identity...It is an argument about which hopes to allow ourselves and which to forgo" [Rorty 1997:13].

As a writer of Dalit discourse, Louis has to be clear about this. Battling out at the level of empirical social science alone will not do. For every Dalit atrocity, may be there is a story of mobility or a happy narrative on electoralism. But, the politics is clear. The way one tells the story is the way of one political choices. But, there is another question. Is internationalising caste only 'political mischief'? Is it a form of disgust for the nation or can one love one's country and still go to the UN. There are no easy answers but we must all face these questions and in doing so we might realise one needs textbook sociology but also something more. We need creative myths to articulate our politics. May be for Béteille textbook sociology is an adequate myth but for Louis it is not enough.

One senses this in Louis' encounter with André Béteille. Béteille's work has been the staple diet of a generation of sociologists often read as an antidote to Srinivas and Dumont. In our minds he is one of the few sociologists who has a nuanced sense of conflict. Yet, Louis is dismissive of him as typical of the integrated colonial upper caste mindset. Louis accuses Béteille of being official, correct, hegemonic and of projecting himself as a noble, righteous person. But Dalit discourse need not differentiate itself from Béteille's work to create its autonomy. Academics will fight to keep concepts from polluting each other. Such a taxonomical clarity can be life giving. But, what we see is a conflation of levels. For Béteille the attempt to defeat the fallacy of race is the political victory of precious kind. "We cannot throw out the concept of race by the front door when it is used for asserting social superiority and bring it back again through the back door to misuse it in the cause of oppressed. The metaphor of race is a dangerous weapon whether it is used for asserting white supremacy or making demands on the basis of disadvantaged groups" [Béteille 2001]. Béteille's point is valid within the claims of a western centric sociology.

Louis' reply is that these categories are western and do not take into account local and regional ideas of the kinship between caste and race, especially the centrality of colour in caste cosmologies. Louis' answer is really not at the level of concepts but at the level of the politics of knowledge. Once you see caste as 'parochial' and create a conceptual distance between caste and race, caste is reduced to local politics even if it encompasses 240 million people. There is a universality to race as an abhorrent category. Racism is recognisable as a universal pathology while caste is read as local aberration. Unfortunately local aberrations do not usually command universal attention of UN or international agencies but merely regional or national politics. Béteille's conceptual wardenship, in fact, academic sociology in general aids the Indian state in constructing a convincing case against 'internationalising caste'. Béteille does not see it. He is like a sociologist who has read Max Weber's science as a vocation' but not 'politics as a vocation'. Béteille is agitated by conceptual conflation and throws his academic might behind exorcising it. But the atrocity as violation play little role in his academic sociology. It is this unevenness that leads Louis to condemn Béteille. What one misses in Béteille's sociology is any empathy for the Dalit movement, especially any compassion for the victim of an atrocity in a separate letter to the editor.

But beyond this there is a more fundamental politics in Louis' paper that we must tease out to establish his idea of a Dalit discourse. For Louis, the politics of electoral democracy, Constitutionalism, or development has little place for the Dalit as citizen. Dalit, as being or space doesn't exist in the dominant discourse. Consider even social indicators. Louis report that "The UNDP *Human Development Report 2001* ranks India as one of the 72 countries which is reported to have made real progress. Incidentally progress in IT is seen as significant but Dalit atrocities are not a part of a *Human Development Report*" [Louis 2001]. The media focuses on electoral battles between Sonia Gandhi and Sushma Swaraj in Bellari but pays little heed to Dalit discrimination there. As politics, as economics, as justice the Dalits do not figure except as acts of protest. Even protest is seen as intrusion and not a legitimate act of political discourse, there is little place for Dalit as discourse or tactics. It is true that Dalits in many ways are not given true status as citizens in India. But does caste work the same way for middle class or other backward castes? Or is there an emerging split – level view of caste with Dalits feeling oppressed and Mandalism and its reforms leaving one with a feel good feeling about India? Maybe what Dalit discourse needs to do is distinguish between a Dalit and a Mandalist perspective on caste exploring similarities but more importantly differences. One is forced to manoeuvre for international attention because only external politics might be able to leverage current paradigms. Dalit discourse is therefore a challenge to the current paradigms of Constitutionality, rights and democracy indicating there is little space for manoeuvre within the current definitions of politics. The lack of space stems from two factors. It emerges from the lack of political will among the elite and the sheer marginalisation and impoverishment of Dalits in everyday life. Democracy and development work for those above the Dalit domain. In fact, it is not academic sociology that Dalit politics challenges but Mandalist politics. Dalit discourse is an unconscious sparring with Mandalist worldviews. At the risk of being provocative let me formalise tactics and strategies (see table below).

Dalit Discourse	*Mandalism*
⋆ Universalist discourse	⋆ regional discourse
⋆ a theory of freedom	⋆ affirmative action
⋆ a critique of state	⋆ committed to statist action within national politics
⋆ globalised	⋆ uses the politics of caste as vertical groups
⋆ anti-caste	⋆ generally within a social framework
⋆ combination of isms	⋆ uneasy relationship with tribalism and feminism
⋆ easy alliance of tribals, Dalits, feminism	⋆ focuses more on politics of exploitation or relative deprivation
⋆ based more on politics of humiliation	⋆ uses current public space
⋆ current public spaces appear constricting	⋆ content with vote - bank politics
⋆ resistance to vote-bank politics, move to autonomous articulation	⋆ Within a Hindu or secular frame sees itself as a paradigmatic part of current politics
⋆ mix of Hindu+ Christian and Buddhist and secular enlightenment ideologies	
⋆ challenges current frames of politics	

One has to be clear that the Durban conference is a rite of passage, a transition from one kind of politics of another. At one level, Durban and the months of preparation before it, are like a thought experiment, an attempt to create what appears like outrageous hypothesis to rework the problem of caste. At another level, Dalit politics seems like a sideshow to the great celebration of condemning race at Durban. The Indian activists have to return to the everyday drama of caste oppression. But here Dalit activists must apply more critical rules for self-reflection and self-criticism. They could hold open seminars explaining their strategy, its possibilities, the extent of networking done. This also tempers down the ugly backlash that will follow from those who felt left out of the Durban Crusade, realising one faction's possible failure might be another faction's opportunity. But there is a wider learning process involved here. One needs to understand how NGOs or other groups in civil society can insert themselves into global politics. More critically one needs to gauge how adept the Dalits were as a lobby in UN backroom politics and also ask whether Dalit activism might become a prey to donor driven politics of foundations and other international agencies. For a Dalit discourse and a Dalit politics: autonomy at every level is a crucial a priori.

More specifically the media halo of Durban should move to 'Dalit discourse' and this we desperately need. Let me specify one well-wisher's expectations both in terms of academic sociology and political strategy.

In a deep and fundamental way, the Dalit discourse is a search for a different politics beyond Mandalism which narcissistically sees itself as a new stage in Indian democracy. Mandalism works within the paradigms of Indian democracy, the Constitution, socialism, the nation state, affirmative action and electoralism. The search for a new Dalit discourse seeks to push beyond it using Durban as text and pretext for a new politics of freedom. An atrocity cannot be domesticated as mere human rights violation. It has to be a theory of freedom where literature and political theory combine in a new way.

The Dalit battle is not complete only as a reaction to atrocity and human rights. The Dalit problem is not merely a human rights problem. It demands a theory of freedom which is something more infinite, multivocal and inexhaustible. We have to ask: What is Dalit discourse as a reflection on freedom? When Dalit politics and literature blend what does one expect to hear? One can articulate it in terms of a notion of time, self and measure. The Dalit problem is not a human rights problem. To borrow from Jean Luc Nancy, rights cannot exhaust the self [Nancy 1988:66-80]. Freedom, in fact, is prior to rights. Secondly, freedom, goes beyond equality as measure freedom with an inch tape as welfare measures and UNIDO reports often do. Freedom demands an excess and secondly each act of freedom is a new beginning. As Nancy argues, each theory of freedom displaces the current idea of the political [Nancy 1988:77]. When a Dalit discourse opens up we don't need to be only severe grammarians but also react as poets, exploring, sipping, gulping the surprises, the new possibilities in the logos called freedom. In this context, waiting itself becomes an obscenity, because the idea of 'waiting' for freedom carries with it a pernicious pedagogy. It suggests that Dalits or bonded labour or tribals are not yet 'mature' and 'need to wait' till freedom is 'granted to them'. Freedom does not need the permission of the Brahmin, the imprimatur of the dominant caste. In that sense the Dalit notion of freedom will displace the current idea of political whether as affirmative action, welfarism or electoral democracy or even self-congratulatory Mandalism. Any new theory of freedom should fill these above categories with a fear and trembling. In recent times the works of Nagaraj and Ilaiah came close to triggering that.

The sociologist Zygmunt Bauman differentiates between a metaphysics of freedom and a sociological notion of freedom. Bauman (1988) argues that since sociology arose "within a western, modern, capitalist frame, sociological idea of freedom comes pre-packed, pre-interpreted; that is to say, complete within common sense beliefs which had already made the experience intelligible..." The Dalit theory of freedom needs both. In Dalit eyes, caste rather than being amoeboid or Brownian seems like a panopticon, with the dominant castes playing the supervisory role. Every act of the Dalits is rendered visible, every act of transgression real or imagined subject to violence. An atrocity is that excess of force which reacts to the very fact of Dalit being. If atrocities are excessive, so must the Dalit notion of freedom. It can't be merely a measured search for equality or a demand for compensation. Bauman talks of the sociogenesis of freedom [Bauman

1988:29-30]. The term refers to the departures, large and small, which led to successive modifications in the discourse of freedom. In this sense 'Durban and Dalit Discourse' is an attempt to emphasise the need for discontinuity, an essay on the exhaustion of current political strategies. Post-Durban, one has to move from negativity to more positive idea of freedom stemming from a Dalit theory of culture.

One needs a theory of rationalism that can account for the magical. Dalit theories must also deconstruct the deep violence of Indian society especially the symbolic violence upholding the caste system. What Dalits are suggesting is the rewriting of the current social contract where citizenship does not exist for marginal. One wishes a Dalit discourse had reread the Constitution, pre-empted the national review of Constitution from producing another ineptly welcome document.

Within such a discourse, the notion of representation changes. It is not the elected notion of the MLA as a democratically elected middleman. For Dalits, Constitutionalism goes beyond electoralism to a representation of worldviews. A Constitution is a geology of 'jun sunwais', a spectrum of cognitive panchayats where health or work are Constitutional issues understood as 'worldviews'. The current Constitution is a visual one. It emphasises the life and the requirement of literacy. A Dalit Constitution would need to look at how the five senses are represented in the Constitution. A Constitution based on sight only wants people to look equal. Even oppression is visual. One talks of social distancing, contamination, violation. What would happen if instead of a Constitution based on sight and hearing, we had a Constitution based on smell and touch? The body of the body politic would change. Sexuality could be rescued from the depressiveness of dominant caste models. Violence would be understood differently. A Constitution that understand smell and touch, understand scavenging and dirt better [Classen et al 1994. For the relation between sight and the enlightenment Romanyshy 1989].

Gopal Guru once told me a story. A group of students from TISS had gone to survey (itself a visual metaphor) a Dalit slum. They were sitting in front of a house with an old Dalit when a pig came running, frolicking like a little dog, and ran right up and kissed the old man. The crowd scattered running pell-mell and the pig frightened by the crowd's reaction also fled. Guru had his own competent interpretation of the story but I wish to propose a slightly different reading. In a Mcluhanese sense, our social scientists wanted to see Dalits, but not touch or smell them. Our notion or rights and exploitation is based on the sense of sight. A lot of Dalit exploitation is explained in visual metaphors of distancing and exclusion. As Louis himself notes, Dalits always live at the borders of the village. Even dirt is visually defined as matter out of place. What I wish to suggest is that the Constitution looks at right and violations in visual, spatial metaphors. Sight dominates the sense of the Constitution. As a result, untouchability, which evokes touch or smell, is something the Constitution forbids but does not fully understand. A Dalit view of the Constitution should refigure the relation between the senses.

It is in this context that one must look at Soli Sorabjee's frivolous piece on toilets and other things [Sorabjee 2001]. Sorabjee begins sensibly enough with his observations on the regional preparatory meeting for the World Conference on Racism at Teheran, warn about conflating caste and race. As a Parsee, he waxes nostalgic on his Zoroastrian roots. All very sensible. Then he suddenly takes off on toilets contending that apart from high sounding tests like a free press, rule of law, independent judiciary, one needs pragmatic tests like clean toilets for evaluating the civilisation of a country. The stench of Indian toilets is overwhelming and Sorabjee salutes ASI and Sulabh for the agreement to maintain toilets in 31 world heritages sites. He even quotes Shabana Azmi's request to the MPs present that they see the Sulabh site at Safdarjung before leaving. He then talks of a 24-carat gold toilet in Hong Kong. For Sorabjee smell is still a visual thing something he must distance himself from. Sorabjee focuses on toilets but has little to say about scavenging, the polluting nature of it, its stigmata, the odour of such an occupation. Sorabjee, I believe, is a jazz fan and he knows that jazz allows for improvisation. What I wish to say is that the Dalit tactic is politically a kind of jazz. It is a pity Sorabjee does not understand it.

A Dalit discourse also needs a different notion of power. Constitutions worldwide seemed to be based on what Philippe Dandi called "the primitive western discourse of power" [quoted in Bauman 1988:45]. Dandi remarks that such a discourse holds that it "shall conquer and subjugate nature, rule over the laws of physics and have power over things. This neutrality is also expressed in our desire to treat people as things. We see each other as instruments to mould and manoeuvre as if people are things." The Dalit discourse on power must go beyond a modernity that makes people things. For this it needs a notion of citizenship, which is more than a bundle of entitlements. A citizen is a repertoire of skills, of competencies. As a thing, he can be obsolescent, as bundle of skills, he can constantly reinvent himself. There is a lot more one can list out. For instance, what is the Dalit theory of knowledge and how would it change the current definitions of democracy? Would the Dalit version of the self alter current notions of sexuality or violence?

My comments are only a set of wishful expectations. But once Durban is over, another drama begins, a drama that may eventually add a sense of the political beyond the 'good boy' theories of democracy the World Bank and our electoral pundits are inflicting on us today. Prakash Louis' paper if read with the works of D R Nagaraj (1993),[2] Kancha Ilaiah (1996)[3] might help trigger the Dalit discourse as a new chapter in the history of freedom in India.

Notes

[This paper is part of a two-part response to the debate. The first paper 'Race for Caste' was published in *EPW,* Vol XXXVI, No 27, July 3, 2001, pp 2512-16]

1. Ritu Priya does a superb hatchet job in 'Critique of a Critical Appraisal', *Lokayan Bulletin,* July-October 1990, 8:4/5, pp. 101-16.
2. Nagaraj's unpublished work might have deeper inklings of this sensitivity.
3. Ilaiah's book is more than suggestive but often operates through the logic of inversion.

References

Bauman, Zygmunt (1988): *Freedom*, Open University Press, Milton Keyes, p.3.

Béteille, André (2001): 'Race and Caste'. *The Hindu*, March 10.

Chorover, Stephen I. (1979): *From Genesis to Genocide*, MIT Press, Cambridge.

Classen, Constance, David Howes, Anthony Synnott (1994): *Aroma: The Cultural History of Smell*, Routledge, London.

Ilaiah's Kanchan (1996): *Why I am Not a Hindu?* Samya, Calcutta.

Louis, Prakash (2001): *Casteism is More Horrendous than Racism: Durban and Dalit Discourse*, Indian Social Institute, New Delhi.

Nagaraj, D.R. (1993): *The Flaming Feet,* South Forum Press, Bangalore.

Nancy, Jean-Luc (1988): *The Experience of Freedom*, Stanford University Press, Stanford (see particularly pp. 66-80).

Romanyshyn, Robert (1989): *Technology as Symptom and Dream*, Routledge, New York.

Sellers, Susan (ed) (2001): *Helene Cixous Reader*, Routledge, London.

Sorabjee, Soli (2001): 'Racism, Name Changing and Toilets', *The Times of India*, March 4.

Visvanathan, Shiv (1990): 'Mandal's Mandala', *Seminar*, 375, November, 99 31-35.

Wertheim, Fredrick (1966): *A Sign for Cain*, Robert Hale, London.

Discriminated Groups in Asia and Africa

Chapter 33

Caste Discrimination

SMITA NARULA

The UN World conference Against Racism, Racial Discrimination, Xenophobia and Related Intolerance (WCAR) held in South Africa in September 2001 will be remembered for many things: controversy over reference to Israel and the plight of Palestinians, a growing demand for reparations to modern-day victims of colonialism and slavery, and of course, the US and Israel walkout. The conference will also be heralded, however, as a watershed for the Dalit movement and for the rights of so-called low caste or outcaste populations throughout the world.

The Dalit caucus at the non-governmental conference that preceded the UN meet was over 160 members strong. Led by India's National Campaign on Dalit Human Right, it was joined by lower caste activists from Nepal, Japan, Sri Lanka, and Senegal. As one of the largest and best organised caucuses, it enjoyed strong solidarity from other groups at the conference, including the Roma, Africans and African-Americans, anti-apartheid activists and even South African Indians. They joined the many protests and processions that were lit up by campaign posters and led by a moving cultural drumming and performance team. Some even joined the hunger strike by Dalit activists in the conference's final days.

The campaign to include caste discrimination at world conference documents also drew strong support from international human rights organisations, numerous governments, UN Secretary General Kofi Annan, and even India's own National Human Rights Commission that took a strong and principled stand against the position of its own government in stating that the conference was a singular opportunity to deal with the vexed problem of caste discrimination.

Dalit activists at the conference learned that while oppression can vary in geography, name and degree, the mechanism to ensure the systematic exclusion of entire populations based on their race, ethnicity and caste are largely the same. The world learned about the endemic abuse meted out at the hands of higher caste populations, often with the complicity of local and state governments, and about the appalling and widespread practices of untouchability, manual scavenging, forced prostitution and other caste-based abuses in India.

The world also learned that despite the Indian government' insistence that these are internal domestic matters, caste discrimination is both a global phenomenon and of global concern. It affects 240 million people in Asia and close to 260 million people worldwide, a population greater than that of the United States. To this day it continues to suffer under what is often a hidden apartheid of segregation, modern-day slavery, and other extreme forms of discrimination, exploitation and violence. Caste imposes enormous obstacle to their full attainment of civil, political, economic, social and cultural rights.

In the run up to the conference, journalists, anthropologists, political parties, and others in India joined an increasingly mainstream debate on caste discrimination as an issue of international concern. By mid-August, Indian papers were ablaze with articles on caste versus race, and conferences throughout the country debated the merits of the Indian governments position – a position taken in the absence of consultation with Parliament, or the country's national commissions on human rights, women and Scheduled Castes and Scheduled Tribes.

Indian officials erroneously and simplistically argued that this was a conference about race or racism, and not other forms of discrimination. The very title of the conference under cut this argument, as did conclusions drawn by the Committee on the Elimination of All Forms of Racial Discrimination that 'the situation of Dalits falls within the scope of the Convention on the Elimination of All Forms of Racial Discrimination,' and that the term 'descent' contained in Article 1 of the convention does not refer solely to race and encompasses the situation of Dalits.

Many found it odd, to say the least, that the world's largest democracy would try to stop discussion of a serious human rights abuse that its own Constitution, laws and agencies are designed to address. The government also argued that efforts to raise the caste issue were part of an 'external agenda'.Their position conveniently ignored the efforts of the National Campaign on Dalit Human Rights who, along with hundreds of Indian human rights groups, collectively submitted over 2.5 million signatures to the Indian Prime Minister A.B. Vajpayee in December 1999 demanding the abolishment of untouchability and urging UN bodies to squarely address the issue of caste-based abuse and discrimination.

Intense Indian political lobbying ensured that the situation of Dalit stood alone as the only issue to have been systematically cut out of the governmental conference's documents. The declaration produced by the parallel NGO conference, however, affirmed the conclusions of the Committee on the Elimination of Racial Discrimination and the United Nation Sub commission on the Promotion and Protection of Human Rights that untouchability, bonded labour, manual scavenging and other caste-based abuses are repugnant and insidious forms of racial discrimination.

The conference was a movement builder and an organising tool that connected grassroots NGOs with international actors. It also ensured that the governments of countries where caste discrimination continues to be practiced and condoned will no longer be able to escape scrutiny at home or abroad.

The remainder of this article highlights the common features of caste systems worldwide and concludes with an overview of the ways in which United Nations human rights bodies have addressed the issue of caste discrimination thus far-often only as a result of intense advocacy on the part of non-governmental organisation within and outside of India.

Despite its constitutional abolition in 1950, the practice of 'untouchability' – the imposition of social disabilities on persons by reason of birth into a particular caste – remains very much a part of rural India. Representing over one-sixth of India's population, or some 160 million people, Dalits endure near complete social ostracisation. 'Untouchables' may not cross the line dividing their part of the village from that occupied by higher castes. They may not use the same wells, visit the same temples, or drink from the same cups in tea stalls. Dalit children are frequently made to sit at the back of classrooms. Entire villages in many Indian states remain completely segregated by caste. Dalits are routinely abused, even killed, at the hand of upper castes that enjoy the state's protection. Laws are openly flouted while state complicity in attacks on Dalit communities continues to reflect a well-documented pattern.

But India is not the only country marred by caste abuses. Dalits in other South Asian countries including Nepal, Bangladesh, Sri Lanka and Pakistan also suffer similar fates. The Buraku people of Japan, the Osu of Nigeria's Igbo people, and certain groups in Senegal, Mauritania and Somalia toil under their own caste or caste like systems. Caste is also a prominent social and economic indicator for the widespread South Asian diaspora in the United States, the United Kingdom, South Africa, Malaysia and many other countries around the world.

These communities share many features in common; features that have allowed even the most appalling practices to escape international scrutiny. In many cases, caste system coexist with otherwise democratic structures. In countries such as India and Nigeria, government have also enacted progressive legislation to combat abuses against lower caste communities. Despite formal protections in law, however, discriminatory treatment remains endemic and discriminatory societal norms continue to be reinforced by government and private structures and practices, in some cases through violent means.

Under various caste systems throughout the world, caste divisions also dominate in housing, marriage, and general social interaction-divisions that are reinforced through the practice and threat of social ostracism, economic boycotts, and even physical violence. Often, rigid social norms of purity and pollution are socially enforced through strict prohibitions on marriage or other social interaction between castes. While economic and social indicators other than caste have gained in significance, allowing inter-marriage among upper castes, in many countries strong social barriers remain in place against marriage between lower and higher castes.

Lower caste communities are almost invariably indistinguishable in physical appearance from higher caste communities. This is not, as some would say, a black and white issue. For most outsiders then, the visual cues that otherwise accompany race or ethnicity are often completely lacking. Stark economic disparities between low and high caste communities also get buried under a seemingly homogenous landscape of poverty. Poverty can be quite deceptive. It makes one conclude that all suffer from it equally.

A closer look reveals the discrimination inherent in the allocation of jobs, land, basic resources and amenities, and even physical security. A closer look at victims of violence, bonded labour, and other severe abuses also reveals disproportionate membership in the lowest ranking in the caste order. A perpetual state of economic dependency also allows for abuses to go unpunished, while a biased state machinery looks the other way, or worse, becomes complicit in the abuse.

The language used to describe low and high caste communities are striking in their similarity, despite the variation in geographic origin, with ideas of pollution and purity, and filth and cleanliness prevalent. In turn, these designations are used to justify the physical and social segregation of low caste communities from the rest of society, their exclusion from certain occupations, and their involuntary monopoly over 'unclean' occupations and tasks.

Allocation of labour on the basis of caste is one of the fundamental tenets of many caste system, with lower caste typically restricted to task and occupations that are deemed too 'filthy' or 'polluting' for higher caste communities. High dropout and lower literacy rates among lower caste populations have rather simplistically been characterised as the natural consequences of poverty and underdevelopment. Though these rates are partly attributable to the need for low caste children to supplement their family wages through labour, more insidious and less well documented is the discriminatory and abusive treatment faced by low caste children who attempt to attend school at the hands of their teachers and fellow students.

Many low caste victims of abuse are landless labourers who form the backbone of nations' agrarian economies. Land is the prime asset in rural areas that determines an individual's standard of living and social status. Lack of access to land makes low caste populations economically vulnerable; their dependency is exploited by landlord and allows for many abuses to go unpunished.

The poor remuneration of manual scavenging, agricultural labour, and other forms of low caste employment often force families of lower castes or case like groups into bondage. A lack of enforcement of relevant legislation prohibiting debt bondage in most of the countries concerned allows for the practice to continue unabated.

Lower caste women are singularly positioned at the bottom of caste, class and gender hierarchies. Largely uneducated and consistently paid less than their male counterparts worldwide, they invariably bear the burnt of exploitation, discrimination and physical attacks. Sexual abuse and other forms of violence against women are often used by landlords and the police to inflict political 'lessons' and crush dissent within the community. Lower caste women also suffer disproportionately in terms of access to health care, education, and subsistence wages as compared to women of higher castes.

Caste discrimination's place in the World Conference Against Racism, Racial Discrimination, Xenophobia and Related Intolerance (WCAR) was confirmed by numerous international bodies created by treaties and by the title of the conference itself. In the concluding observations of its forty ninth session held in August/September 1996 (as it reviewed India's tenth to fourteenth periodic reports under the International Convention on the Elimination of All forms of Racial Discrimination, 1965 [ICERD], the Committee on the Eliminations of Racial Discrimination (CERD) affirmed that 'the situation of Scheduled Castes and Scheduled Tribes falls within the scope of the convention.

The committee has clearly stated that the terms 'descent' contained in Article 1 of the convention does not refer solely to race, and encompasses the situation of Scheduled Castes and Tribes. In

March 2001, CERD's 'concluding observations' on Japan's report noted that discrimination based on descent constitutes racial discrimination, and that 'the terms "descent" contained in Art. 1 of ICERD has its own meaning and is not to be confused with race or ethnic or national origin.' In the same month, while reviewing Bangladesh's report, the committee reaffirmed that 'the term "descent" does not solely refer to race or ethnic or national origin and [that it] is of the view that the situation of castes falls within the scope of the convention.'

Similar conclusions were drawn by the UN special rapporteur on racism, racial discrimination, xenophobia and related intolerance in his January 1999 report. In 1997, the Human Rights Committee noted that members of Scheduled Castes endured 'severe social discrimination, and suffered 'disproportionately from many violations of their rights under the [ICCPR].' In reviewing Nepal's report in August 2000, CERD 'remain [ed] concerned at the existence of caste-based discrimination, and the denial which this system imposes on some segments of the population of the enjoyment of the rights enshrined in the convention.' In January and February 2000, serious concerns over the treatment of Dalit children and Dalit women in India were also expressed by the Committee on the Rights of the Child and the Committee on the Elimination of Discrimination Against Women in their reviews of India's periodic reports under the children's rights and women's rights conventions.

In August 2000 the UN Sub-commission on the Promotion and Protection of Human Rights passed resolution 2000/4 on discrimination based on work and descent. The resolution, aimed at addressing the issue of caste, reaffirmed that discrimination based on work and descent is prohibited under international human rights law. The sub-commission also decided to further identify affected communities, examine existing constitutional, legislative, and administrative measures for the abolition of such discrimination, and make concrete recommendations for the effective elimination of such practices.

In August 2001, sub-commission expert R.K.W. Goonesekere presented his working paper on work and descent-based discrimination to the sub-commission's fifty-third session. The paper was submitted pursuant to sub-commission resolution 2000/4. Because of time and other constraints, Goonesekere limited the paper's focus to the Asian countries of India, Nepal, Pakistan, Sri Lanka, and Japan but stated that further study of African countries in particular was warranted. The presentation of the paper, and the ensuing debate among sub-commission experts that followed, marked the first time that caste discrimination was discussed as a major source of human rights violations worldwide by a UN human rights body. The sub-commission also determined by consensus to extend the study to other regions of the world where work and descent based discrimination continues to be experienced.

This important resolution under-scored the notion that caste systems are inherently economic and social in their consequences and that the exclusion of lower caste communities extends to the economic and social realms of wages, jobs, education, and land.

Despite blockage of discussion of the issue of caste in the major intergovernmental fora of the WCAR process, several preparatory meetings for WCAR highlighted the need to address caste-based discrimination. These include the Asia-Pacific experts seminar in Bangkok, the European NGO meeting in Strasbourg, the African experts seminar in Addis Ababa, the NGO forum in Tehran, the Asia-Pacific NGO meeting in Kathmandu, the global conference against racism and caste-based discrimination in New Delhi, and various satellite conferences, including the Bellagio consultation.

India wasn't alone in coming to the world conference with an anti-agenda. Many governments, including the United States, used all the economic and political influence at their disposal to ensure that racial injustices in their own nations would not be addressed at the conference, or that they would not be bound by remedies outlined in the conference's programme of action. The conference's failures are well documented but its successes are not, successes that are largely a result of the work of NGOs from around the world who came together at numerous preparatory meetings and at the conference itself to speak in a united, singular voice as victims of longstanding oppression.

Ultimately, however, success will be measured by the extend to which governments live up to commitments they make to their own citizens. India actively supported the anti-apartheid struggle, has ratified all major human rights conventions, and has enacted progressive legislation to tackle caste related problems of bonded labour, manual scavenging, untouchability, and other atrocities against Dalit community members. What is lacking is enforcement.

Only with the honest implementation of the ICERD and of domestic laws designed to abolish the vestiges of the caste system and to protect the economic, social, cultural, civil and political rights of all, can the process of attaining economic and physical security and human dignity begin.

Concerted international attention and the commitment of resources to assist national governments in this important work are also long overdue. For at least a quarter billion people worldwide, the end of apartheid in South Africa did not signal the end of segregation and servitude in their own lives. This important conference was the start of a historic process and should bring us closer to this important global goal.

34

Caste and Social Origin

Descent-Based Discrimination in Asia

SUKHADEO THORAT AND UMAKANT

For the last several years the Dalit NGOs and other organisations have been lobbying with the UN Human Rights Commission and also with the Government of India to include the issue of descent and work-related caste-based discrimination of about 260 million Dalits or untouchables of South Asia (India, Nepal, Sri Lanka, Pakistan, Bangladesh) and similar social groups like Burakumin in Japan. The main argument of Dalit groups has been that the Dalits in South Asia suffered from intense discrimination in multiple spheres, namely, social cultural, economic, religious and political, arising out of the practice of the caste system and social origin. And, since the main concern of UN Conference is 'discrimination', the descent and work-related discrimination based on the caste and social origin should be recognised and included on the agenda of this conference.

The continuous efforts by Dalit groups and other organisations have led to some success. The Committee on the Elimination of All Forms of Racial Discrimination (CERD), while defining 'racial discrimination', has observed:

> "In this Convention, the term 'racial discrimination' shall mean any distinction, exclusion, restriction or preference based on race, colour, descent, or national or ethnic origin which has the purpose or effect of nullifying or impairing the recognition, enjoyment or exercise, on an equal footing of human rights and fundamental freedoms in the political, social, cultural or any other field of public life [Article 1 (1)]."

The CERD further observed on India's Periodic Report in August 1996 (CERD/C/304/Add. 13, para 14) that caste falls within the ambit of CERD and clarified that the term 'descent' mentioned in Article 1 of CERD does not solely refer to race. The Committee affirms that the situation of the Scheduled Castes (SCs) and Scheduled Tribes (STs) falls within the scope of the Convention. The Committee also has shown its concern about the forms of discrimination against the SCs and STs in its concluding observations (CERD/C/304/Add.13, para 23).

One of the important developments was that in its 52nd meeting the Sub-Commission for the Promotion and Protection of Human Rights (in resolution 2000/4) declared that discrimination based on work and descent is a form of discrimination prohibited by the international human rights conventions and decided to entrust R.K.W. Goonesekere with task of preparing a working report on the topic of discrimination based on work and descent and identify the communities suffering from these types of discrimination. The report, which was submitted and discussed on August 9 and 10, 2001 observed:

> "The discrimination based on work and descent is a long-standing practice in many societies throughout the world and affects a large portion of the world's population. Discrimination based on descent manifests itself most notably in caste- or tribe-based distinctions. These distinctions, determined by birth, result in serious violations across the full spectrum of civil, cultural, economic, political and social rights. Likewise, the nature of person's work or occupation is often the reason for, or a result of, discrimination against the person. Persons who perform the least desirable jobs in a society are often victims of double discrimination, suffering first from the nature of the work they must perform and suffering again by the denial of

their rights because they perform work that is unacceptable. In most cases, a person's descent determines or is intimately connected with the type of work they are afforded in the society. Victims of discrimination based on descent are singled out, not because of a difference in physical appearance or race, but rather by their membership in an endogamous social group that has been isolated socially and occupationally from other groups in the society."

The report further observed:

> "The most widespread discrimination on the basis of work and descent occurs in societies in which at least a portion of the population is influenced by the tradition of caste, including the Asian countries of Bangladesh, India, Nepal, Pakistan and Sri Lanka."

In the closing minutes of the 3rd Preparatory Committee meeting at Geneva on 10 August 2001, discussing the agenda to be finalised for the World Conference Against Racism, the Chair of the Working Group on Programme of Action ruled that the para 109 is on the agenda of the WCAR.

This is the only para pertaining to caste discrimination, which had been intensely lobbied for by many Dalit groups from Asia as well as other human rights organisations all over the world.

Para 109 reads as:

> "To ensure that all necessary constitutional, legislative and administrative measures including appropriate form of affirmative action are in place to prohibit and redress discrimination on the basis of work and descent and that such measures are respective and implemented by all states authorities at all levels."

This para 109 pertains to discrimination on the basis of caste being practised against the Dalits in South Asia, Burakumin in Japan, and also Osu in Nigeria and other similarly discriminated castes in Senegal and Southern Mauritania.

Three interrelated issues regarding the descent and work-based discrimination arising out of the caste and social origin need to be examined. First, the caste system involves intense discrimination based on descent and work, rather the very foundation of the caste system is based on the principle of inequality and discrimination in descent and work. Secondly, the efforts made by governments in most of these countries in terms of making provision in their constitutions and in passing laws and also in developing policies to mitigate this problem also need to be examined. Thirdly, despite these efforts, the discrimination of the Dalits and other groups based on descent and work continues on large scale because of failure of efforts, particularly on the part of the state, and finally the government should accept the discrimination arising out of caste system and give international commitment to overcome the problem.

Caste System and Untouchability – How Does It Involve Descent and Work-Based Discrimination: Case of India, Nepal, Sri Lanka and Pakistan

The Hindu social order, particularly its main pillars, viz., the caste system and untouchability, presents a unique case. As a system of social, economic and religious governance, it is founded not on the principle of the liberty (or freedom), equality and fraternity, the values which formed the basis of universal human rights, but on the principle of inequality in every sphere of life.

In this context, the three unique features of the caste system need to be understood. In social sphere, the caste system involves:

(a) Artificial division of people in social groups (castes). The social cultural, civic and religious rights of a member of the caste are predetermined in advance by birth into that caste and are hereditary and fixed.
(b) An unequal distribution of these rights across caste groups.
(c) Provision of a mechanism of social and economic ostracism, or penalties to ensure rigid adherence to the system.

In the sphere of economic rights or occupations, the Hindu social order also lays down a scheme of unequal distribution:

(a) It fixes the occupations or work for each caste by birth and its hereditary continuation.
(b) Unequal distribution of these economic rights related to property, trade, employment, wages, education etc., among the caste groups.

(c) Hierarchy of occupations based on social stigma of high and low as some occupations are considered high and some low in social standing.

These features imply that the Hindu social order is based on three interrelated elements, namely, predetermination of social, religious and economic rights of each caste based on birth; the unequal and hierarchical (graded) division of these rights among the castes; and social stigma associated with work or occupation and provision of strong social, religious and economic ostracism.

In Ambedkar's view, the doctrine of inequality is the core and heart of the Hindu social order. What is important is that the philosophical elements in Hinduism also directly or indirectly support the system. This leaves no difference between legal philosophy (and law) and moral philosophy (morality). What is legal also becomes moral. They're being no distinction between the legal and the moral, morality become social and binding on all (cited in Ambedkar 1987).

In this framework, the concept of 'human rights' under the Hindu social system takes a specific and distinct meaning. It becomes clear that unlike other human societies, the Hindu social order in its classical form does not recognise the individual and his distinctiveness as the centre of the social purpose. The unit of the Hindu society is not the individual. Even the family is not regarded as a unit of society except for the purposes of marriages and inheritance (Ambedkar, ibid). The primary unit of society is caste. There is no room for individual merit and the consideration of individual justice. Any rights that an individual has are not granted to him personally; these are granted to him because he belongs to a particular caste. Similarly, if an individual suffers from a lack of rights, it is not because he deserves it by his conduct. The disability is imposed upon the caste and as a member of the caste that is his lot.

The other implication is that the caste system also involves the principle of gradation and hierarchy in social and economic relations. This hierarchically interlinked character of the caste system implies a concept of 'human rights' and 'humanhood' which is different and unique. In this particular order of hierarchy the Brahmins are not only placed at the top but are considered to be 'superior social beings' worthy of all special rights and privileges.

At the bottom the untouchables are treated as 'sub-human beings' or 'lesser human beings' considered unworthy of any rights. Untouchables are treated as inferior social beings and therefore not entitled to any individual rights, i.e., civic, religious, political and economic. In fact, the disabilities are so severe that they are physically and socially isolated and excluded from the rest of the society. Isolation and exclusion of untouchables is a unique feature of the Hindu social order. Classes or social groups are common to all societies, but as long as they do not practise isolation and exclusiveness, they are only non-social in their relations towards one another. "Isolation and exclusiveness" makes them anti-social and inimical to one another (Ambedkar, ibid). This explains as to why high castes are antagonistic to untouchables.

In brief, the institutions of caste and untouchability involve gross disabilities for the Dalits based on the birth or descent. Firstly, they suffer from forced exclusion and isolation. Because of the untouchability and unaccessibility, they are physically excluded from the high caste locality in rural area. Secondly, they are socially excluded from the rest of the community due to restriction on intercaste marriages or endogamy. Thirdly, they are not entitled to any civic, social, cultural and religious rights.

As we shall see in the next section the impact and consequences of the caste system and untouchability can be seen wherever the Hindus have gone such as Nepal and Sri Lanka.

Constitutional Provisions and Other Laws to Prevent Discrimination

All the countries in the South Asia including Japan have accepted the problem of discrimination arising out of caste system and therefore made provision in their constitutions against caste-based discrimination and also enacted laws to prevent discrimination based on work and descent. The sections of the Indian Constitution on "Fundamental Rights" and the "Directive Principles" emulate the UN Declaration. The Indian Constitution reads:

> "[It is solemnly resolved] to secure to all citizens justice: social, economic and political, liberty of thought, expression, belief, faith

> and worship. And equality of status and of opportunity, and to promote among them all fraternity, assuring the dignity of individual and unity."

> The Constitution also states:

> "The state shall not discriminate against any citizen on grounds only of religion, race, caste, place and birth or any form."

> In the Directive Principles it adds:

> "The state shall promote with special care the educational and economic interests of the scheduled castes/tribes and shall protect them from social injustice and all forms of exploitation."

In accordance with these constitutional provisions, a number of measures have also been initiated by the Government of India for providing protection to the untouchables (SCs). These measures are in the nature of both protective and developmental. In the protective sphere, the untouchability was legally abolished and its practice in any form forbidden by the Untouchability Offence Act of 1955. Nearly two decades later, in 1976, the 1955 Act was reviewed in order to make it more stringent and effective, and the Protection of Civil Right Act, 1955 (PCR Act) was enacted. In 1989, the government enacted yet another Act, namely, the Scheduled Castes/Tribes Prevention of Atrocities Act in order to prevent atrocities against members of the SCs/STs. The need for this additional Act was felt because under the circumstances, the PCR Act, 1955 and normal provisions of the Indian Penal Code had been found to be inadequate to provide safeguards to SCs/STs against several crimes.

In the economic, educational and political spheres provisions have been made through the reservation and representation to improve their access and participation. The provision of reservation in various constitutional bodies, in government services, in admission to educational institutions and in several other areas are some of the promotional measures under this category. It must be mentioned that discrimination in private sphere, social or economic, is not covered by this legislation.

In Sri Lanka, the Constitution prohibits discrimination on the ground of caste [Article 12(2)] and prohibits subjecting a person by reason of his caste to any disadvantage with regard to access to shops, public restaurants, etc., and places of public worship of his own religion. However, there are no affirmative action/provisions as in India. But much earlier to the provision in the Constitution, the Prevention of Social Disabilities Act was passed in 1957, recognising that social disadvantages were imposed on people based on the accident of birth or the work they perform. The Act made it an offence for any person to discriminate against another on the ground of his caste in the matter of access to shops, public eating houses and hotels, public wells, hairdressing salons, laundries, cemeteries, places of worship, or for purposes of education and employment. In 1971, the Act was amended to strengthen its priorities and to impose heavier punishment. Initially, there were some prosecutions in the North but there was a tendency for the police not to take action against violations. In the celebrated temple-entry case, the Act was challenged as interfering with customs and ancient usages that prohibited defilement of a Hindu temple by the entry of low caste persons. This argument was rejected by both the Supreme Court and Privy Council.

In Nepal, untouchability was declared illegal in 1963 but the practice was not made punishable until the onset of multi-party democracy in 1990. The Constitution of 1990 guarantees the fundamental rights of the people and makes any discrimination against untouchables punishable by law. The National Code that prohibited Dalits from entering temples and religious sites was declared invalid by the Supreme Court in 1993. The government is committed to implement policies aimed at the advancement of Dalits. Thus, the Independent Downtrodden and Oppressed Community Council was formed in 1998 with the objective of coordinating policies and supervising programmes to benefit Dalits. The Ninth Five-Year Plan adopted several specific policies and programmes for the socio-economic development of the Dalits, including education, health, sanitation, training and capability enhancement, and employment.

Caste and Social Origin: Contemporary Evidence on Descent and Occupation-Based Discrimination in Asia

India

It is in this context we now present empirical evidence on the violation of human rights in different spheres, with respect to the Scheduled Castes (SCs). The annual reports of the Commission for Scheduled Castes and Scheduled Tribes provide the data on the registered cases of untouchability and atrocities against the SCs. The average number of cases registered under Untouchability Offence Act (or Protection of Civil Rights Act) were 480 during the 1950s, 1,903 during the 1960s, 3,240 during the 1970s, 3,875 during the 1980s and 1,672 during the first half of the 1990s. During the nine-year period between 1981-86 and 1995-97, a total of two lakh cases of atrocities on the SCs were registered, which means on an average three thousand cases of atrocities were committed on the SCs annually.

The break-up of the atrocities for the year 1997 shows 504 cases of murder, 3,452 of grievous hurt, 384 of arson, 1,002 of rapes and 12,149 cases of other offences. The data for a period between 1981 and 1997 showed that on an average annually about 508 scheduled caste person were murdered, about 2,343 hurt, 847 subjected to arson, 754 became victims of physical violence and about 12,000 were subjected to other offences.

There are very few empirical studies, which have tried to study the phenomenon of economic discrimination. Banerjee and Knight (1991) and also Deshi and Singh (1995) have brought out the significant presence of caste and untouchability-based economic discrimination in urban job market. Banerjee and Knight (1991), in their study of the Delhi urban job market during 1975-76, observed that "use of the standard methodology showed that there is indeed discrimination by caste", particularly job discrimination. They further observed that "discrimination appears to operate at least in part through traditional mechanism, with untouchables disproportionately represented in poorly-paid dead-end jobs".

Among the regional studies, the studies on Andhra Pradesh and Karnataka also provide evidence about economic discrimination in occupation, employment, wages and loan and other economic spheres.

The study on Andhra Pradesh (Venkateswarlu 1990) indicates that when untouchables wanted to switch over from their traditional occupation in the rural area to some other occupation, they were abused or beaten. The Karnataka study (Khan 1995) revealed that nearly 85% of the respondents continued with their traditional occupation and only 15% could make a switch. In the urban areas, however, 56% expressed a shift in the traditional occupation. The Orissa study for 1987-88 (Tripathy 1994) observed nearly 96% of respondents in one village and all the formerly untouchable respondents in the second village were discriminated against in wage payment whereas 28% in one village and 20% in another faced discrimination in the share of rent. Discrimination in interest rate charged by the moneylender was found in both villages.

We will add to these studies by looking at some complementary data, and putting some similar or related questions: How far do the traditional customary restrictions related to ownership of sources of income imposed on the low-caste untouchable continue? Has their access to agricultural land and capital in rural and urban areas improved? We have selected data on the comparative situation of the Scheduled Castes (SCs) and others in rural and urban areas in the late 1980s and early 1990s. Some sources also go back to the 1960s, 1970s and early 1980s.

Since more than 60% of the SC workers in rural areas and more than one-third in urban areas depend on wage employment, their earnings are determined by the level of employment and wage rates. It seems most possible that the SC workers suffer from discrimination in employment. The unemployment rate of SCs is much higher than that of other workers and they suffer from high underemployment as compared to other sections in Indian society. Higher unemployment rate of SC workers (which is twice that of others) indicates a possible existence of caste-based discrimination against SC workers in hiring.

Another reflection of deprivation because of discriminatory caste practices is found in the proportion of persons falling below a critical minimum level of consumption expenditure, what is called the 'poverty line'. In 1993-94, about half of SC households were below the poverty line in rural areas as compared to only less than one-third for the general population. The poverty level among the SCs was thus high compared to others. What is striking is the variation in poverty ratio among wage labourers across occupation groups. The incidence of poverty was about 60% among agricultural labourers followed by 40% among non-agricultural labourers. The level was relatively low for persons engaged in self-employed activities in agriculture (37.71%) and in the non-agricultural sector (38.19%). For each of these occupation groups, however, the proportion of SC households was much higher than their counterparts among the non-SC/ST groups.

In urban areas, about half of the SCs were below the poverty line in 1993-94, as compared to only one-third among the others. Further, the incidence was astonishingly high among the casual labourers as nearly two-thirds of them were poor. The disparities in the level of urban poverty between the two social groups were relatively higher in the case of self-employment and regular salaried and wage workers but less in the case of casual labourers.

This indicates that by the early 1990s still half of the SC population was below the poverty line both in rural and urban areas. The 1993-94 figures revealed that the SCs were at least twenty-five years behind the other groups in terms of level of poverty.

This macro-level comparative account of the economic position of the formerly untouchable and upper-caste persons covering relevant economic indicators provides convincing evidence of the continuing economic inequalities associated with caste. It is thus beyond doubt that the historical impact of traditional caste-based restrictions on the ownership of property, employment and occupation are still visible in significant measure, the access of the formerly untouchables to income-earning capital assets and employment is limited, and their segregation into manual labour is overwhelmingly high. The two prime economic attributes of the caste system thus seem to be present in sizeable measure, even today.

Nepal

Nepal has a predominately Hindu population and a caste system similar to that of India. About 21% of the population of 22 million constitutes the service castes (untouchables/Dalits), which are engaged in traditional occupations with low status value. They range from artisans and singers to castes doing unclean work like scavenging and removing dead animals. What unites them is that they are subject to hurtful discrimination – segregation, exclusion from public institutions such as hotels, restaurants and milk cooperatives, or denied free access to water, schools and temples, on the one hand, and deprived of rights, facilities and opportunities given to others to improve their conditions, on the other.

While there has been some change, Dalits complain that untouchability has not been eliminated, that there is unequal distribution of resources, that many of them lack agricultural land and that they remain economically and socially depressed. The government has acknowledged: "For an overwhelming majority of people the caste system continues to be an extremely salient feature of personal identity and social relationships and, to some extent, determines access to social opportunities."

The present statistics shows that 78% of Dalits are in an extreme poor situation with lack of land, housing, food, education and employment. Dalits do not own even 1% of agriculture land of the country. The literacy rate among them is 10% as against 50% national average. In 1992, in five selected districts of Nepal, over 90% of males and 97% of females among Dalit castes were illiterate, 90% of Dalits were victims of untouchability.

Dalits in Nepal also suffer several kinds of human rights violations, which are very much similar to their predicament in other parts of South Asia. These would include untouchability and residential segregation, denial of access to temples and many other public facilities, no access to public water taps, community forest resources and other kinds of humiliations which are faced by the Dalits on everyday basis.

Though the Government of Nepal has established a National Dalit Commission for the uplift of Dalits, however, the Constitution's Directive Principles, which should benefit Dalits, have been poorly implemented. Many discriminatory laws still remain on the law books and no special legislation has been passed for protection of Dalits. The National Dalit Commission lacks financial as well as political autonomy and that is why very little has been accomplished by this Commission. Whereas, on the other hand, the ongoing civil war has also seriously aggravated the plight of Dalits.

Sri Lanka

In Sri Lanka, there are two caste systems, one for the Sinhalese and the other for the Tamils. Although they both have their origin in India, the Sinhalese caste system is not linked to the Hindu *varna* system. It was an aspect of a feudal society, which divided people according to descent and blood or according to their hereditary roles and functions. Social distance was practised but the notion of pollution hardly existed. As an American scholar concluded, "The absence of the Hindu concept had rendered the Sinhalese caste system mild and humanitarian when judged by Indian standards" (Ryan 1953, cited in Goonesekere's paper).

The exception is the caste of Rodiyas or Rodi (meaning 'filth') from very early times. They suffered "untouchability with a vengeance". They were always a small community of about 500 families living mainly in the central highlands in their own colonies of huts devoid of amenities.

In recent times, allegation of discrimination based on descent is made by Tamils of Indian origin employed mainly as tea estate workers in the hill country. With regard to wages, housing, sanitation, health and education facilities, they were an oppressed group. Improvements have slowly been made as a result of government policies and powerful trade union action. Integration with the rest of society is more difficult owing to prejudice, but this is breaking down. There are signs of upward mobility through education and non-discriminatory laws. Caste distinctions exist among themselves and complaints have been made that workers (mostly Dalits) are kept out of trade union offices by high caste supervisors. The citizenship laws enacted after independence rendered Indian Tamils, who numbered about one million, stateless, and they were denied voting rights. Subsequent laws based on agreements between the governments of India and Sri Lanka have enabled them to acquire citizenship by registration without any distinction being made between them and others who are citizens by descent.

Pakistan

In Pakistan, there are about 36 castes declared to be SCs under the Declaration of Scheduled Castes Act, 1956. Since they are part of a tiny minority, i.e., 5% of the country's population, and due to lack of education they continue to stick to different forms of Hinduism. The caste-Hindus continue their domination mainly in southern part of Pakistan, especially former Mirpur Khas division, where more than one million Dalits dwell as landless peasants and labourers. The incidents of atrocities and caste-based discriminations on Dalits are increasing day by day in Tharparker – a district where about 35 % people belong to different Dalit communities among a million people. In Tharparker violence against Dalits is treated normally as a very minor issue, even by the law enforcement machinery, whether be it police, the prosecution, the medico-legal fraternity or even the judiciary. Non-registration of crimes against Dalits is one of the main problems here. Political influence over the police, caste, class and gender biases is rampant. It is extremely difficult for helpless Dalits to file complaints, particularly against the powerful individuals or perpetrators of violence against them.

In Babrario village, a Dalit boy Sadhu Meghwar was done to death and thrown into a well by caste-Hindus. The poor relatives of the deceased were threatened not to pursue the case, which was dubbed as a suicide case by the local police and subsequently closed. Another Dalit boy in Diplo tehsil who defended his sister from being raped at gun point by the scion of an influential caste-Hindu political family was tortured severely and forced to keep silence. Cases like these and even other kinds of caste discrimination occur at regular intervals.

The Legal Framework Order, 2002 enacted by the President Musharraf failed to ensure true representation of Dalits in the Legislative Assemblies as per their population ratio among Dalits. Dalits who form about 70% of the total Hindu population in Pakistan are completely marginalised and live at the mercy of their caste-Hindu and Muslim masters. The Human Rights Commission of Pakistan has also compiled various kinds of human rights abuses against Dalit bonded labourers who are popularly known as Haris.

In areas of Swat, in northern Pakistan, there had been a system of stratification of unequal social groups (*qaum*) that can be compared to the Hindu caste system, except that the people are Sunni Muslims. The concept of ritual pollution is absent, and is replaced by notions of privilege and shame. The groups are such as are to be found in an agricultural community, and at the bottom are despised people – sweepers, washermen, barbers and those who work with the guts of animals. There is pollution by occupation but caste status by birth does not prevent change of occupation. In ritual activities, there is equality but in everyday situations a distinction exists.

Japan

Japanese have also a section called Burakmin who suffer from the discrimination based on decent, work and employment. They consisted of *eta* (extreme filth) and *hinin* (non-human). The *eta* were assigned such duties as disposing of dead cattle, leather production, being security guards and sweeping while *hinin* made their living as security guards, executioners and performers. The Buraku, as they are now subjected to intense prejudice and discrimination, forbidden to marry or have physical contact with common people as such contact was seen as 'polluting' the higher classes. They were an outcaste population confined to living in hamlets, now officially classified as Dowa districts. The people of a Dowa district consist of the original *eta* and *hinin* people and others who have moved there. The official figures are 4,442 Dowa districts with a total population of 1.2 million Burakumin, but the unofficial figures are 6,000 and 3 million, respectively. The discrimination is not only against those who work in traditional occupations but also to others who belong to these communities and are actually doing other kinds of work.

Beginning with the Emancipation Edict, 1871, many laws have been enacted addressing the Buraku issues. Article 14 of the Constitution of 1946 states: "All people are equal under the law and there shall be no discrimination in political, economic or social relations because of race, creed, sex, social status or family origin." But, a government report in 1965 conceded that the Burakumin are "placed in such an inferior position economically, socially and culturally that their fundamental human rights are grossly violated even in present-day society and that, in particular, their civil rights and liberties which are assured to all people as a principle of modern society are not guaranteed in reality". The state's responsibility to solve the Buraku problem was accepted and special laws were passed in 1969, 1982 and 1987. The Law for the Measures for Promotion of Human Rights Protection, 1996 established a committee to analyse the extent of Buraku discrimination and make recommendations for human rights education and relief measures for victims. The Law on the Promotion of Human Rights Education and Human Rights Awareness Raising, 2000 was the result of a national campaign for the enactment of a fundamental law for Buraku liberation.

The present situation of Burakumin with respect to economic condition, employment, education and human rights is far behind the other sections of the Japanese society. The percentage of Buraku households on welfare in 1993 was 7 as against a national average of 2.1. The percentage of the Buraku income tax payers was 58 as against 81 among others. The proportion of regular employees among Burakus was 58 as against 65 among others while the percentage of temporary workers was higher than others. The percentage of Buraku people, who earned 3 million yen annually, is much less than the national average. The Burakumin experience the discrimination in marriages too. About 24%, 6.8%, 16.4%, 21.2% and 23.6% face discrimination in marriages, employment, school life, workplace and daily life in community respectively. A survey shows that 53.7% non-Buraku parents would oppose marriage for obvious reasons with Burakumin.

Concluding Observations

The official evidence revealed that in rural India, in several spheres, if not in all, the social behaviour of the high-caste Hindus is still governed by the norms and codes of the traditional caste system, although there are changes in some spheres of social relations. The settlements of the untouchables in rural areas are away from the high-caste locality, endogamy (which is the backbone of the caste system) continues, entries for the untouchables in private houses and temples in rural areas are limited, and common sharing of tea and food is also extremely limited. Pressures and restrictions on voting and political participation also prevail. The restriction on the change of occupation and discrimination in employment, wage rate, share of rent, rate of interest charged and in sale of items from shops owned by the untouchables is still observed to some degree in the rural areas, where three-fourths of the untouchables live.

The work and descent-based discrimination is far more intense in Nepal. Even in Sri Lanka and Pakistan, some groups are subjected to discrimination. In Japan, the problem of discrimination against Burakumin still continues.

This goes to show that the enforcement and practice of universal human rights in society is not conditioned by the formal supportive legal framework (such as the Constitution and other laws) alone. Often, cultural, social, religious and economic notions make the enforcement and practice of human rights difficult. Non-formal institutions, such as social, religious and economic, involve a framework of social behaviour of their own, which may not be in consonance with the principles enunciated by the United Nations, or the Constitution of a nation in which case different sets of values may result in conflicts. The values of the classical Hindu caste system with its ideas of unequal rights and untouchability and social system in these Asian countries present such a case which makes the enforcement and practice of secular human rights difficult. And, it implies that unless inequalities imbedded in the social, economic and cultural structures of the society are not addressed, the legal measures will make much less difference in providing access to human rights to the Dalits in India and elsewhere in Asia too.

The Dalit organisations have urged that the governments in these countries should accept the ground realities of widespread practice of discrimination in work as well as social relations based on descent and associated with caste and social origin/status. It should be accepted as an issue under the provision of UN and therefore on the agenda of WCAR. The governments should also make commitments that they would implement the existing laws and programmes in a much more effective way. The required political will should not be found wanting on this score. There has been a big gap between law and practice and the governments should ensure and develop time-bound programmes to provide access to social, cultural, economic, civic and political rights to a large chunk of humanity who are still struggling to lead a life of normal human being.

References

Ambedkar, B.R., 1987. in "Philosophy of Hinduism" in Vasant Moon (Ed.) *Dr. Babasaheb Ambedkar, Writings and Speeches*, Volume 3, Government of Maharashtra, Bombay.

Banerjee, Biswajit and J.B. Knight, 1985. "Caste Discrimination in Indian Urban Labour Market", *Journal of Developing Economics*.

Dalits in Nepal, *Dalit International Newsletter*, June 2004.

Deshi, A.K. and H. Singh, 1995. "Education, Labour Market Distortions and Relative Earning of Different Religious: Caste Categories in India", *Canadian Journal of Development of Studies*, December 21.

Deepak, Lal, 1988, *The Hindu Equilibrium*, Clarendon Oxford.

Goonesekere, R.K.W., Working Paper on "Discrimination Based on Work and Descent", E/CN.4/Sub.2/2001/16, June 14, 2001.

Khan, Mumtaz Ali, 1995. *Human Rights and the Dalits*, Uppal Publishers, Delhi.

Parvathamma, 1984. *Scheduled Castes and Tribes: A Socio-economic Survey*, Ashish, Delhi.

Report, National Commission for Scheduled Castes and Scheduled Tribes, 1998, Government of India, New Delhi.

Roshani M. Gunewardene, "The Caste System: A Violation of Fundamental Human Rights", *Human Rights Law Journal*, Vol. 11, Nos. 1-2, 1990.

Scheduled Caste Federation of Pakistan, see www.pakdalits.tk

Shah, Ghanshyam, 1998. "Caste and Untouchability: Theory and Practice". Paper presented at the Seminar "Ambedkar in Retrospect", Jawaharlal Nehru University, New Delhi.

Thorat, S.K., 1996. "Ambedkar on Economics of Hindu Social Order: Understanding its Orthodoxy and Legacy", in Walter Fernandes, *The Emerging Dalit Identity*, Indian Social Institute, New Delhi.

Tripathy, R.B., 1994. *Dalits: A Sub-Human Society*, Ashish, Delhi.

Venkateswarlu, D., 1990. *Harijan-Upper Class Conflict*, Discovery, Delhi.

Post-Durban Reflections

Chapter 35

What Next for India's Dalits?

MARI MARCEL THEKAEKARA

India's Dalits are downcast because the World Conference Against Racism at Durban dropped not just the word caste but watered down and diluted the issue of racism entirely. Indian diplomats worked overtime in Durban to eliminate references to work and descent. And succeeded to some extent. So it is likely that there will be some rejoicing in New Delhi's official circles.

But is a victory of diplomatic wheeling and dealing really a victory for India? Just because the word caste has not been included in the UN lexicon, is it really a vindication of the Governments position that caste is no longer a problem in India? One has only to read today's or tomorrow's newspaper to realise that caste is alive and well. Kicking, beating, raping and murdering Dalits with impunity.

In spite of the world leaders buckling under pressure from India, the National Campaign on Dalit Human Rights (NCDHR) has much to celebrate. Against all odds, it took the issue of caste to Durban and got the whole world to sit up and take notice. The need for and relevance of doing that has been hotly debated. The point is for us in India, caste is something we take for granted. The average, middle class city dweller doubts that atrocities exist in this day and age. They think reporters and activists exaggerate, make up the stories. Everyday, in every newspaper, there is a news item about Dalits raped, murdered, humiliated or molested and the readers eye, stated and cynical, passes over it in search of something different, something appealing.

Just before the Durban conference, the National Human Rights Commission admitted that the situation for Dalits was intolerable and lent its support to the NCDHR. Men and women of integrity and honour dropped out of the official Government delegation chosen to go to Durban. Their consciences won.

In Durban, Mohini Giri, former Chairperson of the All-India Women's Conference, stood in conscience, by the Dalit caucus. "Ms. Giri what are you doing with them," annoyed officials asked her. "My dear, do you know what we are doing to my Dalit women everyday in our country," the feisty lady rejoined. "How can I not stand with them?" the Indian spokesperson belittled the Dalits data, dismissing their atrocities reports and figures as manufactured or merely anecdotal in spite of the fact that all statistics were meticulously sourced from the National SC-ST Commission reports, and UNDP and Government of India Census figures. Our indifference, our cynicism, and our blasé approach to one of the most shameful situations of the century, was jolted because our izzat (honour) was threatened. Our government protested. A bit too much. But with little effect.

Whether the Government of India decides to admit the fact or not, the Dalits took caste to the centre stage at Durban. Their cultural troupe in somber black epitomised the mood of India's Dalits. The stylised, staccato movements to the beat of furious drummers both male and female brought the entire Kingsmead stadium to a halt. The drummers and dancers seemed to carry the anguish of their people. They had an intensity and passion that communicated their angst and their sorrow. Words were not needed.

The UN Human Rights Commissioner, Mary Robinson, the South African President, Thabo Mbeki, and the Cuban President, Fidel Castro, publicly stated that it was time for the Dalits to get justice. And though certain sections of the media went to town on the UN Secretary-General, Kofi Annan, rebuking a small group led by an uncouth politician, it was Kofi Annan who assured the Dalits of his support and invited Paul Divakar of the NCDHR to address the 12 Presidents and world leaders opening session. Divakar used the opportunity brilliantly. He made a succinct but moving presentation of the plight of India's 160 million Dalits. And he had his elite audience completely rivetted. At the end of the presentation, Castro, in his usual inimitable style, threw UN protocol out of the window and urged the leaders to take up the cause of the Dalits, Romas, migrant workers and Palestinians.

The actual UN Conference was a pointless game played out by diplomats and politicians. Like most UN Conferences, it was an endless round of meaningless, reciprocal back scratching. There is little genuine concern or even decent morality in the way serious issues are treated. It is governed by each country's politics, clean or dirty, and trade and political alliances rule the roost. So the outcome is not a real victory or loss for any one and certainly does not help the wretched of the earth that Mbeki pleaded for.

If it proved anything, the Durban Conference proved that racism was alive and well. The passion and commitment reflected in Robinson's, Mbeki's and Castro's speeches inspired the NGO gathering. For the diplomats it was business as usual. Each trying to protect his turf, to hide his country's shame.

UN Conferences come and go but hardly anyone in India notices them. This conference grabbed the headlines of every Indian newspaper and TV station and brought caste back into the news with a vengeance. Dalits have seized the opportunity, and used the Durban WCAR to rally people around the issue which for too long has been ignored. It is what activists are meant to do. More importantly, throughout the country, the Dalit Campaign has created a new awareness about human right in States such as Rajasthan, Uttar Pradesh and Bihar. Journalists, artists, poets, writers and academicians have joined with Dalit activists to mobilise people to rise and fight for their rights.

If the Government of India is wise, it will use this opportunity to eradicate the evils of the caste system instead of going against the tide. How can we do this? We can do this by actually punishing perpetrators of atrocities. It is not enough to hide behind the fact that we have enacted legislation to punish them – legislation becomes meaningless if it is not implemented. When the police go after criminals, terrorists or naxalite, they do so with a vengeance. Why can they not treat caste criminals with equal severity? A common thief may be beaten or tortured to death in one of our police stations. But criminals who molest, rapes or even murder Dalits get away scot-free in spite of the presence of a draconian Prevention of Atrocities Act.

If we want to stop the murder of Dalits we need to have people who care in positions of power. There are police officers, judges and collectors whose integrity and courage are well known. These people together with Dalit police, IAS and judicial officials should be in position in sensitive areas where atrocities abound. For this we need political will.

At every point, our government hides behind the fact that we have had reservation and radical legislation for 50 years. We do indeed have the world's most powerful, inspiring Constitution. But that is cold comfort to the women who watched her family burnt alive in Chintamani, Karnataka, a year ago.

If the Prime Minister, Atal Behari Vajpayee, and his colleagues in high places could turn their attention to this problem, there would be no need to hide our dirty linen at international conference. It is a hollow victory for New Delhi. Because, whether we admit it or not, the tiniest African country, indigenous people from New Zealand and South America, and obscure little European kingdoms have listened in horror to the tales of what we do to our Dalits.

It is time to live upto the ideals of our Constitution. To face reality and change our cruel society. Or posterity will judge us severely and all the empty fanfare about our great and glorious culture will be consigned to the dustbin of history. It is after all, only what we deserve.

But whether we like it or not, admit it or not, Indian Dalit won in Durban.

Chapter 36

Post-Durban Reflections

Color Line – Caste Line

N. PAUL DIVAKAR

Paragraph 73 of the Draft Programme of Action prepared for the World Conference Against Racism (WCAR) meeting held in Durban, South Africa, urges States "to ensure that all necessary constitutional, legislative, and administrative measures, including appropriate forms of affirmative action, are in place to prohibit and redress discrimination on the basis of work and descent, and that such measures are respected and implemented by all State authorities at all levels. "This paragraph could not be included in the final WCAR Programme of Action Declaration because of the delay tactics employed by the Government of India. Rightly understanding this paragraph to be a declaration of war against caste hierarchy, discrimination and atrocities against the 240 million Dalits in India, the government first tried to delete, then to dilute, and finally to delay discussion of this paragraph so that it had to be set aside, along with 50 other paragraphs dealing with the slave trade and reparations, the Middle East conflict, sexual orientation, and a few more on which the Conference could not arrive at a consensus.

The might of the Indian government crushed the aspirations of 260 million people across the world who had raised the issue of their 3000 year old discrimination and disempowerment before the world assembly for human equality, dignity and rights. Protectors turning Perpetrators! The scene was no different from that experienced every day by Dalits at the hands of local landlords, police, courts and bureaucrats. Although the Government of India tried to delete its well-guarded secret of systematic violation of human rights from the text of the declaration, that secret stood exposed before the world community, Indian civil society, and human rights bodies present at the WCAR. The NGO declaration devoted 20 paragraphs to caste discrimination and the Youth Declaration included it as well. That clearly reflected a large gap between the aspirations of civil society and the politics of governments.

The Government of India's Role

The Government of India started its vicious propaganda long before the Conference began. Throughout the preparatory period the government used Dalit leaders, bureaucrats and politicians to assure the United Nations human rights bodies that caste discrimination is a thing of the past, that constitutional mechanisms have laid it to rest, citing the fact that the President of India as well as the Speaker of Parliament come from Dalit communities. Government spokespersons also argued that since caste is different from race, it did not properly belong on the WCAR agenda. There was much media debate and expert opinion which branded the activists as anti-national, as stooges of Christian missionaries and agents of the West. There were, however, some dissenting voices. Devaki Jain and André Béteille resigned from the Committee set up by the Government. Justice Ramaswamy from the National Human Rights Commission acknowledge the continuing practice of caste discrimination and called the WCAR an appropriate platform to discuss the issue.

The National Campaign and the Durban Conference

About 180 Dalits and their supporters were able to attend the WCAR through the preparatory work done by the National Campaign on Dalit Human Rights (NCDHR). For over two years prior to the Conference, since the 50th anniversary of the Universal Declaration of Human Rights in 1998, the NCDHR was involved in an extensive campaign within India, protesting human rights violations against the Dalit community, the lack of political will in implementing constitutional and legal provisions to safeguard them, as well as the bias against Dalits in development and decision-making processes. Through its active participation in the process of preparation leading up to the Durban conference, the NCDHR succeeded in making caste discrimination an issue commensurate with the intensity and expansion of discrimination against 260 million people across the world and in the subcontinent. "260 million reasons why caste should be an agenda for the WCAR" amply projected the issue. The International Dalit Solidarity Network, comprising of civil society and human rights organisations, lobbied their own governments to support the Dalit cause. They kept the issue alive on the agenda and gave it rebirth three times during the conference when the Government of India tried to scuttle it.

The Balance Sheet at Durban

So has the attempt of the Dalits failed or succeeded in Durban? Because Paragraph 73 was not included in the final Declaration, especially the Government of India feels vindicated and has declared our effort a failure. Some sections of media have testified to the brashness and shame of the Dalits. However, for the Dalits, and for those concerned about building a truly egalitarian and democratic society in India, the WCAR was a beginning. Dalits certainly did not expect caste discrimination to be the central issue at the WCAR, but Dalits certainly did feel betrayed by a government that has pledged to give its people liberty, equality, justice, fraternity, and especially to protect and promote the rights of the marginalised.

WCAR is not an event, but a process. It is a process towards the building of a "Global society free of racism, racial discrimination, xenophobia and related intolerance." Caste certainly is institutionalised xenophobia and related intolerance. We are proud to carry on the legacy and struggle of Dr. Babasaheb Ambedkar who for the first time raised the issue of caste in the international forum. After about seventy years, this issue has been placed at the centre-stage of global human rights violations. As Mary Robinson, High Commissioner for Human rights, shared in her discussion with the Dalit delegation at

Durban, the issue has become an agenda for the world community, whether it is in the declaration or not. A Dalit was able to address the Round Table Conference of the Heads of States in the United Nations for the first time and relate, first hand, the atrocities and violations experienced day in and day out by his fellow human beings.

WCAR stands out as the "victims conference" (Mary Robinson). To Dalits in every way it has been so. At the forum organised during the conference by ICERD, Manimmegalai, the young widow of Murugesan, the beheaded *Panchayat* president from Tamil Nadu, raised her voice concerning the anguish of Dalit women whose husbands and sons are murdered while exercising constitutionally bestowed political power. Hajamma testified to the continuing cultural and religious practices where by dominant castes continue to sexually exploit Dalit women as Devadasis [Dalit women who are dedicated to temples and then sexually exploited]. Ninety percent of the Dait participants in Durban were grass roots activists, academics and movement leaders who continue to experience caste discrimination. We spoke to the media, displayed our posters, distributed handouts, organised workshops and seminars, shared our dance and music, and even undertook a relay fast for two days during the Conference. We lobbied intensely with various governments and UN officials throughout the Conference, and were able to communicate our plight and aspirations as only victims and victors can.

Post-Durban

Was it just an exotic experience? Does it makes any difference to the lives of the millions of Dalits in our villages, slums, schools, and colleges? What have we communicated to those on the other side of the caste-line? The Dalits who returned from Durban have become heroes in the eyes of the Dalit community. Media reports of the Conference were followed as none before by the Dalits in India. Meetings and debates were organised by students, employees and activists in many states and districts as Dalit issues become visible on the world stage. Educated and employed Dalits were eager to contribute to the process. Politicians are coming forward furtively to support the process. The Government of Andhra Pradesh announced various measures to tackle untouchability and human rights violations against Dalits described in the previously-shelved report of the Justice Punnayya Commission Against Untouchability. It has also openly acknowledged the existence of untouchability and discriminatory practices against Dalits and initiated a state-wide campaign against these abuses. One can see posters on buses and billboards promoting the campaign. The Government of Madhya Pradesh has called for a National workshop on "Transforming India through a Dalit Paradigm." Caste has become a critical point in analysis and debates on national issues.

WCAR is not the end but the beginning of a global debate on the hidden apartheid in Indian society through the institution of caste. Equality, dignity, liberty and fraternity will prevail over politics and authoritarianism. We believe in the power of the oppressed to break boundaries. The big question is "on which side of the line are we standing".

Chapter 37

Caste at the World Conference Against Racism

PETER N. PROVE

The issue of caste-based discrimination (and the similar forms of discrimination referred to by the UN Sub-Commission on the Promotion and Protection of Human Rights as "discrimination based on work and descent") was not addressed in the Declaration and Programme of Action adopted in Durban. Despite this lack of official recognition, the issue of discrimination based on caste and related forms of discrimination reached unprecedented levels of international prominence and media exposure during the WCAR and the preceding NGO Forum, due to the high degree of organisation and visibility of the Dalit caucus.

The only, albeit implicit, reference to caste-based discrimination and related forms of discrimination in the draft documents used as the basis for negotiations at Durban was paragraph 73 of the Draft Programme of Action, which read as follows: "The World Conference Against Racism, Racial Discrimination, Xenophobia and Related Intolerance... urges States to ensure that all necessary constitutional, legislative and administrative measures, including appropriate forms of affirmative action, are in place to prohibit and redress discrimination on the basis of work and descent, and that such measures are respected and implemented by all State authorities at all levels."

This paragraph was supported and introduced into the draft text by the delegation of Switzerland. Despite (a) the very circumspect language of this paragraph, (b) the fact that both the UN Committee on the Elimination of Racial Discrimination and the UN Sub-Commission on the Promotion and Protection of Human Rights had already addressed this issue in several different national contexts, and (c) India's own constitutional commitment to the abolition of untouchability and the eradication of discrimination, the Indian government insisted on interpreting this paragraph as singling out India for a politically motivated attack, and mounted a major international diplomatic effort to have it removed. The Government of India was widely rumoured to have secured the USA's agreement to exercise its considerable influence to ensure this result, in exchange for which the Indian delegation would promote among developing countries perspectives amenable to the US position on the contentious issues of reparations and Israel/Palestine.

These rumours seemed well-founded when Switzerland, previously a strong and forthright supporter of the paragraph and of the issue, pre-emptively announced its intention at the very beginning of the WCAR to withdraw its support for paragraph 73. Privately, Swiss representatives cited "extreme pressure, not only from India" as being behind the radical revision of their position. The USA was implicated by a number of diplomats as being responsible for applying this pressure.

Despite strong and active support from Denmark and the Netherlands, the European Union's position on the matter always remained equivocal. The Presidency (Belgium) was reported to be disinclined to antagonise India, seeing India as a potential ally on "other key issues" (i.e., reparations and Israel/Palestine). Determined lobbying by NGO representatives succeeded in gathering support from key Latin American, African and Arab countries, as well as from the Holy See and from Canada, but too little and too late to prevent paragraph 73 from being dropped with the other paragraphs still in square brackets at the ends of the World Conference.

In the end result, the Declaration and Programme of Action of the World Conference Against Racism lack a single, even implicit, reference to the daily reality of entrenched discrimination experienced by an estimated 250 million Dalits in South Asia, 3 million Burakumin in Japan, and an unknown number in parts of Africa – a form of discrimination which since 1996 has been repeatedly acknowledged by the UN Committee on the Elimination of Racial Discrimination as falling under the 'descent' limb of the definition of "racial discrimination" contained in Article 1.1 of the International Convention on the Elimination of All Forms of Racial Discrimination.

Despite this failure on the part of the political gathering, the World Conference Against Racism (and its preparatory processes) had provided a common focus which helped to promote unity and coordination among Dalit groups and solidarity networks around the world. The World Conference, and the pressure to address caste-based discrimination in that context, also provoked an unprecedented public debate in India which received intensive media coverage both within the country and internationally. Efforts by the Government of India to keep the matter off the international agenda only served to intensify the public debate, nationally and internationally. As a result of Durban, the international recognition of the issue of caste-based discrimination was very much enhanced. The challenge will now be to maintain and build upon the increased national and international awareness of the issue, and to capitalise on the level of open debate which the international campaign has provoked in the national context (especially in India) to press for further domestic reforms.

It is also evident from Durban that the key to internationalising the issue of caste-based discrimination successfully is the recognition of this form of discrimination as not being limited to one country or even to one region, but as a human rights problem of global significance. (The situation of the Burakumin in Japan and of marginalised castes in some African societies has been shown to be closely analogous to that of the Dalits of South Asia). Perhaps precisely for this reason, the Government of India persists in describing the campaign against caste-based discrimination as a politically-inspired attack on India per se. International solidarity networks between groups discriminated against on the basis of caste, which were very much strengthened in the Durban process, will continue to be of significant mutual benefit, and should be further developed.

After Durban, however, the risk is that the enthusiasm and the energy which the WCAR attracted will dissipate, and that the coordination among affected groups that was so evident there will evaporate again in fragmentation and competition. That would be a tragedy. It is critical that new common priorities be identified and campaigns developed that will add strength to the Dalit drumbeat that sounded so loud in Durban.

Sources of Articles

(1) UN Bodies and the Dalits: A Historical Review of Interventions, **N. Paul Divakar and Ajai M.,** Unpublished Paper prepared in February 2001.

(2) (UN) Touchable in Durban, **Martin Macwan**, *Seminar*, 508, December 2001.

(3) The Official Position, **Soli J. Sorabjee,** *Seminar*, 508, December 2001.

(4) Race and Caste, **André Béteille,** *The Hindu*, 10th March 2001.

(5) Caste is Not Race: But, Let's Go to the UN Forum Anyway, **Dipankar Gupta,** *The Times of India*, 18th August 2001.

(6) Dalits and Durban, **P. Radhakrishnan,** *The Hindu*, New Delhi, 27th August 2001.

(7) Caste Consciousness: Initiate an Open Discussion in Durban, **André Béteille,** *The Times of India*, New Delhi, 30th August 2001.

(8) Caste, Race, Politics, **Dipankar Gupta**, *Seminar*, 508, December 2001.

(9) Caste in the Mirror of Race, **D.L.Sheth** , *Seminar*, 508, December 2001.

(10) Race and Caste: Anthropological and Sociological Perspectives, **T.K. Oommen,** Paper Presented in a National Seminar Organised by the National Human Rights Commission and National Law School (Bangalore), 3-4 August, 2001.

(11) Silence of the Lambs: Durban and the Indian Elite, **Subhash Gatade,** *Mainstream*, July 21, 2001.

(12) UN Conference Against Racism: Is Caste Race?, **Ambrose Pinto,** *Economic and Political Weekly*, July 28, 2001.

(13) Hidden Apartheid, **Teesta Setalvad**, *Communalism Combat*, April 2001.

(14) Discrimination that Must be Cast Away, **Swami Agnivesh and Valson Thampu,** *The Hindu*, 3 June 2001.

(15) We, The Other People, **K.G. Kannabiran,** *The Hindu*, New Delhi, 8 June, 2001.

(16) Annihilating Caste, **Mari Marcel Thekaekara,** *The Hindu*, New Delhi, 10 June, 2001.

(17) Durban, Caste and Indian Democracy, **Kancha Ilaiah,** *The Hindu*, New Delhi, 11 June, 2001.

(18) Caste, the Academy and Dalit Women, **Kalpana Kannabiran,** *The Hindu*, New Delhi, 20 June, 2001.

(19) India's Apartheid, **Rajeev Dhavan,** *The Hindu*, New Delhi, 24 August 2001.

(20) Debate on Discrimination: Casteism is Racism of Another Sort, **Arjun Sengupta,** *The Times of India*, New Delhi, 29 August, 2001.

(21) Facing Up to the Facts, **Kuldip Nayar,** *The Hindu*, New Delhi, 31 August 2001.

(22) Caste, Race and Human Rights, **M.N. Panini,** *Economic and Political Weekly*, 1 September, 2001.

(23) The UN Racism and Caste, **Gail Omvedt,** *The Hindu*, 9 & 10 April, 2001.

(24) Caste and the World Conference Against Racism, **David Haslam,** *Dalit International Newsletter*, June 2001.

(25) Racial Discrimination as a Grave Violation of Human Rights, **P.N. Bhagwati,** *PUCL Bulletin*, July 2001.

(26) Caste at Durban: Why and How, **A.S. Narang,** *Mainstream*, July 21, 2001.

(27) UN's Record on Caste Rights, **Siraj M. Sait,** MRG Briefing, August 2001. This paper was prepared by the author under the title "Inheriting a Life Without Dignity: A Call to the United Nation to Address Caste-Based Discrimination" for Minority Rights Group International, London. The title has been changed for this volume on the author's suggestion.

(28) Regaining Our Lost Faith, **Prakash Louis,** *Seminar*, 508, December 2001.

(29) Caste and the UN Meet, **Kancha Ilaiah,** *The Hindu*, New Delhi, 21 August 2001.

(30) Politics of Representation, **Gopal Guru**, *Seminar*, 508, December 2001.

(31) The Race for Caste: Prolegomena to the Durban Conference, **Shiv Visvanathan,** *Economic and Political Weekly*, 7 July, 2001.

(32) Durban and Dalit Discourse, **Shiv Visvanathan,** *Economic and Political Weekly*, 18 August, 2001.

(33) Caste Discrimination, **Smita Narula**, *Seminar*, 508, December 2001.

(34) Caste and Social Origin: Descent Based Discriminations in Asia, **Sukhadeo Thorat and Umakant,** Unpublished Paper. This paper is a modified version of the presentation made at WCAR, Durban, South Africa, August 2001.

(35) What Next for India's Dalits?, **Mari Marcel Thekaekara,** *The Hindu*, New Delhi, 13 September 2001.

(36) Post-Durban Reflections: Color Line – Caste Line, **N. Paul Divakar,** *Dalit International Newsletter*, February 2002.

(37) Caste at the World Conference Against Racism, **Peter N. Prove**, *Dalit International Newsletter*, February 2002.

Contributors

Ajai M. was an Intern Advocate with NCDHR and currently he is a practising lawyer.

Ambrose Pinto, former Executive Director of Indian Social Institute, New Delhi, is now the Principal of St. Joseph College, Bangalore. A very keen campaigner of human rights of Dalits, Adivasis, minorities and other disadvantaged sections of Indian society.

A.S. Narang is on the faculty of Political Science at Indira Gandhi National Open University, New Delhi. He regularly writes on issues concerning human rights.

André Béteille, a very prominent sociologist, recently retired from the department of sociology, Delhi School of Economics. Apart from many books, he has also published many articles in reputed journals in India and abroad.

Arjun Sengupta, a former Member of Planning Commission, Government of India, taught International Politics at Jawaharlal Nehru University, New Delhi. Has also been a member of the Economic Advisory Council to the Prime Minister. He is the author of several books and articles on economic as well as human rights issues.

David Haslam, convenor of Dalit Solidarity Network in United Kingdom, has played an important role in spreading awareness about Dalit human rights globally.

Dipankar Gupta, a Professor of Sociology at Jawaharlal Nehru University, New Delhi, has to his credit many books and articles. He has also been commenting regularly on various issues of national/international importance in the print as well as visual media.

D.L. Sheth has been associated with the Centre for the Study of Developing Societies, Delhi, and has contributed books and articles on various social and political issues.

Gail Omvedt, a Sociologist/cultural anthropologist and also a social activist, has contributed several articles and books. Some of her prominent publications are: *Dalit Vision, Dalit Democratic Revolution, Buddhism in India: Challenging Brahmanism and Caste and Ambedkar: Towards an Enlightened India*.

Gopal Guru was Professor of Political Science at Pune University and Delhi University and now at Jawaharlal Nehru University, New Delhi. He has contributed enormously on the issues related to Dalit social and political movement.

K.G. Kannabiran, President of People's Union for Civil Liberties (PUCL) has been a long-time advocate of people's rights against State repression and has also sided with various people's movement for a world free of exploitation and injustice.

Kalpana Kannabiran, a sociologist at NALSAR, University of Law, Hyderabad, and also a womens' right activist, has been contributing regularly in social and political movements of the deprived and the disadvantaged.

Kancha Ilaiah, Professor of Political Science, Osmania University, has been regularly writing on various socio-political issues affecting the Dalit Bahujans. His important publications are: *Why I am Not a Hindu, God as a Political Philosopher: Buddha's Challenge to Brahminism and Buffalo Nationalism: A Critique of Spiritual Fascism*. He has also written various articles which have been published in reputed journals and newspapers.

Kuldip Nayar, a senior journalist, a diplomat, a former Member of Rajya Sabha and champion of human rights, has always voiced his concern on human rights violations by the State, and on other issues of national and international importance.

M.N. Panini, a Professor of Sociology at Jawaharlal Nehru University, has been regularly writing and commenting on various social, cultural and political issues.

Mari Marcel Thekaekara, a freelance journalist and a social activist, she has been regularly contributing articles in newspapers on human rights situation of Dalits. She is the author of a book *Endless Filth*.

Martin Macwan, a social activist, founder Director of Navsarjan Trust, Ahmedabad, a former Convenor of National Campaign on Dalit Human Rights, recipient of Robert F Kennedy International Award for Human Rights, and now the Chairman of Indian Institute of Dalit Studies, New Delhi, has been tirelessly campaigning for Human Rights of Dalits since last 25 years or so. A prolific speaker and a writer too, he has been contributing in a very effective way the cause of Dalit Human Rights.

N. Paul Divakar, a social activist, a human right activist and the current Convenor of the National Campaign on Dalit Human Rights, is not only credited with starting organisations working for social and economic empowerment of Dalits in Andhra Pradesh and elsewhere, but also for highlighting the Human Rights situation of Dalits both nationally and internationally.

P.N. Bhagwati, former Chief Justice of the Supreme Court, an authority on jurisprudence and law, a champion of judicial activism, defender of human rights of common people, has advocated the cause of the disadvantaged in a forceful and effective manner.

Peter N. Prove, a human rights activist based in Geneva, he has been actively working on various fronts and in various locations to highlight the cause of the disadvantaged in Asia, Africa and Europe.

Prakash Louis is currently the Executive Director of Indian Social Institute, New Delhi. He has also been with the grassroot movements and organisations for a long time. In recent years he has been continuously highlighting the issues affecting the disadvantaged sections of society through his books, articles and columns.

P. Radhakrishnan, a Professor at Madras Institute of Development Studies, Chennai, has to his credit books and articles on socio-economic issues.

Rajeev Dhavan a well-known Supreme Court Lawyer, has been advocating the cause of human rights not only through legal interventions by fighting cases on behalf of the victims but has also been continuously writing on socio, legal and political issues affecting the lives of common people.

Shiv Visvanathan, Social Scientist working with Centre for the Study of Developing Societies, Delhi, has to his credit several writings on social, ideological and political issues.

Siraj M. Sait, senior Lecturer in Law and Human Rights, University of East London, UK, and formerly State Prosecutor against caste atrocities in Tamil Nadu, has been advocating the cause of Dalits, minorities and other disadvantaged sections of society.

Smita Narula, formerly with the Human Rights Watch and now Executive Director, Center for Human Rights and Global Justice, School of Law, New York University, has been tirelessly advocating the cause of Dalits and other disadvantaged groups in India and elsewhere. She is the author of *Broken People: Caste Violence Against India's Untouchables*.

Soli J. Sorabjee, a lawyer of eminence and former Attorney General of India, has been on various committees and panels of the United Nation.

Subhash Gatade, a social activist, a writer, editor of a Hindi Journal – "Sandhan", has been regularly highlighting the social, economic, political, ideological and human right issues related to Dalits, Adivasis, minorities and other disadvantaged sections of society.

Sukhadeo Thorat is a Professor of Economics at Jawaharlal Nehru University, New Delhi. Currently he is the Director of Indian Institute of Dalit Studies, New Delhi. He has written extensively on the problem of Dalits, caste discrimination, Ambedkar's economic thinking, human rights issues, agricultural development, rural poverty, rural labour and child labour, problem of slums. He has so far published seven books and about forty articles in national and international journals.

Swami Agnivesh, the founder chairperson, Bandhua Mukti Morcha, a front dedicated to liberate bonded labour, has been tirelessly campaigning for the rights of poor, common man, disadvantaged and religious minorities.

T.K. Oommen, a noted sociologist, former President of the International Sociological and also former President of Indian Sociological Society, in his long and distinguished career as an academician at Jawaharlal Nehru University, New Delhi, has contributed immensely on various sociological and anthropological issues relevant to India in particular and global society in general. He is the author of several books and articles.

Teesta Setalvad, a journalist, Joint Editor of "Communalism Combat", a human right activist, has been fighting against communal and obscurantist forces. Through her powerful writings and forceful interventions she has highlighted the sufferings of Muslims, Dalits, women and other disadvantaged sections of society.

Umakant, a Doctorate from Jawaharlal Nehru University, New Delhi, is currently working as Associate Fellow at Indian Institute of Dalit Studies, New Delhi. He has written on the issues related to Dalit politics, Dalit leadership and human rights issues. He has also been involved in human rights activities related to Dalits.

Valson Thampu, a prominent Christian leader, a theologian, an activist and a writer. He retied as Professor of English Literature at the St. Stephen College, Delhi. He been voicing his concern against religious obscurantism, caste and communal violence.

Appendix

Statement by the National Human Rights Commission, India at WCAR

JUSTICE K. RAMASWAMY

This World Conference holds, in reality, a mirror to the soul of each of us.

First, I would like to say that our Commission fully concurs with the Statement on behalf of National Institutions that has been read out by our South African colleague.

The Indian Commission has considered it its duty to listen attentively to those in our country who have been the victims of historical injustices, and who are hurting because of discrimination and inequality. I refer in particular to those who, under our Constitution, comprise the Scheduled Castes and Scheduled Tribes - the Dalits and Adivasis of India - with the protection of whose human rights our Commission is itself deeply involved. It was to hear their voices, and to benefit from an exchange of views with them, and with eminent jurists, academics and human rights activists, that our Commission organised two major consultations in August 2001, in Bangalore and Delhi respectively, as steps preparatory to the formulation of the views of our Commission for this Conference. May I now outline the views of our Commission on certain of the issues before the Conference that are particularly germane to my country?

- There can be no doubt that in India - as everywhere else in the world - history and society has been scarred by discrimination and inequality.

- It was in recognition of this - and to end such injustice - that our Constitution contained powerful provisions to combat all forms of discrimination, including notably those forms, which were based on race, caste or descent. These provisions of the Constitution are justifiable.
- It can with good reason be said that India has embarked on a programme of affirmative action, which is, perhaps, without parallel in scale and dimension in human history. It is all the more remarkable for being undertaken in a country that has demonstrated an unshakeable faith in the capacity of its people to effect fundamental social, economic and political change through the processes of democracy.
- Our Commission believes it is essential that all Member States, including India respect the international human rights regime established under the auspices of the United Nations and observe the discipline of the treaties to which they are States Party.
- In the light of this, our Commission is of the opinion that the exchange of views on human rights matters, whether at the national, regional or international level, can all contribute constructively to the promotion and protection of such rights and that this Conference provides a singular opportunity to the international community to deal openly and courageously with the vexed issues of discrimination and inequality as they exist all over the world, in all of their variety, including the forms of discrimination that persist in India and all other countries. In such a context, it is not so much the nomenclature of the form of discrimination that must engage our attention, but the fact of its persistence that must cause concern. Given this perception, the Commission is of the view that the debate on whether race and caste are co-terminus, or similar forms of discrimination, is not the essence of the matter. The Constitution of India in Article 15 expressly prohibits discrimination on either ground, and that Constitutional guarantee must be rigorously implemented. In this connection, the Commission believes deeply in the value of engaging Governments, non-governmental organizations, national institutions, and all concerned elements of civil society in the process of fighting discrimination, and urges that this process be conducted at all levels in a spirit that is genuinely interested in the furtherance of human rights, and not vitiated by self-righteousness or by political and other extraneous considerations.

In furtherance of its statutory responsibilities, the Commission has thus accorded the highest priority to ending discrimination against Scheduled Castes and Scheduled Tribes and in seeking to eradicate, in particular, two pernicious practices which largely affect members of these communities: these relate to manual scavenging and bonded labour.

The Commission has also taken up the issue of the rights of persons displaced by mega projects and large dams, many of who are tribals.

In the final analysis, the Commission believes that the promotion and protection of the human rights of the weakest sections of society are clearly related to their full and proper empowerment. That is why the Commission has urged the adoption and implementation of policies at the Central and State levels that will open the doors of opportunity to them. In addition, the Commission has continued to receive and redress numerous individual complaints that it has received daily from persons, notably Dalits and Adivasis; these have alleged acts of discrimination, "untouchability", violence against the human person, atrocities of various kinds, and high-handedness by public servants and others.

Economic upliftment and empowerment of Dalits is the most effective tool to combat casteism. More avenues must be opened for the economic betterment of the disadvantaged.

The Commission is acutely aware that the journey to end discrimination, injustice and inequality will be long and often frustrating. But it is convinced that, in this mission, the Constitution of the Republic has shown the way. Legislative and affirmative action programmes are firmly in place, but unquestionably need to be far better implemented. The Commission is convinced that discrimination on any of the grounds contained in the Constitution of India, and these include race, caste and descent, constitute an unacceptable assault on the dignity and worth of the human person and an egregious violation of human rights. The commission holds the view that the instruments of governance in our country, and the energetic and committed non-governmental sector that exists, can unitedly triumph over the historical injustices that have hurt the weakest sections of our country, particularly Dalits and Scheduled Tribes. This is above all a national responsibility and a moral imperative than can and must be honoured.

September 5, 2001

Index

Abdullah, Omar, 230
Agnivesh, Swami, xxvi, 142-148, 251
Ajai, M., xxix, xxx
Ambedkar Mission, 188, 189
Ambedkar, Bhim Rao, 7, 57, 79, 93, 111, 137, 138, 144, 161, 248, 260, 263
anthropometry, 105, 106
  see racial superiority
Apartheid, 144
Appadurai, Arjun, 76
Atishudra
  theory of, 136, 137

Babb, L.A., 78
Bamiyan, Buddha, 139
Bansode, Harish, 235
Bayley, Susan, 102
Berreman, Gerald D., xxv
Berwa, Laxmi, 188
Béteille, André, xxiv, xxv, 49-52, 62, 65-68, 113, 143, 190, 191, 265, 268, 271
Bhagwati, Justice, 14
Bhambri, C.P., 82
Bhopatkar, Gauri, 251
Boas, Franz, 49, 51
bon-ton society, 74
Bobbio, Norberto, 262, 263
Bonded Labour (Abolition) Act, 1976, 20, 21
bonded labour, 20
Brockington, John, 100
Buraku of Japan, 86, 95, 111, 211, 213, 286

caste
  and Dalit position, 17-19
  and its omission from UDHR, CERD, 5, 8
  civil and political rights in, 215; economic, social and cultural rights, 216-217
  Durban Conference and Debate, xxii-xxvi
  Is it Race?, xxii, 120-130
  policies to eliminate discrimination, 176-177
  politics of, 181-183
caste and race, 145
  in Indian Constitution, 126-129

caste and social origin, 300
 in India, 300-302
 in Japan, 306, 307
 in Nepal, 302-303
 in Pakistan, 305
 in Sri Lanka, 304
caste discrimination, 209-210
 UN's response on (1948-2002), xvii-xxii
 historical overview: emerging recognition in UN, 5-16;
 and Indian government's position, 16-17;
 various concerns on, 34-36; and concept of racism, 47;
 major issues needing national attention on, 36-38;
 and untouchability: *Chamars,* Buraku (Japan), Peekchongas (Korea), Ragyappas (Tibet), 86
 and UN, 123-126, 129, 130, 140, 141
 and racial discrimination, 214
 Constitutional recognition of, 147, 149
caste division
 in the *Dharmashastra,* 176-177
caste rights
 against torture and inhuman treatment, 216
caste-is-race thesis, 69
caste system
 and untouchability, 295-297
casteism and racism, 168-171, 176-179
Chattopadhyaya, B.D., 78
Children's Rights, 219
Charover, Stephen, 269
civil society to twice born (CSTB), 242
civic internationalism, 262
Committee on Elimination of Racial Discrimination (CERD), xiii, xvi, xvii, 3, 4, 111, 112, 114, 167
Cox, Oliver Cromwell, 60

Dalit discourse, 267
Dalit oppression
 approach of judiciary on, 115-117
Dalit(s)
 and manual scavenging, 19-20, 32
 embracing of Buddhism by, 232
 exclusion by media of, 243-244
 plight of women, 11
 meaning of, 252
 use of international forums by, xxvi-xxx
 who are they?, 4-5
 economic situation of, 21-23
 and poverty, 23, 24
 and access to education/health, 24-25
 untouchability and atrocities on, 25-26
 and employment, 23
 economic discrimination and exclusion of, 25-27
 reservation of jobs for, 43-47
Dumont, Louis, 251, 253, 266, 271
Dandekar, V.M., 66
Dandi, Philippe, 277
de Gobineav, Count Joseph Arthur, 105
'Depressed Classes', 6
 and *swaraj*, 7, 8
devdasis, 32
discrimination
 against women, xviii, xix
 and Constitutional provisions, 297-299
 based on work and descent, xx, xxi, xxxiv, 111, 113, 211, 212
 definition of (racial), xvi

renewed discussion on current status of, xxx-xxxii
UN framework on, xv-xvii
Divakar, N. Paul, xxix, xxx, 260, 261, 315
Du Bois, W.E.B., xxix, xxx
Durkheim, Emile, 258
Durrenmatt, Friedrich, 250

Eide, Asbjorn, xxxiv, xxxv
Elimination of All Forms of Racial Discrimination (ECERD), 134
Elliot, Walter, 101

Farrakan, Louis, 75
Field, Leigh, 72
Forbes, James, 100

Galanter, Marc, 63
Gandhi, Maneka, 110
Gehlot, Ashok, 154
Goonesekere, R.K.W., xx, xxxiii, xxxiv, 13, 43, 46, 48, 118, 141, 289
Golwalkar, M.S., 103
Guha, B.S., 50, 51, 161
Gupta, Dipankar, xxiv, xxvii, 53-56, 69-83, 59
Guru, Gopal, 251, 263
Gutman, Herberg G., 76

Haldane, J.B.S., 66
Hall, Ronald, 75
Hellman-Rajanayagam, 104
Herskovitz, Melville, 75
Hock, Hans Henrich, 71
Human Genome Project, 162
human right abuses
on Chakmas, 205
on hill tribes of Thailand, 204
on indigeneous peoples in Indonesia, 205
Hunter, W.W., 101, 102
Hutchinson, Harry, 75

Ibbetson, Denzil, 102
Ignatieff, Michael, 262
Ilaiah, Kancha, 126, 275, 278
Inden, Ronald, 99
International Dalit Solidarity Network (IDSN), 59, 196

Kashi Nath, 101
King, Martin Luther, 251
Kunadi, Savitri, 114

Louis, Prakash, 266, 267, 271

Macwan, Martin, xxviii, 31-39, 251, 259, 265
Majumdar, D.N., 72, 73
Mandela, Nelson, 144, 187
manual scavenging, 19
Manusmriti, 193
Mathew, Ajai, 260, 261
Mandalism, 272-74
Marriot, McKim, 266
Mate, S.M., 263
Mishra, Ranganath, 237
Montagu, Ashley M.F., 49, 268
Myrdal, Grunnar, 60
Max Muller, 98

Nagaraj, D.R., 275
Nagy, Rosemary, 209
Naicker, Ramaswamy (Periyar), 104
Nancy, Jean-Luc, 275
National Campaign on Dalit Human Rights (NCDHR), 195
National Campaign on Dalit Human Right (NCDHR), xiv, 133, 154
National Federation of Dalit Women (NFDW), 162, 163

National Human Rights Commission (NHRC), 172-175, 205
Nayyar, Kuldeep, 143
Nipata, Sutta, 192
Nirula, Smita, xxxiii, 190
Nussbaum, Martha, 262

Omvedt, Gail, xxvi, 126, 187-193, 251
Oommen, T.K., xxv, 97-108, 98, 106, 126

Pandey, Gyanendra, 103
Parrish, Charles H., 75
Periyar (Ramaswamy Naiker), 104, 161
Phule, Jotirao, 252
Phule, Jotiba, 161
Phule, Savitribai, 161
Pillai, R.V., 14
Pinheirio, Paulo Sergio, 210
Pinto, Ambrose, 265
Prakasam, Gnana, 251

race verses caste
  difference, 86-90, 99-100
racial discrimination, 85-87
  definition of, 207, 208
racial superiority
  anthropometry science on, 105
racism and racial discrimination
  First and Second World Conference on, 201
  Third World Conference on, 202, 203, 205
  UN General Assembly on, 201
Radhakrishanan, P., xxvi, 57-64, 78
Rajkishore, 113
Ramaswamy, Justice K., 229
Rao, C.R., 72, 73
Ray, Ajit K., 72
Rege, Sharmila, 161
Rex, John, 165
Risley, Sir Herbert, 50, 102, 161, 263
Robinson, Mary, 202, 207, 230, 314
Rorty, Richard, 270, 271
Russel, Kathy, 75

Said, E.A., 99
Samuel, John, 251
Sanskritization, 76-77
Saraswati, Swami Dayanand, 102, 144
Sawarkar, V.D., 103
Scheduled Caste and Scheduled Tribe (Prevention of Atrocities) Act, 1989, 107, 150, 166, 205
Sellers, Susan, 269
Setalvad, Teesta, xxvi
Sheth, D.L., xxiv, xxvii, 85-96, 113, 266
Shah, A.M., 78, 82
Sharma, K.L., 76
Shinde, V.R., 263
Shroff, G., 78, 82
Sorabjee, Soli, xxvi, 134, 143, 189, 277
Srinivas, M.N., 251, 253, 258, 266, 271
State Legal System (SLS), 106, 107
Surje, Sira, 72
swaraj, 6

Teltumbde, Anand, 231, 233
Thampu, Valson, xxvi
Thekaekara, Mari Marcel, xxxiii, 153-155
Thomas Theorem, 108
Thorat, Sukhadeo, xxix, 137
Tilak, Lokamanya, 103

UN Human Rights Systems, 212-214
Universal Declaration of Human Rights (UDHR), xvii
Untouchability (Offences) Act, 1955, 107

Vajpayee, A.B., 285, 316
Varna, 72
varanasankara, 108
Varna Vyavastha (system), 104, 105, 144
Venkateswarlu, 26
Verma, J.S., 237, 239

Warhade, Yogesh, 188
Ward, William, 101
Weber, Max, 272
Wertheim, Fredrick, 269
White, J., 101
Wilson, Midge, 75
Women's Rights, 218
World Conference Against Racism(WCAR), xiii, 85, 111, 120, 133, 134, 139, 142, 153, 156, 199
  addressing Dalit issue in, 27
  major agenda themes in, 31
  objectives of, 208, 209

xenophobia, 202, 203, 205

Yokota, Yozo, xxxiv, xxxv